POEMS 1955-2005

Titles by Anne Stevenson

POETRY

Living in America (Generation Press,
  University of Michigan, USA, 1965)
Reversals (Wesleyan University Press, USA, 1969)
Travelling Behind Glass: Selected Poems 1963-1973
  (Oxford University Press, 1974)
Correspondences, a Family History in Letters
  (Oxford University Press, 1974)
Enough of Green (Oxford University Press, 1977)
Sonnets for Five Seasons (Five Seasons Press, 1979)
Minute by Glass Minute (Oxford University Press, 1982)
A Legacy (Taxvs Press, 1983)
The Fiction-Makers (Oxford University Press, 1985)
Wintertime (MidNAG, 1986)
Selected Poems 1956-1986 (Oxford University Press, 1987)
The Other House (Oxford University Press, 1990)
Four and a Half Dancing Men (Oxford University Press, 1993)
The Collected Poems 1955-1995
  (Oxford University Press, 1996; Bloodaxe Books, 2000)
Granny Scarecrow (Bloodaxe Books, 2000)
A Report from the Border (Bloodaxe Books, 2003)
Poems 1955-2005 (Bloodaxe Books, 2005)

LITERARY CRITICISM & BIOGRAPHY

Elizabeth Bishop (Twayne, USA, 1966)
Bitter Fame: A Life of Sylvia Plath
  (Viking, 1989; Houghton Mifflin, USA, 1989)
Between the Iceberg and the Ship: Selected Essays
  (University of Michigan Press, 1998)
Five Looks at Elizabeth Bishop
  (Bellew/Agenda Editions, 1998)

POETRY CASSETTE

The Poetry Quartets 6 (The British Council/Bloodaxe Books, 2000)
  [shared with Moniza Alvi, Michael Donaghy, Anne Stevenson and George Szirtes]

Anne Stevenson

P O E M S 1955-2005

BLOODAXE BOOKS

ISBN: 1 85224 721 5 hardback edition
       1 85224 699 5 paperback edition

First published 2004 by
Bloodaxe Books Ltd,
Highgreen,
Tarset,
Northumberland NE48 1RP.

www.bloodaxebooks.com
For further information about Bloodaxe titles
please visit our website or write to
the above address for a catalogue.

Bloodaxe Books Ltd acknowledges
the financial assistance of
Arts Council England, North East.

Cover printing by J. Thomson Colour Printers Ltd, Glasgow.

Printed in Great Britain by
Bell & Bain Limited, Glasgow, Scotland.

For Peter Lucas

The Inn

It appeared to be an inn for actors, so our boss
Asked for a room with four beds. The landlady,
Quaint in a lace mobcap, shook her lustrous
Green ribbons at his trilby hat. Only three
Beds were free. The fourth was let to her lover.
My sister and I were laying our charms in rows
On our childhood bed when into that oak-ribbed chamber
Burst the lovers in eighteenth-century clothes;
Her furbelowed fish scales, and his velvet pelt.
Hearing their panting and bird-like cries, I knew
If I looked too closely they would turn to dust.
As I would, dreaming, if I couldn't reach you,
Solid, asleep in this inn we've carefully built
Of seasoned faith and uncorrupted trust.

ACKNOWLEDGEMENTS

Poems 1955-2005 replaces all previous selections of Anne Stevenson's work. It includes poems first collected in the following books: *Living in America* (Generation Press, University of Michigan, 1965); *Reversals* (Wesleyan University Press, 1969); *Travelling Behind Glass: Selected Poems 1963-1973* (1974), *Correspondences: A Family History in Letters* (1974), *Enough of Green* (1977), *Minute by Glass Minute* (1982), *The Fiction-Makers* (1985), *The Other House* (1990) and *Four and a Half Dancing Men* (1993), all from Oxford University Press; *The Collected Poems 1955-1995* (Oxford University Press, 1996; Bloodaxe Books, 2000); *Granny Scarecrow* (2000) and *A Report from the Border* (2003), both from Bloodaxe Books. The arrangement of poems is thematic and also includes some poems from the pamphlet *Winter Time* (MidNAG, 1986), as well as new poems and previously uncollected earlier poems. The original sources are given after the poem titles in the index of titles and first lines at the back of the book. The texts follow those of *The Collected Poems 1955-1995* rather than the earlier collections, with some corrections and later amendments.

The author is grateful to the following journals and anthologies in which her uncollected and new poems have appeared. 'American Rhetoric for Scotland', written in 1969, was published in *Scotland's Poets and the Nation*, ed. Douglas Gifford and Alan Riach (Scottish Poetry Library/Carcanet, 2004). 'At Kilpeck Church' was published in *The Kilpeck Anthology*, ed. Glenn Storhaug (Five Seasons Press, 1981). 'Spring Again' and 'Killing Spiders' were included in *Mairi MacInnes: A Tribute* (Shoestring Press, 2005). 'Killing Spiders' also appeared in *Roundy House* (Wales) and in the *TLS*. The *TLS* published 'In the Museum of Floating Bodies and Flammable Souls' in 2005. Thanks are due to the *Guardian Saturday Review* for '17.14 Out of Newcastle' and three of the 'Grim Sonnets'; to *PN Review* for 'Forgotten of the Foot' to *London Magazine* for 'A Riddle for Peter Scupham' and 'As I Lay Sleeping'; to *Literary Imagination* (Athens, Georgia, 2005) for 'In the Weather of Deciduous Souls'; to *Metre* for 'Photographing Change' and to *Poetry Review* for 'Variations on a Line by Peter Redgrove' and 'Christmas Comfort and the Green Man'. 'Fool's Gold' appeared in *Fashioned Pleasures*, ed. William Thompson (Parallel Press, University of Wisconsin/ Madison Libraries, 2005) .

The author wishes to express special thanks to the sponsors of the Northern Rock Writers Award, 2002, for making it possible for her to complete this book through their exceptional financial generosity.

CONTENTS

Prologue

17   Making Poetry
18   Saying the World
18   The Sun Appears in November
19   From an Unfinished Poem
20   The Fiction Makers
22   Gannets Diving
22   North Sea off Carnoustie
23   Moonrise
24   If I Could Paint Essences
25   Swifts
26   In the Tunnel of Summers
27   A Report from the Border
28   Small Philosophical Poem
28   Vertigo

I   *The Way You Say the World*

30   Living in America
30   Sierra Nevada
32   Still Life in Utah
32   Ann Arbor
33   Going Back
36   The Dear Ladies of Cincinnati
37   Harvard
38   Nightmare in North Carolina
38   A Summer Place
40   Ruin
41   New York
41   A Hot Night in New York
42   Journal Entry: Ward's Island

44   England
46   The Women
47   Fen People
47   A River
48   In Middle England
50   Travelling Behind Glass
56   From the Motorway
57   Branch Line
58   A Tourist Guide to the Fens
59   Coming Back to Cambridge

61   Temporarily in Oxford
62   Lockkeeper's Island
63   By the Boat House, Oxford
64   Walking Early by the Wye
65   Burnished

66 Himalayan Balsam
67 Whose Goat?
68 Earth Station
69 The Wrekin

POEMS FROM CWM NANTCOL

71 Binoculars in Ardudwy
72 The Unaccommodated
73 *Phoenicurus phoenicurus*
74 Pity the Birds
75 A Present
76 The Wind, the Sun and the Moon
77 Under Moelfre
77 Attacking the Waterfall
78 Why Take Against Mythology (1)
79 Why Take Against Mythology (2)
80 Spring Poem
80 Without Me
81 May Bluebells, Coed Aber Artro
82 Leaving

83 Pennine
83 Shale
84 A Prayer to Live with Real People
85 Household Gods
86 Forgotten of the Foot
88 Demolition
88 Spring Song
89 November
90 From My Study
96 Winter Time
97 Salter's Gate
98 Claude Glass
99 Jarrow
100 North Easter
101 Skills
102 Night Walking with Shadows
103 Spring Again
104 17.14 Out of Newcastle

106 American Rhetoric for Scotland
108 East Coast
108 *Fire and the Tide*
108 *Summer*
108 *The Bench*
108 *Boating Pool at Night*
109 *Winter Flowers*
109 *The Lighthouse*
110 *Night Wind, Dundee*
110 *Aberdeen*

110 The Mudtower
111 The Fish Are All Sick
111 The Man in the Wind
112 Cramond
113 Inverkirkaig

114 Buzzard and Alder
114 Cold
115 Path
116 Resurrection
117 Enough of Green
118 In the Weather of Deciduous Souls

II *Seven Ages*

121 Epigraph from *Reversals*
122 The Spirit Is Too Blunt an Instrument
123 The Victory
123 Stabilities
124 Poem for a Daughter
124 To My Daughter in a Red Coat
125 In March
125 With My Sons at Boarhills
127 In the Nursery
127 To Phoebe
128 Little Paul and the Sea
128 Four and a Half Dancing Men
130 The Holly and the Ivy
131 The Doctor
131 A Surprise on the First Day of School
132 Innocence and Experience
133 At Thirteen
134 Incident
134 Suicide
135 Transparencies

137 Sous-entendu
137 Love
138 Politesse
139 Aubade
140 Reversals
140 Two Love Poems
141 Wanted
141 Posted
142 Drought
142 After the End of It
143 An Impenitent Ghost
144 'All Canal Boat Cruises Start Here'
145 This

146 In the House
147 Night Thoughts and False Confessions
148 The Suburb
149 The Takeover
150 The Mother
150 Generations
151 Five Poems of Innocence and Experience
151 *The Crush*
151 *The Marriage*
152 *The Affair*
152 *The Demolition*
153 *Old Scholars*
153 The Other House
155 Old Wife's Tale
155 Eros
156 Questionable
156 False Flowers
158 On Watching a Cold Woman Wade into a Cold Sea

159 Musician's Widow
160 The Professor's Tale
161 Stone Fig
VISITS TO THE CEMETERY OF THE LONG ALIVE
162 Hadrian's
162 A Sepia Garden
165 Bloody Bloody
167 Black Hole
168 Lost
168 A Tricksy June
169 Granny Scarecrow
170 To witness pain is different form of pain
170 Who's Joking with the Photographer

172 After Her Death
172 Apology
173 The Loss
173 Hands
175 The Minister
176 Siskin
177 The White Room
178 Elegy
179 When the camel is dust it goes through the needle's eye
180 A Marriage

III

181 Haunted
182 Green Mountain, Black Mountain

189 *Correspondences: A Family History in Letters*

IV *Problematica*

260 The Garden
261 The Unhappened
261 The Grey Land
262 On Not Being Able to Look at the Moon
263 About Crying
264 The Three
265 The Sirens Are Virtuous
266 Icon
266 Respectable House
267 Meniscus

268 Thales and Li Po
268 Cain
269 He and It
270 And even then
270 Inquit Deus
271 Cloven hoof's-bane
272 The Garden of Intellect

273 Trinity at Low Tide
273 Negatives
275 Love Stories and a Bed of Sand
276 A Love Sequence
277 Calendar
278 Washing the Clocks
279 An Angel
281 Washing My Hair
282 Naming the Flowers

V *The Art of Making*

285 Morning
286 Theme with Variations
287 To Write It
287 The Price
288 In Passing
289 Ah Babel
289 From the Men of Letters
290 The Figure in the Carpet
291 A Riddle for Peter Scupham
291 The Morden Angel
293 Re-reading Jane
294 John Keats, 1821-1950
295 At the Grave of Ezra Pound

296 Dreaming of Immortality in a Thatched Hut
296 The Exhibition
298 The Blue Pool

299   Seven Poems after Frances Bacon
299   1 *Study for a Portrait on a Folding Bed*
299   2 *Study of a Dog*
299   3 *Three Figures and Portrait*
300   4 *Seated Figure*
301   5 *Portrait of a Lady*
301   6 *Triptych*
302   7 *Study for a portrait of Van Gogh*
303   Brueghel's Snow
304   Hans Memling's *Sibylla Sambetha*
304   In the Museum of Floating Bodies and Flammable Souls
305   Whistler's *Gentleman by the Sea*
306   Painting It In
307   After you left
308   Red Hot Sex
310   The Miracle of Camp 60

313   Journal Entry: Impromptu in C Minor
316   Kosovo Surprised by Mozart
317   Hearing with My Fingers
318   Arioso Dolente
320   Post Scriptum

VI *Verses*

323   The Traveller
324   In Winter
325   Opera Piece
325   Two Quatrains
325   *Lesson*
325   *Television*
326   Ailanthus with Ghosts
327   A Ballad for Apothecaries

330   After the Fall
330   At Kilpeck Church
332   The Parson and the Romany
333   The Theologian's Confession
334   Carol of the Birds

335   Celebrity
336   A Quest
337   Ballad of the Made Maid
338   Oysters
339   Cashpoint Charlie
340   Skin Deep
341   Fool's Gold
341   Prophylactic Sonnets

343 Four Grim Fairy Tales
343   1 *Rapunzel*
343   2 *Sleeping Beauty*
344   3 *Was Cinderella Ever Happy?*
344   4 *If Wishes Were Fishes*

345 Giving Rabbit to My Cat, Bonnie
346 Epitaph for a Good Mouser
346 Clydie Is Dead!
348 Where the Animals Go

VII *Border Crossings*
351 Talking Sense to My Senses
351 On Going Deaf
352 What I Miss

353 In the Orchard
353 Melon meaning melon
354 Terrorist
355 Late
356 A Luxury
358 Christmas Comfort and the Green Man

359 It looks so simple from a distance…
359 Graves with Children
360 Two Countries
361 The Watchers
362 From the Primrose Path
363 A Cradle of Fist
364 New York Is Crying
365 Toy
366 Killing Spiders
367 As I Lay Sleeping
368 Photographing Change

VIII *In Memoriam*
371 Sonnets for Five Seasons
371   *This House*
371   *Complaint*
372   *Between*
372   *Stasis*
373   *The Circle*
374 Dreaming of the Dead
375 Waving to Elizabeth
376 A Dream of Stones
    TWO POEMS FOR FRANCES HOROVITZ
377 Red Rock Fault
378 Willow Song

TWO POEMS FOR JOHN COLE
380 Dinghy
381 Cambrian

382 Poem for Harry Fainlight

THREE POEMS FOR SYLVIA PLATH
383 Nightmare, Daymoths
384 Letter to Sylvia Plath
387 Hot Wind, Hard Rain
388 The Name of the Worm
389 Invocation and Interruption
391 A Parable for Norman
394 Comet
395 Freeing Lizzie
397 The Writer in the Corner
398 Passifloraceae

TWO POEMS FOR NERYS JOHNSON
399 Portrait of the Artist in an Orthopaedic Halo Crowned with Flowers
399 Passing Her House

401 Variations on a Line by Peter Redgrove

403 INDEX OF TITLES AND FIRST LINES

Prologue

Making Poetry

'You have to inhabit poetry
if you want to make it.'

And what's 'to inhabit'?

To be in the habit of, to wear
words, sitting in the plainest light,
in the silk of morning, in the shoe of night;
a feeling bare and frondish in surprising air;
familiar... rare.

And what's 'to make'?

To be and to become words' passing
weather; to serve a girl on terrible
terms, embark on voyages over voices,
evade the ego-hill, the misery-well,
the siren hiss of *publish, success, publish,
success, success, success.*

And why inhabit, make, inherit poetry?

Oh, it's the shared comedy of the worst
blessed; the sound leading the hand;
a wordlife running from mind to mind
through the washed rooms of the simple senses;
one of those haunted, undefendable, unpoetic
crosses we have to find.

Saying the World

The way you say the world is what you get.
What's more, you haven't time to change or choose.
The words swim out to pin you in their net

Before you guess you're in the TV set,
Lit up and sizzling in unfriendly news.
The mind's machine – and you invented it –

Grinds out the formulae you have to fit,
The ritual syllables you need to use
To charm the world and not be crushed by it.

This cluttered motorway, that screaming jet,
Those crouching skeletons whose eyes accuse;
O see and say them, make yourself forget

The world is vaster than the alphabet,
And profligate, and meaner than the muse.
A bauble in the universe? Or shit?

Whichever way, you say the world you get.
Though what there is is always there to lose.
No crimson name redeems the poisoned rose.
The absolute's irrelevant. And yet...

(1994)

The Sun Appears in November

When trees are bare,
when ground is more glowing than summer,
in sun, in November,
you can see what lay under
confusing eloquence of green.

Bare boughs in their cunning
twist this way and that way,
trying to persuade with crooked reasoning.
But trees are constrained from within
to conform to skeleton.

Nothing they put on
will equal these lines of cold branches,
the willows in bunches,
birches like lightning,
transparent in brown spinneys, beeches.

From an Unfinished Poem

The idea of event is horizontal,
the idea of personality, vertical.
Let fiction take root
in the idea of the cross between them.

The mind of the world
is a vast field of crosses.
We pick our way through the cemetery
calling out names and stories.

In the event
the story is foretold,
foremade in the code of its happening.

In the event
the event is sacrificed
to a fiction of its having happened.

The Fiction Makers

(i.m. Frances Horovitz)

We were the wrecked elect,
the ruined few. Youth,
youth, the Café Iruña
and the bullfight set,
looped on Lepanto brandy
but talking 'truth'.
Hem, the 4 a.m. wisecrack,
the hard way in,
that story we were all at the end of
and couldn't begin –
we thought we were living now
but we were living then.

Sanctified Pound, a knot
of nerves in his fist,
squeezing the Goddamn iamb
out of our verse,
making it new in his
archaeological plot –
to maintain 'the sublime'
in the factive? Couldn't be done.
Something went wrong
with 'new' in the Pisan pen;
he thought he was making now,
but he was making then.

Virginia, Vanessa,
a teapot, a Fitzroy fuss,
'Semen?' asks Lytton,
eyeing a smudge on a dress.
How to educate England
and keep a correct address
on the path to the river through
Auschwitz? Belsen?
Auden and Isherwood
stalking glad boys in Berlin –
they thought they were suffering now
but they were suffering then.

Out of pink-cheeked Cwmdonkin,
Dylan with his Soho grin.
Planted in the fiercest of flames,
gold ash on a stem.
When Henry jumped out of his joke,
Mr Bones sat in.
Even you, with your breakable heart
in your ruined skin,
those poems all written
that have to be you, dear friend,
you guessed you were dying now,
but you were dying then.

Here is a table with glasses,
ribbed cages tipped back,
or turned on a hinge to each other
to talk, to talk,
mouths that are drinking or smiling
or quoting some book,
or laughing out laughter as candletongues
lick at the dark.
So bright in this fiction
forever becoming its end,
we think we are laughing now,
but we are laughing then.

Gannets Diving

The sea is dark
by virtue of its white lips;
the gannets, white,
by virtue of their dark wings.

Gannet into sea.

Cross the white bolt
with the dark bride.

Act of your name, Lord,
though it does not appear so
to you in the speared fish.

North Sea off Carnoustie

You know it by the northern look of the shore,
by salt-worried faces,
an absence of trees, an abundance of lighthouses.
It's a serious ocean.

Along marram-scarred, sandbitten margins
wired roofs straggle out to where
a cold little holiday fair
has floated in and pitched itself
safely near the prairie of a golf course.
Coloured lights have sunk deep into the solid wind,
but all they've caught is a pair of lovers
and three silly boys.
Everyone else has a dog.
Or a room to get to.

The smells are of fish and of sewage and cut grass.
Oystercatchers, doubtful of habitation,
clamour *weep*, *weep*, *weep*, as they fuss over
scummy black rocks the tide leaves for them.

The sea is as near as we come to another world.

But there in your stony and windswept garden
a blackbird is confirming the grip of the land.
You, you, he murmurs, dark purple in his voice.

And now in far quarters of the horizon
lighthouses are awake, sending messages –
invitations to the landlocked,
warnings to the experienced,
but to anyone returning from the planet ocean,
candles in the windows of a safe earth.

Moonrise

While my anxiety stood phoning you last evening,
My simpler self lay marvelling through glass
At the full moon marbling the clouds, climbing
In shafts, a headlamp through an underpass,
Until it swung free, cratered, deadly clear,
Earth's stillborn twin unsoiled by life or air.

And while our voices huddled mouth to ear,
I watched tenacity of long imagination
Cast her again in a film of the old goddess,
Chaste of the chase, more virgin than the Virgin,
Lifting herself from that rucked, unfeeling waste
As from the desert of her own ruined face.

Such an unhinging light. To see her. To see that.
As no one else had seen her. Or might see that.

If I Could Paint Essences
(Hay on Wye)

Another day in March. Late
rawness and wetness. I hear my mind say,
if only I could paint essences.

Such as the mudness of mud
on this rainsoaked dyke where coltsfoot
displays its yellow misleading daisy.

Such as the westness of west here
in England's last thatched, rivered
county. Red ploughland. Green pasture.

Black cattle. Quick water. Overpainted
by lightshafts from layered gold
and purple cumulus. A cloudness of clouds

which are not like anything but clouds.

But just as I arrive at true sightness of seeing,
unexpectedly I want to play on those bell-toned
cellos of delicate not-quite-flowering larches

that offer, on the opposite hill, their unfurled
amber instruments – floating, insubstantial, a rising
horizon of music embodied in light.

And in such imagining I lose sight of sight.
Just as I'll lose the tune of what
hurls in my head, as I turn back, turn

home to you, conversation, the inescapable ache
of trying to catch, say, the catness of cat
as he crouches, stalking his shadow,

on the other side of the window.

Swifts

Spring comes little, a little. All April it rains.
The new leaves stick in their fists; new ferns still fiddleheads.
But one day the swifts are back. Face to the sun like a child
You shout, 'The swifts are back!'

Sure enough, bolt nocks bow to carry one sky-scyther
Two hundred miles an hour across fullblown windfields.
Swereee swereee. Another. And another.
It's the cut air falling in shrieks on our chimneys and roofs.

The next day, a fleet of high crosses cruises in ether.
These are the air pilgrims, pilots of air rivers.
But a shift of wing, and they're earth-skimmers, daggers
Skilful in guiding the throw of themselves away from themselves.

Quick flutter, a scimitar upsweep, out of danger of touch, for
Earth is forbidden to them, water's forbidden to them,
All air and fire, little owlish ascetics, they outfly storms,
They rush to the pillars of altitude, the thermal fountains.

Here is a legend of swifts, a parable –
When the Great Raven bent over earth to create the birds,
The swifts were ungrateful. They were small muddy things
Like shoes, with long legs and short wings,

So they took themselves off to the mountains to sulk.
And they stayed there. 'Well,' said the Raven, after years of this,
'I will give you the sky. You can have the whole sky
On condition that you give up rest.'

'Yes, yes,' screamed the swifts, 'We abhor rest.
We detest the filth of growth, the sweat of sleep,
Soft nests in the wet fields, slimehold of worms.
Let us be free, be air!'

So the Raven took their legs and bound them into their bodies.
He bent their wings like boomerangs, honed them like knives.
He streamlined their feathers and stripped them of velvet.
Then he released them, *Never to Return*

Inscribed on their feet and wings. And so
We have swifts, though in reality, not parables but
Bolts in the world's need: swift
Swifts, not in punishment, not in ecstasy, simply

Sleepers over oceans in the mill of the world's breathing.
The grace to say they live in another firmament.
A way to say the miracle will not occur,
And watch the miracle.

In the Tunnel of Summers

Moving from day into day,
I don't know how,
eating these plums now
this morning for breakfast,
tasting of childhood's
mouth-pucker tartness,
watching the broad light
seed in the fences,
honey of barley,
gold ocean, grasses,
as the tunnel of summers,
of nothing but summers,
opens again
in my travelling senses.

I am eight and eighteen and eighty
all the Augusts of my day.

Why should I be, I be
more than another?
Brown foot in sandal,
burnt palm on flaked clay,
flesh under waterfall
baubled in strong spray,
blood on the stubble
of fly-sweet hay.
Why not my mother's, my
grandmother's ankle
hurting as harvest hurts
thistle and animal?
A needle of burning;
why this way or that way?

They are already building the long straw cemetery
where my granddaughter's daughter has been born and buried.

A Report from the Border

Wars in peacetime don't behave like wars.
So loving they are.
Kissed on both cheeks, silk-lined ambassadors
Pose and confer.

Unbuckle your envy, drop it there by the door.
We will settle,
We will settle without blows or bullets
The unequal score.

In nature, havenots have to be many
And havelots few.
Making money out of making money
Helps us help you.

This from the party of good intent. From the other,
Hunger's stare,
Drowned crops, charred hopes, fear, stupor, prayer
And literature.

Small Philosophical Poem

Dr Animus, whose philosophy is a table,
sits down contentedly to a square meal.
The plates lie there, and there,
just where they should lie.
His feet stay just where they should stay,
between legs and the floor.
His eyes believe the clean waxed surfaces
are what they are.

But while he's eating his un-
exceptional propositions, his wise
wife, Anima, sweeping a haze-gold decanter
from a metaphysical salver,
pours him a small glass of doubt.
Just what he needs.
He smacks his lips and cracks his knuckles.
The world is the pleasure of thought.

He'd like to stay awake all night
(elbows on the table)
talking of how the table might not be there.
But Anima, whose philosophy is hunger,
perceives the plates are void in empty air.
The floor is void beneath his trusting feet.
Peeling her glass from its slender cone of fire,
she fills the room with love. And fear. And fear.

Vertigo

Mind led body
to the edge of the precipice.
They stared in desire
at the naked abyss.
If you love me, said mind,
take that step into silence.
If you love me, said body,
turn and exist.

I

The Way You Say the World

Living in America

'Living in America,'
the intelligent people at Harvard say,
'is the price you pay for living in New England.'

Californians think
living in America is a reward
for managing not to live anywhere else.

The rest of the country?
Could it be sagging between two poles,
tastelessly decorated, dangerously overweight?

No. Look closely.
Under cover of light and noise
both shores are hurrying towards each other.

San Francisco
is already half way to Omaha.
Boston is nervously losing its way in Detroit.

Desperately the inhabitants
hope to be saved in the middle.
Pray to the mountains and deserts to keep them apart.

Sierra Nevada
(for Margaret Elvin, 1963)

Landscape without regrets whose weakest junipers
        strangle and split granite,
whose hard, clean light is utterly without restraint,
        whose mountains can purify and dazzle
and every minute excite us, but never can offer us
        commiseration, never can tell us
anything about ourselves except that we are dispensable...

The rocks and water. The glimmering rocks, the hundreds
        and hundreds of blue lakes
ought to be mythical, while the great trees, soon as they die,
        immediately become ghosts,
stalk upright among the living with awful composure.
        But even these bones that light
has taken and twisted, with their weird gesticulations
        and shadows that look as if
they'd been carved out of dust, even these
have nothing to do with what we have done or not done.

Now, as we climb on the high bare slopes,
        the most difficult earth
supports the most delicate flowers: gilia and harebells,
        kalmia and larkspur, everywhere
wild lupin's tight blue spires and fine-fingered
        handshaped leaves.
Daintiest of all, the low mariposa, lily of the mountain,
with its honey stained cup and no imperfect dimension.

If we stand in the fierce but perfectly transparent wind
        we can look down over the boulders,
over the drifted scree with its tattered collar of manzanita,
        over the groves of hemlock,
the tip of each tree resembling an arm
        extended to a drooping forefinger,
down, down, over the whole, dry, difficult
        train of the ascent, down to the lake
with its narrow, swarming edges where little white boats
        are moving their oars like waterbugs.

        Nothing but the wind makes noise.
The lake, transparent to its greeny brown floor,
        is everywhere else bluer than the sky.
The boats hardly seem to touch its surface. Just as
        this granite cannot really touch us,
although we stand here and name the colours of its flowers.

The wind is strong without knowing that it is wind.
        The twisted tree that is not warning
or supplicating, never considers that it is not wind.
        We think
if we were to stay here for a long time, lie here
        like wood on these waterless beaches,
we would forget our names, would remember that
        what we first wanted
had something to do with stones, the sun,
the thousand colours of water, brilliances, blues.

Still Life in Utah

Somewhere nowhere in Utah, a boy by the roadside,
gun in his hand, and the rare dumb hard tears flowing.
Beside him, the greyheaded man has let one arm slide
awkwardly over his shoulders, is talking and pointing
at whatever it is, dead, in the dust on the ground.

By the old parked Chevy, two women, talking and watching.
Their skirts flag forward, bandannas twist with their hair.
Around them, sheep and a fence and the sagebrush burning
and burning with a blue flame. In the distance, where
mountains are clouds, lightning, but no rain.

Ann Arbor
(A Profile)

Neither city nor town, its location,
even, is ambiguous.
Of North and East and Middlewest it is
and is not; in every sense,
a hopeless candidate for the picturesque.
Trees and a few grand accidentally preserved
eyesores save it from total suburbanisation,
give it the mildly authentic complexion
of secondhand furniture.

No setting for tragedy,
it is the scene, nonetheless, for more
than its surfeit of traffic would suggest.
Entrances and exits are frequent enough
to be anonymous as each year the young
adolesce in its residences, the usual
academic antipathies liven the cocktail parties;
hard done by, driven from their garrets,
thin graduate students gripe in the beer joints,
leaving their wives to cope with babies
and contemporary interior decoration.

In all the tongues of the world
its tone is Germanic and provincial.
Yugoslavs, Hindus, Japanese
fraternise in the supermarkets
where beansprouts and braunschweiger
are equally available.
Love is frequently experienced over
jugs of California claret, politics are important,
and culture so cheap and convenient
that every evening you expect thin strains of Mozart
to issue from half a dozen windows.

The women who do not run for alderman
paint pictures, write poetry or give expensive parties
for the members of visiting symphony orchestras.
Their children are well-fed, rude and intelligent,
while, alone in immense mysterious houses, witches
remember the coaches of the first city fathers.

A microcosm, a mosaic, always paradoxical,
with scenery it has little to do.
And if you venerate antiquity or feel wiser
where there is history, you will, of course,
prefer Cambridge, though even there
the proportion of good people to bad architecture
is probably about the same.

(1961)

Going Back
(Ann Arbor, October 1993)

It hazes over,
blurred by forty years,
a nerveless place,
like the idea of pain,
like love affairs
that at the time *were* time.

An intimate alias,
half mine,
floats on these streets,

33

identifies each elm
that isn't there,
breathes in these
shapeless, lax,
companionable homes,
hand-built midwest America
that clones itself
in leafy, bypassed towns
steepled, asleep on
ochre-coloured lawns,
named for the dead that still
fadingly mark a street, a school,
its sledding hill and park.

And next? When I next come?
More will be gone.
The underwater palimpsest
may be all but illegible,
may even release me
from haunted erasures,
more haunting survivals –
Mrs Winter's
witch's den of cures
now flaunts a showy extension
with red doors.
How strong, in spite of that,
its tell-tale reek of compost,
eau de chat.

Behind a veil of murky conifers,
screened by her purple-brown veranda,
Miss Elizabeth Dean, at ninety-four
(a hundred and thirty-four?)
entices, still, with an *epergne*
of ripple-ribboned candies
young neighbours she'll outlive;
as she outlived the elms
(those smoky autumns
drugged with burning leaves)
as she at last outlived
all her contemporaries.

She willed her virgin wealth
to the city's trees. And who,
among our PhDs and kindly
Democratic wives would
forty years ago have guessed that,

thanks to old Miss Dean,
while maples last,
Ann Arbor will remain an
arbour, releasing from October's
gentle hospice leaves like hands
that beg to go, let go,
let go, regretfully, a salmon one,
a crimson one, a yellow one,
brimming the sidewalks and shallow gutters
with yet another generation,
another kickable pile.

A mobile municipal vacuum-leafer
roars with gluttony outside
the Newcombs' house,
its chocolate porch no longer
painted chocolate;
now by the Bursley's grander brick,
no longer Mr & Mrs Bursley's.
At sixteen, waking on our sleeping porch,
I wrote a sonnet to the morning
'walking like a dancer'
on Miss Dean's shimmering, weedless,
surely eternal front lawn.

Our house wants paint.
The porches have been glassed in.
With the side fence gone,
how shrunken the little summer house.
New owners shut their white blinds
tight as eyelids, but I see through
to that famous 'L',
living-room bought for two
pianos to live in.
It brought up two girls – three –
too carefully, too musically.

Is it a brace or a fetter,
never to be set quite free
from vanished elms we took for granted,
angel-food cake and mother's
League of Women Voters,
mother and faithful Mother Destler,
Mrs Florer, deaf, next door,
and further down, remote as Greek,
foundering in sadness I crossed
to get away from, Mister Blake?

The Dear Ladies of Cincinnati

'Life is what you make it,' my half-Italian
        grandmother used to say.
And remembering how that purposely ludicrous voice
        pulled down the exalted
ceilings of my great aunt's castle in Cincinnati,
        I know that brave cliché
as a legacy from her father. His western dream
        was a palace of chequered aprons.
Ambition? All colour and doom as he roared through
        four fortunes, strewing
sheep, gold, horses and diamonds like sawdust
        over Kentucky. Before he died
he squandered his last square hundred
        on a silver tureen,
a peacock big as a weathervane on its lid.

Then what could his five chaste daughters do
        but divide up his maxims
and marry as well as they could? Uselessness
        was the use they made
of their half raw beauty, so they all found husbands who,
        liking their women gay,
preserved them in an air-tight empire made of soap
        and mattresses. There, for years,
they manufactured their own climate, generated events
        to keep everybody laughing.

Outside, the luck of Republicans fluctuated.
        Stocks were uncertain. Sadness
perplexed them. But the aunts kept their chins up
        trying on hats, called everybody 'sugar',
remembered the words of hit tunes they'd been courted to,
        avoided the contagion of thought
so successfully that the game kept time to the music
        even as the vanishing chairs
put my grandmother out and sent my sad over-dieted
        uncles upstairs
trailing cigar-brown panelling into their bedrooms.

Yet the eyes in the gilded frames
        of their portraits have
nothing unpleasant to say. The red wax roses
        are dusted but not arranged.

The vellum Catullus crumbles behind glass doors
        in the bookcase, frail as the oakleaf
fifty years dead in its cloudy, undulating pages.

And the ladies, the ladies still sit
        on the stone verandah,
in the bamboo chairs upholstered
        with chintz geraniums,
with the white-painted wrought-iron
        furniture still in bloom,
laughing and rocking and talking
        their father's language
while the city eats and breathes for them
        in the distance,
and the river grows ugly
        in their perpetual service.

Harvard

We have seen ghosts of the once green peacocks
Walking through the stubble of the cut wheat,
Spreading their shady tails among the stalks.

Each certain of its magnificence, they meet,
But out of kindness do not tell each other
Of their sickly feathers, of their dim beaks.

Nightmare in North Carolina

Arriving in North Carolina after midnight,
Watched by the sheet-white sockets of the town,
Listened to by white men propped against the street light,
She found the one hotel and took a room.
Its walls were green. The hard bed wore a scroll
Of painted roses where the pillows met.
The air conditioner on the window sill
Roared and roared as the moth-white faces
Of her lovers poured down from the gilded pelmet
And disappeared in the jaws of the open suitcases.
'Wait!' she cried, but the windows were stuffed with newspapers,
Horror-black headlines, buckling and billowing in.
She rose, trampling furiously. The papers and lovers
Dissolved. Were her lovers dead?
In their place stood an old man, wart on his chin,
Bundles of yellow newspapers up to his knees.
'Our paper comes out once a week,' he said,
Shuffling behind the counter with the keys.

A Summer Place
(Vermont, 1974)

You know that house she called home,
so sleek, so clapboard-white,
that used to be some country jobber's blight
or scab on our hill's arm.
You can see the two cellars of the barn –
stones still squatting where the fellow stacked them.

He worked the place as a farm,
though how, with stones for soil, she never knew.
Partly she hoped he'd been a poet, too.
Why else hang Haystack mountain and its view
from northwest windows?
It was the view she bought it for. He'd gone.
The house sagged on its frame. The barns were down.

The use she saw for it was not to be
of use. A summer place. A lovely
setting where fine minds could graze
at leisure on long summer days
and gather books from bushes, phrase by phrase.
Work would be thought. A tractor bought for play
would scare unnecessary ugly scrub away.

A white gem set on a green silk glove
she bought and owned there.
And summers wore it, just as she would wear
each summer like a dress of sacred air,
until the house was half compounded of
foundations, beams and paint – half of her love.

She lived profoundly, felt, wrote from her heart,
knew each confessional songbird by its voice,
cloistered her garden with bee balm and fanning iris,
sat, stained by sunsets, in a vault of noise,
listening through cricket prayer for whitethroat,
hermit thrush. And couldn't keep it out:
the shade of something wrong, a fear, a doubt.

As though she heard the house stir in its plaster,
stones depart unsteadily from walls,
the woods, unwatched, stretch out their roots like claws
and tear through careful fences, fiercer than saws.
Something alive lived under her mind-cropped pasture,
hated the house. Or worse, loved. Hungering after
its perfectly closed compactness.

She dreamed or daydreamed what it might have come to,
the house itself wanting the view
to take it, and the view's love gathering into
brambles, tendrils, trunks of maples, needing
her every window, entering, seeding.
Fear of attack kept her from sleeping,
kept her awake in her white room, pacing, weeping.

But you see the place still stands there, pretty as new.
Whatever she thought the mountain and trees would do,
they did, and took her with them, and withdrew.

Ruin

Well, they're gone, long gone,
and the land they called theirs
owns them now, without knowing
anyone cares.

What they lived to be doing
has been done, long done.
It's as if looking back
were to look further on.

For their money and saws
and queer human knack
they gained a few acres,
achieved this wreck.

Beneath choke-cherry, broadfern,
bramble and mullein –
boulders they'll build from,
bedrooms they'll lie in.

New York

This addiction.
The ones who get drunk on it easily.
The romantic, sad-hearted,
expensive inhabitants
who have to believe there is no way out,
who tear at themselves and each other
under the drumbeats while everyone
dances or weeps
or takes off clothes hopefully,
half sure the quivering bedstead
can bring forth leaves,
that love, love, love
is the only green in the jungle.

A Hot Night in New York

Midnight air's unbreathing steam
Shifts, with a sound of whips, to rain
As diamond-studded traffic meets
Its image doubled in the streets.

Shisssssh as meteors plunge and spray.
Crescendo, now glissando, they
Cool and evolve a deeper night
From sibilant liquorice and light.

(2001)

Journal Entry: Ward's Island

(Toronto, 1989)

On the last day of the poetry festival
I took the harbour ferry to the island.
Two dollars to crawl across the iced silk
of my view from the hotel window
from the giant stalagmites of the waterfront
to Ward's back woods.

A sunny Sunday, cobalt, with feathery clouds.
Wind at minus eighteen degrees centigrade
knifing the lake. I felt on my face
the grinding of its blade, but water tossed light
like fishscales in our wake, so I stayed on deck
in my boots and visible breath
watching the city recede.

Silver, jet, gold, porphyry, jade.

Splendid in the sun, with their mineral eyelids
the tall banks winked goodbye from a haze of piers.
After fifteen, twenty-five minutes
that might have been fifty years,
with a backwash of waves and a shrill
admonitory hoot, fussily we arrived.
Someone's sleeve threw a rope,
someone's caked gloves tied it.
I skidded down a gangway from the boat
to where Ward's little wilderness survives.

Outcast, silent, down-at-heel, deserted.
Whose shacks of rotting clapboard, synthetic brick?
Whose mud yards? Whose buggies and broken toys?
Whose chairs left out for a snow picnic, maybe?
Who stacked the wood so neatly? Who tarred the roofs?
Whose smoke? Whose cat? Whose bandaged porch? Whose story?

Talking to myself. In that place even the cat
seemed disposed to be sad and scarce.
Perhaps he was old Ward's ghost
scuttling by in the fur of his past.
I heard my footsteps one by one talk back.
Along a windswept municipal boardwalk:
evergreens, benches, tourist views of the lake.

On the other side, the open side, colder.
I saw how ice had hugged and hugged each boulder.
The beach was studded with layered, glittering skulls.
I kept on walking with whatever it was I felt –
something between jubilation and fear.

There appeared to be no traffic at all
on that sea no one could see over;
only to the airport frail, silver insects
sailed from the beautiful air.

Turning, I cut through woods to the canal.
Two boys in red and blue padded anoraks
skated swiftly between frozen-in boats.
They'd set up rusty oil cans for goal posts,
and the faint click, click of their hockey sticks
knitted me a coat.

Still, I caught the next ferry back.
A gaunt youth in a baseball cap and two burly men
settled themselves and their boredom
in the too hot cabin,
there to spread newsprint wings and disappear.
I paced the warmth, rubbing life into my hands.
The city advanced to admit us, cruel and dear.

* * *

England
(for Peter Lucas, 1966)

Without nostalgia who could love England?
Without a sentimental attachment to tolerance
Who could delight in this cramped corner country
In no quarter savage, where everything done well
Is touched with the melancholy of understanding?

No one leaves England enamoured,
But England remembered invites an equivocal regret.
For what traveller or exile, mesmerised by the sun
Or released by spaciousness from habitual self-denial,
Recalls without wistfulness its fine peculiarities
Or remembers with distaste its unique, vulnerable surfaces?

Summer and the shine of white leaves against thunder.
Ploughland where the wind throws the black soil loose
And horses pull clumsily as though through surf,
Or stand, hoofs clapped to the earth like bells,
Braced in their fields between churches and seagulls.
England. Cool and in bloom.
Where sky begets colours on uneasy seasons
And hills lie down patiently in the rain.

Americans like England to live in her cameo,
A dignified profile attached to a past
Understood to belong to her, like the body of a bust.
The image to the native is battered but complete,
The cracked clay flaking, reluctantly sloughed away,
Inadequately renewed on her beautiful bones.

The stinginess of England. The proliferating ugliness.
The pale boys, harmful, dissatisfied, groping for comfort
In the sodium darkness of December evenings.
Wet roofs creeping for miles along wet bricks.
Lovers urgently propping each other on the endless
Identical pavements, in the vacant light
Where the cars live, their pupilless eyes
Turned upward without envy or disapproval.

Someone must live in the stunted houses behind the stucco.
Someone must feed from the tiny sick shops.
Someone must love these babies.
                            Unbelievable
In the murk of her cottage, the eighty-year virgin

Fussing over bottles and cats; the uncharitable cold;
Light falling in squares from the frugal windows
Of public houses; schoolgirls dragging in crocodile
Through damp lanes behind the converted castle,
Querulous in the big wind. In the same wind
That gathers them, with pylons and steeples and
Gas drums, with domes and scaffolding and graveyards
And small kempt gardens by the railway, helplessly,
Recklessly, untidily into the temporary spring.

Anglers appear, umbrellas and transistors
On the paths by the silted canals; and Sunday couples
Spread like wet clothes on the bank.
Days unobtrusively seep into the nights,
Days that drew the daffodil after the crocus
And lit the rose from the embers of the hyacinth
Thrust nettle and thistle through ribs of abandoned machinery
And dye green the trunks of elaborate beeches.
Then the hills fill with gold wheat.

September. Already autumnal.
Lost days drift under the plane trees.
Leaves tangle in the gutters.
In Greenwich, in Kew, in Hampstead
The paths are dry, the ponds dazed with reflections.

Come with me. Look. The city,
Nourished by its poisons, is beautiful in them.
A pearly contamination strokes the river
As cranes ride or dissolve in it,
And the sun dissolves in the hub of its own explosion.

The seconds flare and are gone.
The season is gone that was a long time coming.
Fulfilment is like bread, and
The cornfields lie naked in the burnt shires.
But we must believe the blunt evidence of our senses
As any physicist the map of his calculations,
As any child the reasonable comfort of his mother
That the leaves are beautiful because they are dying,
That the trees are only falling asleep.

The Women

(Halifax, Yorkshire, 1955)

Women, waiting for their husbands,
Sit among dahlias all the afternoons,
While quiet processional seasons
Drift and subside at their doors like dunes,
And echoes of ocean curl from the flowered wall.

The room is a murmuring shell of nothing at all.
As the fire dies under the dahlias, shifting embers
Flake from the silence, thundering when they fall,
And wives who are faithful waken bathed in slumber.
The loud tide breaks and turns to bring them breath.

At five o'clock it flows about their death,
And then the dahlias, whirling
Suddenly to catherine wheels of surf,
Spin on their stems until the shallows sing,
And flower pools gleam like lamps on the lifeless tables.

Flung phosphorescence of dahlias tells
The women time. They wait to be,
Prepared for the moment of inevitable
Good evening when back from the deep, from the mystery,
The tritons return and the women whirl in their sea.

Fen People

They are already old when the fen makes them,
Faces without feature,
Flesh with the mud
And the slatternly weather,
Green water pulled from the weirs.

Fine rain smudges their level years,
Is food for their cabbages,
Smoke for their fires,
Veils for their eyes.
They keep to themselves behind shrouded glass.

Through their low doors no strangers pass.
Their viscid souls
Spawn a dejection
Too flat for pity.
It is not even grief that takes their voices
And leaves them glazed and lost in their houses.

A River
(for Edward Lowbury)

The line between land and water
Forms itself without thought.
Land ends where on the river
No one can walk,
Though the deep, familiar
Path looks hard as silver,
Though land can be held there
Firm in precise inversion
As an eye holds rock.

Neither side of the river
Is a mountain, and no mind
Hesitates, moving from one
Bank to the other,
To cross the line.

Solid boats grow
In the ploughed slime.
Ducks with their hungry beaks
Break the water.

Where's an end to illusion?
Swans, clusters of pale stems,
Finger the air;
Their tuberous bodies
Flower momentarily.
The river is full of fungi,
Its scabby trunk
Breathes sour putrefaction
Out of the fen.

At night, the land slips softly
Into the river in vague
Columns of light, as the line
Between land and water
Forms in the eye
Of any casual observer
Who crosses the line
Between himself and object
Ceaselessly, without thought.

In Middle England

For bungalows,
For weeded parlours,
For trained souls pinched in the bud,
The window boxes apologise.

Amid highbred
Miniature kindnesses,
The spinster gardens
Make polite, inaudible remarks.

Yes, for the
UnEnglish tourist
Who lives without tea
In a terrific country,

Who cannot,
In England, sufficiently
Diminish himself,
The gardens

Are unnecessary
As ubiquitous. The wilted
Curtains, the cold
Mercenary bathrooms,

He thinks,
Would be cheaper without them.
The blossoming carpets
And the teacups

And the shelves of
Useless, ornamental porcelain
Affect, he considers,
The price of his dinner.

He swears
And departs for Madrid.
Later, in Chicago or Dallas,
Will he ever think gently

Of the ladies
Planted in pairs in
Identical houses? Of the
Jars of lilac-coloured soap?

Of the mournful
Decanters full of perfume or
Disinfectant? Of the roses,
The desolate neatness? The despair?

Travelling Behind Glass

Then I spent a long time
living in the mountains
but left them and their silence
unexplored. It was no use
looking to them for mercy.
Caves are not mouths.
Stones are not breasts.
The sun is not an eye.
A scum of blue lichen
may be the only living
possession of the mountains.
Now I am safe behind glass
and driving south.
These are the plains.

How well I know them,
comforters and friends,
miles that unfold and hold me,
warm, wet and hedged
and swarming with vegetables;
fat people, farm people
tuning the land with their ploughs
before playing it,
plucking their fields like instruments.

The valleys repeat until
they are like the sea. They
copy its aerial complexion;
islands of ochre and blue
flatten themselves beneath me
into their map. Surf-like scrub
embroiders the clean continents.
Farmhouses, lighthouses, lie
as if applied by a hand.

I would ask such a sea
to be accommodating,
to warm me, obey me,
accept me like an arm;
in time to release me
entirely, as nothing at all.
As belonging to nothing at all.

I imagine a life here,
felicitous,
a heart at grass,
a mind at ease in its corner;
nothing but at morning and evening
the shadows' predictable crawl
over greenest ground;
seed time and harvest,
in time the night,
and sleep, the good food,
the right nourishment.

And everything could be true:
the walled farmhouses,
the stone bridges,
the towns advancing, daubed,
through washed sunlight;
blown, scudding fragments of crowd
hauled tight by a market-place;
cobblestones lapping,
or floating, a vast cathedral,

possible, until stopping
makes them property:
somebody's chickens and beans,
a countable number of sheep,
telephone wires to the house eaves,
and I with no name in this village,
no one to meet.

                    *

Who is that woman?

That old woman sitting,
no, moving now,
moving her memories...
one black pane, then another,
in the shadow-broken mirror
of her window.

Avoiding her eyes,
I discover my own in her face,
there, beside the parked cars
and passing cars,
between the glass
and the prams gorged with babies;

but never whole babies,
never whole cars;
parts of them missing,
parts of them eaten away
where her room –
or is it my eye? –
has entered with a dresser,
a curtain, a cat
with one haunch through a motorcycle.

I can believe in the cat
and in the motorcycle,
in her and in the
street that intersects her.
But only if the glass were
shattered and the vision
remained could I really
believe in the void between
my time and hers –
in the absence,
pieced out with recollections,
of all her years.

                    *

Sealed in this carapace,
my will
hurtles at seventy,
warm and still
through familiar urban
overspill.
Now and then
some shards, debris,
a tamed, vestigial
century:
gabled mansion,
timbered inn,
salvaged church
in a green pen,
steeple raised
to warn or greet
a city crawling
for its meat,
staccato,
crawling bright and neat,
home to its plural
human street.

                    *

This must be a place to pass through,
on the way somewhere, or away,
Nowhere to make a home in,
though women may have hung
pure passion on the lines,
and men have it in their minds,
come evening, to come back here,
breaking the opaque,
continuously equal membrane
into a solace or anguish of their own.

There is just enough room.
Behind each pair of curtains,
enough and no more,
for the wanting and having,
the having and losing,
for each day keeping its balance
on the shelf between meal and meal,
waking, cooking, eating
to an endless beginning
in the square bed,
trim as a cake or an altar
under its lavender,
cruel as an altar
under its wreath of roses.

And which is the street?
Which the number?
Behind which window
does the woman myself
multiply out of her noon
into three children,
divide and reconstitute
in the flesh of three children
where is just enough room
for this day and the next day,
where the paranoid howl
of the highway
troubles the far side of the glass
without breaking it,
whines behind the frosted window
not touching her at all,
not disturbing for an instant
the monotony of her purpose
or the respectability of her sacrifice?

How easy to accept,
be content
with her invitation...
They were so beautiful,
your children in the park,
rolling down that embankment
into a black knot of rhododendrons.

But how will you describe
the conspicuous hush of the suburbs
when the children have grown up and gone?
Your breasts sag into your ribs.
You dig weeds out of the lawn.
The radio's on.

*

A wider view is this estuary, an entrance.
In the distance,
three erect, steaming chimneys,
part of the steel works;
pylons, six shoulders to each,
six skeletal shivas.

They have taken with indifference
the prim, sacred cities of the old maps,
forcing the small passages.
Mariages de convenance.

A used country, wanting to be used.
Its history, a shell
smashed empty like a castle
on a hill
down which the cracked
chalk ruins spill
an avalanche arrested.
What grovels at the bottom
is a gaggle of roofs.

Cultivate them, children,
play among the roofs as they
creep into their tarred black
necessary pastures.
Between motorway and motorway
and motorway look for a door.

But I have forgotten
what hope it was I came for.
My body's all head,
my two breasts are stones,
and this sun is so dull and estranged
that I know it as a final
dark vision of the valley.

I dreamed I watched
the rubbled pith and core
of a dead, gutted valley
shudder into space
with the candour of any volcano,
while I drove alive and alone
on the oily circumference,
peering at the twittering abyss,
'l'âbime des oiseaux',
until the glass shattered,
into its stars, and stars
scattered, flashing like kingfishers
into the emptiness.

From the Motorway

Everywhere up and down the island
Britain is mending her desert.
Marvellous, we exclaim as we fly on it,
tying the country in a parcel.
London to Edinburgh, Birmingham to Cardiff,
no time to examine the contents,

thank you, but consider the bliss
of sitting absolutely numbed to your
nulled mind, music when you want it,
while identical miles thunder under you,
the same spot coming and going
seventy, eighty times a minute,

till you're there, wherever there
is, ready to be someone in
Liverpool, Leeds, Manchester,
they're all the same to the road,
which loves itself, which nonetheless
here and there hands you trailing

necklaces of fume in which to be
one squeezed breather among
rich and ragged, sprinter and staggerer,
a status parade for Major Roadworks
toiling in his red-trimmed triangle,
then a regiment of wounded orange witches

defending a shamelessly naked
(rarely a stitch of work on her)
captive free lane,
while the inchlings inch on
without bite or sup, at most
a hard shoulder to creep on,

while there, on all sides,
lie your unwrapped destinations,
lanes trickling off into childhood
or anonymity, apple-scented villages
asleep in their promise of being
nowhere anyone would like to get to.

Branch Line

The train is two cars linking
Lincoln and Market Rasen.

Late May. Proof everywhere from
smudged sunny windows
that the European Union
is paying the farmers for rape.

How unembarrassed they are,
wanton patches the colour of heat
dropped like cheap tropical skirts
on the proper wolds.

The trees have almost completely
put on their clothes.
They sway in green crinolines,
new cool generous Eves.

The hawthorn-snow
looks predictably cold, unclenching.

As the train parts green field from gold
a spray of peewits fans up in a bow wave.

Is that a new factory out there
where the sea might be?
A lighthouse? A tall methane candle,
lethal if it were to go out?

The train slowly judders and halts
for no visible reason.

Rooks squabble in a maple.
A blackbird ferries an enormous worm to a nest.
Staring cows bend again to their munching.

Meaningless life, I'm reading in the TLS,
a nexus of competing purposes...

God is impossible.

Life is impossible.

But here it is.

A Tourists' Guide to the Fens

Level Cambridgshire, islands
of England
apportioned by drain and motorway;

dolls-house villages that have lost
their childhood;
roses called *peace* and *blessing*

exclusive to frilly white cottages
under pie-crust thatch.

Can you hear it?
The wind? Or traffic?

The low-hummed roar of saurian lorries
and a soughing avenue of 18th-century limes
sound the same.

In another film,
the heroine escapes with the hero
into rural Cambridgeshire *circa* 1666...

A field of barley, feathered;
a fen full of sky-blue butterfly flax,
undulations like the ocean's

rolling right up to the cameraman's
pollen-dusted loafers.
And when Anthea sets up her easel

to catch in watercolour
a picturesque angle of the almshouses,
she scrupulously omits

electrical wiring and TV paraphernalia
that, in strange time, connect her to

'the brutish, uncivilised tempers of these parts'...
the cottagers' corpses stinking,
unburied by the furrows,

Christ's men in retreat
at the Fever House at Malton,

'there to tarry in time of contagious
sickness at Cambridge
and exercise their learning and studies

until such time
as God pleased to make the city
safe again for commerce and superior minds'.

Coming Back to Cambridge
(England, 1971)

Casual, almost unnoticeable,
it happens every time you return.
Somewhere along the flat road in
you lose to voluptuous levels
between signposts to unnecessary dozing villages
every ghost of yourself but Cambridge.
Somewhere – by Fen Drayton or Dry Drayton,
by the finger pointing aimlessly to Over –
you slip into a skin that lives
perpetually in Cambridge.

It knows where you are.

As you drive you watch a workman
wheel a bicycle around a stile,
hump onto the saddle and
ride off past a field of cows.
A few stop chewing to stare.
And you know where you are even before
the landmarks (beautiful to the excluded)
begin to accumulate.
The stump of the Library.
The lupin spire of the Catholic Church.
Four spikey blossoms on King's.
The Round Church, a mushroom in this
forest of Gothic and traffic and
roses too perfect to look alive.

The river is the same – conceited,
historic, full of the young.
The streets are the same. And around them
the same figures, the same cast with a
change of actors, move as if concentric
to a radiance without location.
The pupils of their eyes glide sideways,
apprehensive of martyrdom to which
they might not be central.
They can never be sure.
Great elations could be happening without them.

And just as the hurrying, preoccupied dons
tread the elevations of their detachment and yet
preserve an air of needing to be protected,
so, also, these wives choosing vegetables in the market,
these schoolchildren in squadrons,
these continental girl-friends and black men,
these beards, these bicycles, these
skinny boys fishing, these lovers of the pubs,
these lovers of the choirboys, these intense shrill
ladies and gaunt, fanatical burnt out old women
are all more than this. Arrogant.
Within the compass of wistfulness.

Nothing that really matters really exists.

But the statues are alive.
You can walk in and out of the picture.
Though the mild façades harden before and
behind you like stereographs, within them
there is much to be taken for granted.
Meals and quarrels, passions and inequalities.
A city like any other, were it not for the
order at the centre and the high
invisible bridge it is built upon,
with its immense views of an intelligible human landscape
into which you never look without longing to enter;
into which you never fall without the curious struggle back.

* * *

Temporarily in Oxford

Where they will bury me
I don't know.
Many places might not be
sorry to store me.

The Midwest has right of origin.
Already it has welcomed my mother
to its flat sheets.

The English fens that bore me
have been close curiously often.
It seems I can't get away from
dampness and learning.

If I stay where I am
I could sleep in this educated earth.

But if they are kind, they'll burn me
and send me to Vermont.

I'd be an education for the trees
and would relish, really,
flaring into maple each October –
my scarlet letter to you.

Your stormy north is possible.
You will be there, engrossed in its peat.

It would be handy not
to have to cross the whole Atlantic
each time I wanted to
lift up the turf and slip in beside you.

Lockkeeper's Island

It is late, but as usual
we will turn away from sleep
and walk by the river.

The houses will withdraw as usual,
seeming to be blind.
The path will seem more dangerous,
flooded with shadows,

crossing the narrow footbridge
over the slipstream,
crossing the inflicted hurry of the weir,
crossing to the lockkeeper's
gated, moated island,
meeting the river's divided darkness there.

We will not talk at all, but as usual
my hand will say to yours,
'A river in the middle of an island
is that island's island, alien element,
daring the tedium of the safe.'

You'll observe, under Orion,
how an island at the centre of a river
is the pupil of its eye.

Everything will be silent on the island
except for the sliding water.
The lockkeeper will be sleeping.
His dog, his wife, his name, his discontents –
they will be silent and asleep.

Only the eye will be awake as usual,
keeping watch on the source,
keeping open a vein of the sea's
dangerous protection,

wild water, out-poured, sluiced forth,
declaring this winter one island between
summer and summer, this night, one island
in an archipelago of nights, this city,
one perilous island set lightly on gold
quivering pillars of itself.

Above the lockkeeper's island,
the absolute moon –
dry island among inaccessible islands –
will drag its magnet,
force its connections.

Between moon and water,
consoling machinery of the land.
No moon will bless this place,
or the houses on it,
or this black latticework of derricks,
or these bridges shaken by trains,
their arguments with darkness.

'Blessing' is a word of ours.

Though nothing will have changed
when we turn away from the river
to the sacrament of sleep.

By the Boat House, Oxford

They belong here in their own quenched country.
I had forgotten nice women could be so nice,
smiling beside large sons on the makeshift quay,
frail, behind pale faces and hurt eyes.

Their husbands are plainly superior, with them, without them.
Their boys wear privilege like a clean inheritance, easily.
(Now a swan's neck couples with its own reflection,
making in the simple water a perfect 3.)

The punts seem resigned to an unexciting mooring.
But the women? It's hard to tell. Do their fine grey hairs
and filament lips approve or disdain the loving
that living alone, or else lonely in pairs, impairs?

Walking Early by the Wye

Through dawn in February's wincing radiance,
every splinter of river mist
rayed in my eyes.

As if the squint of the sun had released light's
metals. As if the river pulsed white,
and the holly's

sharp green lacquered leaves leaped acetylene.
As if the air smouldered from the ice of dry
pain, as if day

were fragmented in doubt. As if it were given
to enter alive the braided rings Saturn
is known by

and yet be allied to the dyke's heaped mud.
I will not forget how the ash trees stood,
silvered and still,

how each soft stone on its near shadow knelt,
how the sheep became stones where they built
their pearled hill.

Burnished

(A Riddle)

Walking out of Hay in the rain, imagining Blake
imagining his own world into existence,
I suddenly turned on him and said with energy,
'How dare you inflict imagination on us!' And he,
'Let worlds die burnished as along this bank.'

'Beautiful,' I said to him, and to a new world
oiled by a cloud, still wet, in its spiny shell.
A gloss of red horse's flank shone in its name.
To hold, it was a smooth pebble
mountain water had been running over. Sculpted round,
it swam like an embryo in my palm.

'Now close your eyes.' I felt the whole world warmed.
It was breathing its native heat in my blind skin.
When I looked again, it was a leather ocean
lapping a small sandy island. No one
appeared to live there. Now where its gleam had been
is a breast with a shrivelled nipple, like a dry wound.*

* A conker, or horse chestnut.

65

Himalayan Balsam

Orchid-lipped, loose-jointed, purplish, indolent flowers,
with a ripe smell of peaches, like a girl's breath through lipstick,
delicate and coarse in the weedlap of late summer rivers,
dishevelled, weak-stemmed, common as brambles, as love which

subtracts us from seasons, their courtships and murders,
(*Meta segmentata* in her web, and the male waiting,
between blossom and violent blossom, meticulous spiders
repeated in gossamer, and the slim males waiting).

Fragrance too rich for keeping, too light to remember,
like grief for the cat's sparrow and the wild gull's
beach-hatched embryo. (She ran from the reaching water
with the broken egg in her hand, but the clamped bill

refused brandy and grubs, a shred too naked and perilous for
life, offered freely in cardboard boxes, little windowsill
coffins for bird death, kitten death, squirrel death, summer
repeated and ended in heartbreak, in sad small funerals.)

Sometimes, shaping bread or scraping potatoes for supper,
I have stood in the kitchen, transfixed by what I'd call love,
if love were a whiff, a wanting for no particular lover,
no child, or baby, or creature. 'Love, dear love,'

I could cry to these scent-spilling ragged flowers,
and mean nothing but 'no', in that word's breath,
to their evident going, their important descent through red towering
stalks to the riverbed. It's not, as I thought, that death

creates love. More that love knows death. Therefore
tears, therefore poems, therefore long stone sobs of cathedrals
that speak to no ferret or fox, that prevent no massacre.
(I am combing abundant leaves from these icy shallows.)

Love, it was you who said, 'Murder the killer
we have to call life and we'd be a bare planet under a dead sun.'
Then I loved you with the usual soft lust of October
that says 'yes' to the coming winter and a summoning odour of balsam.

Whose Goat?

Broken bleats
from a half-built house
by the reefy unfeeling river
prefigure goat.

Where? Whose goat?

Who'd wall a goat up in cinderblocks?
A kind of goat closet full of hairy,
shadowy, strawy, obstinate
hopelessness of goat.

Only a kid, really, but mammy and
all other times undone,
unhappened for her
in the huge push to get out.

So I grieve for her and her
sore forked head
rattling wire mesh like machinery,
for the pale hurt muzzle
pleading between pearl hooves.

It's beech I poke into the helpless
loop of her mouth. She meets
my labrador nostril to nostril, but
they breathe different languages.

I look my own language deep into the well
beneath the letter-box-black slit
in the gold mandala of her eye.
It finds a goat's ghost there,
lonely as snow. She's not
my goat, she's not my goat.

Somebody's collar of hospitality
is called 'I love that goat'.
Somebody's notion of living in the country
is building their own house slowly,
slowly around their own goat.

Earth Station

(Goonhilly Downs)

Tumuli, not hills. Cold earthheaps
with men and women in them,
femurs, teeth, four thousand years old;
easy to consider.

Unlike this briar with its punishing straps
drawing stripes on my reddening wrists now.
Unlike your bootlength, hesitant steps
into unstitched heather.

The wind will not be revealed as wind
until it's story. We say it was
'so strong we had to lean on it to stand'.
But really weather is now.

And it's now we can't know.
We can't hold what we feel,
only say that we felt. And so
learn to suffer.

Two huge silent heads turn away
from this trouble, trained by our needs
not to need, not to feel.
Their commitment to other places?

Easy to consider: earthhopes
with men and women in them,
Philadelphia? California? Dial 0101...

Purr goes the receiver.

Purr purr. Purr purr.

Goonhilly Downs is satellite station in Cornwall; also an iron age burial ground.

The Wrekin

(a version from the Welsh of Dewi Stephen Jones)

Overnight it climbs like a snail
    to a corner of the window,
so that the sun each day
    greets a new form of the same animal.
A birth mound. A tumulus,
    neither watch tower nor turret;
more a muscle slewed to the south-east
    hiding its rounded horns.

I examine a homely shape
    slumped in its shell,
a foot stuck fast to the window pane,
    a slipper clamped in a shackle.
And when night arrives to prise it loose,
    I imagine it sliding back softly
along a wet, silvery track
    to a tunnel in the dark.

For coming and going is its nature,
    like the nature of the coming-and-going
generations who built and bred here,
    leaving raw fingerprints on the land:
  hunters, cultivators, destroyers,
    spillers of blood and seed,
brothers and enemies. Stone, bronze and iron
    precipitates of history.

An omphalos, then, a centre that to many
    was barrow and womb,
threshold for the long perished living,
    household for the ever-present dead.
So the river flows on to the sea,
    and between myself
and the ocean of air above me
    red elder berries shake in the wind.

How long has the mountain been an eye
    fixed above the human flow,
constant through continual change? MARS ULTOR
    stamped on the sestertius;
the Roman villa's buried shrine to Venus,
    traces of a tessellated floor.
Civilisation ghosts the wreck of Uricon,
    a dragon heart incarnadine with war.

Shall we say that at a turning point in history
        a Mount of Olives rose
above our plains? Is it Golgotha again
        where Heledd, in her grief,
was Mary Magdalene? How far or near
        is the mountain on the rim of the world?
What would our lowland lives be like
        without its frame?

Look out again this morning,
        it's a print on dirty canvas,
a stone bridge out of pre-history,
        coloured thickbrown; peat smoke
cresting the ridge and drifting down,
        a shape detached, displaced,
one of my own vertebrae,
        an unearthed bone.

But no, look again, see how
        the heavy lowered eyelid
of the cloud has lifted now.
        And that's the sun,
it must be sunlight striking straight
        down on the rock face,
lighting fires of pure annihilation
        like a lens.

But gifting me with insight, too,
        so I see the mountain,
the circumference of my own small life,
        consumed, extinguished
on my shore; my ocean purged of stars.
        One day I'll set my prow,
strip off my longings, cut the anchor line and go.
        See, I'm almost naked now.

* * *

Binoculars in Ardudwy

(North Wales, 1990)

A lean season, March, for ewes
who all winter camped on the hills.
They're gathered in now to give birth
to children more cheerful than themselves.

There's a farmer, Land Rover, black dog
trotting, now rolling on his back.
At the gate, sheep bunched – one alone
drifting down the steep Cambrian track.

Look now, the sun's reached out,
painting turf over ice-smoothed stone.
A green much younger than that
praises *Twll-nant* and *Pen-isa'r-cwm*.

All this through the lens of a noose
I hold to my focusing eyes,
hauling hill, yard, barn, man, house
and a line of blown washing across

a mile of diluvian marsh.
I see every reed, rust-copper,
and a fattened S-bend of the river.
Then, just as I frame it, the farm

wraps its windows in lichenous weather
and buries itself in its tongue.
Not my eyes but my language is wrong.
And the cloud is between us forever.

Under cover of mist and myth
the pieced fields whisper together,
'Find invisible *Maes-y-garnedd*...,
Y Llethr...*Foel Ddu*...*Foel Wen*.'

The Unaccommodated

Like winter in the hills, the heft of their
lingering, still unburied shadows
in the wind's hoarse uprush
out of heaps of rock they lived in.
     Millennia later,
houses rise stone by stone, neighbour
by aching neighbour; impenitent webs of wall
     from the haunted spills.

Sickness in the dark they lived in.
Candlelight hoarding sweet secrets
     in the mice's corners.
Girls giving birth by rushlight.
The same fires set by the dead
in a theatre of cheekbones and foreheads;
a hand through the night, stitching cloth
     with a stiff thread.

Just as constant, the cold they lived in,
each minute paid down on an open Bible
     one by one by one
in hard brass grudged by the pendulum.
Firelight is the lurch of a hummed,
     lambent, discontinuous meditation,
nimbus of their voices and table talk.
Flick off the mains and you'll be them.

Phoenicurus phoenicurus

Phu-eet! Phu-eet! Mr unresting redstart has something to be
anxious about. A nest of eggs? Babies? Or has he
lost them already to the weasel, scared away yesterday,

slithering (guilty? sinister?) out of a rock hole?
Phu-eet, on and on, a tiny, uptilted, not really hysterical
shriek. Greeting his mate on top of the clothes pole…

gone. Divers? No, rust-tinted streamers, each, so to speak,
with an end of invisible raffia in its beak.
So where is the camouflaged nook or lichenous crack

that has to be wicker-worked, netted inside those flights?
Such showy displays and flash, panic-coloured lights.
Calm down, pretty bird! You've been gulping big bites

from my reading and writing all morning. Stay still!
What wars do you have to survive, with your phoenix tail
in all that Darwinian weather, too small, too frail?

Snug in my nest of vocabularies, safe in my view,
I've had to jump up three, four times, just to
tell Something Awful out there to be careful of you.

Phu-eet, a more and more panicky piping, *phu-eet*!
And not meaning anything I mean. In the grammar of *tweet*
why did we ever say birds should sound *sweet, sweet*?

Pity the Birds

(for Charles Elvin who said, 'Poetry should protest')

Pity
the persistent clamour of a song thrush
I can't see;
the gull's vacant wail, its sea-saw
yodel of injury;
that black and white wagtail bobbing
for a meal of midges;
rapacious Mrs Blackbird shopping on foot
in the hedges;
even yesterday's warbler, lying stiff on the step
to the barn,
olive green wings torn awry by the wind,
eyes gone,
but with tri-clawed reptilian feet still
hungrily curled.

Not one of them gened to protest
against the world.

A Present

(for Lee Harwood)

A grey undecided morning.
No wind.
It's cold, so get dressed quickly.
Step out into the new born air.
Look around.
It's yours, this shifting misty envelope,
a hospital to breathe in,
along with chaffinches and great tits
queueing for the wire feeder;
on the lichened wall beneath,
dunnocks make do with titbits.
Now a thrush in concentrated rushes
combs the pasture.
Those sheep-bitten daffodils
poke up, you'd say, out of nowhere,
though moles know
what's going on down there,
rebuilding under their slagheaps
a secret city.

But your secret's up in the hills,
so pull on your socks, boots, woolly hat
and layers of windproofing.
Fill up your thermos, shoulder your pack.
The ice age planed these mountains down for you
too many millennia ago to be
reasonably thanked.
They're a gift, like your life,
that never thought to be a life.
Moelfre, Rhinog Fawr, Y Llethr, Diphwys,
bald monitors bearded with cloud,
at rest in their Welsh nomenclature.

And like living things, old.
So old they're not likely to look older
when one day you don't remember them;
when lovers and readers you can't know about
get up at six or seven on chill winter mornings
to greet them, choosing, maybe,
certain words of yours to remember you.

Here's a present, the gift of a perfect view
straight back to a future that,
despite the computer, won't change in a hurry.
Shall I tell you what happened
in mid-February, 2099?
A soft cloud clung to the summit of Foel Ddu.
The next day, thickening, it crept down,
and as the wind backed to the east,
veered south, west and north-west,
hail, sleet, sunburst and snow flurry
gave pleasure to a lonely walker, cold
but happy on the high ground,
as the sun handed him a hillside,
bright as ever green moss
shone over stone in the bronze age.
The story in the marsh was a long memory
retelling itself in a shower of gold.

The Wind, the Sun and the Moon

For weeks the wind has been talking to us,
Swearing, imploring, singing like a person.
Not a person, more the noise a being might make
Searching for a body and a name. The sun
In its polished aurora rises late, then dazzles
Our eyes and days, pacing a bronze horizon
To a mauve bed in the sea. Light kindles the hills,
Though in the long shadow of Moelfre, winter
Won't unshackle the dead house by the marsh.
Putting these words on paper after sunset
Alters the length and asperity of night.
By the fire, when the wind pauses, little is said.
Every phrase we unfold stands upright. Outside,
The visible cold, the therapy of moonlight.

Under Moelfre
A poem for a marriage

Whatever it is we share with folds of rock
Is nowhere to own and doesn't own a name.
Its hug was ours before we learned to talk.
When we stop speaking, it will be the same,
For all our anxious bustling and assessing.

Sense says there's only us, the way we dither
Plan, write poems, seriously discuss.
When man and woman come to live together,
Why invoke the presence of a place?
Unless the place, responsive to hard pressing,

Carries in ice age crevices some spoor,
Some truth the planet cherishes, or seed,
That finds a future in the years before.
Deep age in rock, like weather, meets our need
And blesses when it doesn't know it's blessing.

(for Lisa & Fred, and to Sim and Arnold)

Attacking the Waterfall

Curlews long gone from the valley,
and now swallows that used to swoop
and then again swoop,
lightening the load of the sky,
are this summer so few
that the thrill of their sighting,
just one? no, two, is a flicker of hope,
a flare marginal to their dying –
though the rhaeadr still quarrels intimately
with its mountains,
skirmishing, water against water, quick time;
slow time with the sloth of stones.

As a hemisphere skews towards the sun,
the cwm competes, clock time, against migrants
raring to have fun.
Up, counter to the cataract, they swarm,
warrior ants in wetsuits and cocky helmets,
gutsy, braggish, betting on their luck,
pitching their rise against a fall mad Adam
fancied was his own.
For sure, the fall is nature's.
Listen! The old man's raging on. *Shit! Fuck!*
ricochet from the battleground – gunshot,
or a fighter plane, maybe, testing the barriers.

Why Take Against Mythology (1)

That twilight skyline, for example,
the more I look at it,
the more I see a skull
crushed into the hill, nose
chipped flat, jaw
thrust up, full bush of
genitals stirring just
in the right place.

See him? No, stand
here, clear of the house.
Uncork a magnum
of imagination, man!
Inflame your heart
with my enchanted giant.
Figure his resurrection
in your dreams, or art,

But make him art, not fact.
For when daylight comes back
it will tear him apart.
And how could I love,
dear, a Wales
made of ice-cut rock? No tales
in the making of mountains,
no mind in the dark?

Why Take Against Mythology (2)

Why, love, do you persist
in personifying natural events?
That's not imagination, it's arrogance,
locating fate in stars, off-loading
guilt on rocks that were liquid once
eons before our first
purposeless cells
commenced their crawl.

You like to imagine?
Imagine nuclei moiling themselves
alive in steamy crevices,
continents travelling and clashing.
Then, three miles high, a grinding
plain of ice, a Pleistocene caul,
gouging, sculpting, furrowing
this scoop of valley.

Before art, lichens delicately
etched that cliff-face.
Millions of millennia formed
bracken, heather, gorse.
Facts? They'll be minted by imagination
once daft mankind
stops conjuring out of mass and force
false spirit-shadows of his own mind.

Spring Poem
(for John Heath-Stubbs)

Language raked tribute from her screen all winter,
but now comes a day in spring when restless Eve
runs out of words to commit to her lord computer
and in neglect of her career, plays diligently
and with delight on the vacuum cleaner:

Let Cambria vouchsafe to her hard unloving hills
a sharp green glance of enchantment.
Let daffodils be scrubbed until they shine.
Let windows crack open and kick back the April sun.

Let be, let be, too eloquent Eve.
Give up newfangledness for nourishment.

Without Me

A north wind light this morning.
Who will watch it
gilding the hennas of the marsh?
Between the iron gate's upright
and its top rung
death's in her diamond collar.
And if ewes last night
laid glistening pebbles, the pasture
will be pointillist with dung,
with burnished dung-flies busily feeding.

After heavy rain, a flood of sun,
but not for me the rainbows hanging
one   one   one
from lines of crooked fencing
that will rust by noon.
Now, what's that shadow by the pigsty
pecking, looking, pecking?
Fly away, silly bird, fly!
Whose pasture will be grazing
on your white bones soon?

May Bluebells, Coed Aber Artro

No Greek self-pitying hetairos in blue-rinse curls,
       the north's true Hyacinthus non-scriptus
(much written about, nonetheless),
       beloved of Hopkins, who in Hodder Wood
perfectly caught its 'level shire of colour'
       while his companions talked.

West Country 'Crowfoot' or 'Grammer Graegles',
       in Welsh translated 'Cookoo's Boot',
'Blue of the Wood', 'Welcome Summer',
       each silky delicate bell-stalk
carrying its carillon to one side,
       dusky wine-cups, ringers of creamy anthers,
in Cymbeline misnamed 'the azured harebell'
       by Arviragus...

And even in our time,
       self-assigned to resurrection.
Camping gas set burning
       at the lowest visible flame.
Ice-age giant still nourishing
       the trodden mulch and green enchantment
of his daughter beechwood, watering
       one more summer out of hazy veins.

Leaving

Habits the hands have, reaching for this and that,
    (tea kettle, orange squeezer, milk jug,
    frying pan, sugar jar, coffee mug)
manipulate, or make, a habitat,
become its *genii loci*, working on
quietly in the kitchen when you've gone.

Objects a house keeps safe on hooks and shelves
    (climbing boots, garden tools, backpacks
    bird feeders, tennis balls, anoraks)
the day you leave them bleakly to themselves,
do they decide how long, behind the door,
to keep your personality in store?

Good Bishop Berkeley made the objects stay
just where we leave them when we go away
by lending them to God. If so, God's mind
is crammed with things abandoned by mankind
    (featherbeds, chamber pots, flint lighters,
    quill pens, sealing wax, typewriters),

an archive of the infinitely there.
But there for whom? For what museum? And where?
I like to think of spiders, moths, white worms
leading their natural lives in empty rooms
    (egg-sacks, mouse-litter, dead flies,
    cobwebs, silverfish, small eyes)

while my possessions cease to study me
    (*Emma, The Signet Shakespeare, Saving Whales.*
    Living with Mushrooms, Leviathan, Wild Wales).
Habit by habit, they sink through time to be
one with the mind or instinct of the place,
home in its shadowy silence and stone space.

*   *   *

Pennine

Hills? Or a high plateau scissored by rivers?
Strong as grass, a winter's crop of stones
Craters the drive. The black paths trickle.
Randomly, fells erupt in armoured cliffs
That might be houses – might, in this cloud, be
Slack, grit, slag, moss, a memory of mills.

Everything trains to the perpendicular.
Trees stand taller on one green root than another.
The village is slabbed like steps into its slope,
The churchyard paved with graves, thronged with unbalanced
Mitred headstones, an asylum of bishops. The dead
are unsafe. Their graves hardly hold them.

Victorian conscience breathes over church and ruin
A slatey rain. Whoever sent a dove
To star the cross where Thomas Holinrake's buried
Guessed that its message needed marble.
Feathers and blood stab at the lichened walls,
Stonefalls crossing in their long decline.

Shale

that comes to pieces in your hand
like stale biscuit; birth book
how many million years
left out in the rain. Break back

the pages, the flaking pages,
to reveal our own hairline habitations,
the airless museum in which we're
still chained into that still ocean,

while all this burly and stirring water –
motion in monotonous repetition –
washes with silt our Jurassic numbness,
shelves of ourselves to which we will not return.

Bedded in shale, in its negative evidence,
this Venus shell is small – as maybe she was.
The fan-shaped tracery of vertical ridges
could be fine-spread, radiant hair,

or proof of what we take to be
her temper: hot sluttishness loosened
by accident into cold mudslide,
preserving a hated symmetry, a hated elegance.

There is so little sheltered, kept, little
and frail, broken in excavation, half
buried, half broken, poor real child in the boulder
that finds the right shape of its mind

only at the moment of disintegration.
And yet, – this clear cuneiform in rock,
this sea urchin humping its flower under
'low flying phantoms' – this flowing anemone.

A Prayer to Live with Real People

Let me not live, ever, without fat people,
the marshmallow flesh set thick on the muscular bone,
the silk white perms of sweet sixteen-stone ladies,
luscious as pom-poms or full blown perfumed magnolias,
breasts like cottage loaves dropped into lace-knit sweaters,
all cream-bun arms and bottoms in sticky leathers.
O Russian dolls, O range of hills
rosy behind the glo-green park of the pool table,
thorns are not neater or sharper than your delicate shoes.

Let me not live, ever, without pub people,
the tattooed forearm steering the cue like a pencil,
the twelve-pint belly who adds up the scores in his head,
the wiry owner of whippets, the keeper of ferrets,
thin wives who suffer, who are silent, who talk with their eyes,
the girl who's discovered that sex is for she who tries.
O zebra blouse, O vampish back
blown like a lily from the swaying stalk of your skirt,
roses are not more ruthless than your silver-pink lipstick.

And let me live, always and forever among neighbours like these
who order their year by the dates of the leek competitions,
who care sacrificially for Jack Russell terriers and pigeons,
who read very carefully captions in *The Advertiser* and *Echo*
which record their successes and successes of teams they support,
whose daughters grow up and marry friends' boys from Crook.
O wedding gifts, O porcelain flowers
twined on their vases under the lace-lipped curtains
save me from Habitat, and snobbery and too damn much literary ambition.

Household Gods

The room is silent except for the two hearth spirits.

The fire speaks out of the grate like a kindly tongue.
The man speaks out of the square screen like a god.

The fire burns slowly, holding itself back from burning.
The man speaks quickly, hurtling himself into particles.

Hold up your hands to the fire, and they, too, are fires.
Hold your hand up to the screen and feel the premises of illusion.

Wherever you move, the fire pulls you close like a magnet.
Wherever you look, the screen intercepts your escape.

When the fire is worshipped, the resident cats will pray with you.
When the screen presides, it lashes the dog with its scream.

The fire has nothing to tell you; it waits for your thoughts.
The screen has to tell you everything except what you are.

In heaven, they will give you to fire to be consumed into freedom.
In hell, they will play you over and over on the tape of your dead life.

In hell, nothing you have done will be not watched.

Forgotten of the Foot

(Langley Park, County Durham, 1983-84)

Equisetum, horsetail, railway weed
Laid down in the unconscious of the hills;
Three hundred million years still buried

In this hair-soft surviving growth that kills
Everything in the glorious garden except itself,
That thrives on starvation, and distils

Black diamonds, the carboniferous shelf –
That was life before our animals,
With trilobite and coelacanth,

A stratum of compressed time that tells
Truth without language and is the body store
Of fire, heat, night without intervals –

That becomes people's living only when strange air
Fills out the folded lungs, the inert corpuscles.
Into the mute dark, light crawls once more.

*

So the hills must be pillaged and cored.
Such history as they hide must be hacked out
Urgent as money, the buried black seams uncovered.

Rows of stunted houses under the smoke,
Soot black houses pressed back hard against pit
By fog, by smoke, by a cobra hood of smouldering coke

Swayed from the nest of ovens huddled opposite.
Families, seven or ten to a household,
Growing up, breathing it, becoming it.

On winter mornings, grey capped men in the cold,
Clatter of boots on tarmac, sharp and empty,
First shift out in thick frost simple as gold

On the sulphurous roofs, on the stilted gantry,
Crossing to engine house and winding gear –
Helmet, pick, lamp, tin bottle of tea.

*

A Nan or Nora slave to each black grate.
Washing on Monday, the water grimed in its well.
Iron and clean on Tuesday, roll out and bake

Each Wednesday (that sweet bituminous smell
No child who grew up here forgets).
Thursdays, the Union and the Methodist Circle;

Fishday on Friday (fryday), a queue of kids,
Thin, squabbling by the chippy. Resurfaced quarrels
After pay day – hard drinking and broken heads.

Wheels within wheels, an England of working Ezekiels.
Between slag-heaps, coke-tarns and black sludgy leavings,
Forges roaring and reddening, hot irons glowing like jewels.

No more, no more. They've swept up the workings
As if they were never meant to be part of memory.
A once way of being. A dead place. Hard livings

That won't return, grim tales forgot as soon as told,
Streaming from the roofs in smoke from a lost century –
A veil of breath in which to survive the cold.

*

When the mine's shut down, habits prolong the story,
Habits and voices, till grandmothers' old ways pass,
And the terraces fold into themselves, so black, ugly

And unloved that all but the saved (success
Has spared them, the angel of death-by-money) move away.
The town's inhabited by alien, washed up innocents.

Children and animals, people too poor to stay
Anywhere else, stray, dazed, into this slum of Eden.
The church is without saints or statuary.

The memorial is a pick, a hammer, a shovel, given
By the men of Harvey Seam and Victoria Seam. May
Their good bones wake in the living seams of Heaven.

He breaketh open a shaft away from where men sojourn.
*They are forgotten of the foot that passeth by.**

* Job 28.4: The inscription on the Miners' Memorial in Durham Cathedral.

Demolition

(Langley Park, Durham)

They have blown up the old brick bridge
connecting the coal works with the coke works.
Useful and unimposing,
it was ever a chapel of small waters,
a graceful arch toothworked with
yellow bricks notched into red bricks,
reflecting there sudden bright winks
from the Browney – an oval asymmetrical image
that must have delighted, as fisher-children,
these shiftless, solid grey men
who follow so closely the toil of its demolition.

The digger's head drops and grates, now swings up,
yellow fangs slavering rubble and purple brickdust.
Its watchers wear the same grave, equivocal expression.
They might be grieving
(their fathers built it, or their fathers' fathers).
Or they might be meaning
Boys won't be going to the mine no more.
Best do away with what's not needed.
That's Jock Munsey's lad in the cab there, surely.
Good job it's at home, not away on the telly.

Spring Song

The sun is warm,
and the house in the sun
is filthy:

grime like permanent fog
        on the soot-framed windowpanes,
dust, imprinted with cats' feet,
        on the lid of the hi-fi,
dishes on the dresser
        in a deepening plush of disuse,
books on the blackened shelves
        bearing in the cusps of their pages
a stripe of mourning.

The sun is warm,
the dust motes and dust mice
are dancing.

The ivies are pushing green tongues
        from their charcoal tentacles,
the fire is reduced to a
        smoky lamp in a cave.
Soon it will be spring, sweet spring,
        and I will take pleasure in spending
many hours and days out of doors,
        away from the chores and bores
        of these filthy things.

November

All saints and all souls,
martyrdom of the good days.
Daylight is smoke out of the dark's bonfire.
An old sun huddles in unclean caves.
But here, anyway, is this step,
now another step.
In imaginary fields, a tractor
sputters with purposes.
As black coal in our black grate
ignites in uncertain tongues,
birch-blaze thins over clinker
where the coke works were.

From My Study

(Langley Park, Durham, 1990)

With the hot sun palming my back
like a good therapist,
kneading softly through this
unwashed window, with its
view of stout chimneys
threading smoke in cat-tails,
a maypole of wires joining
pebble-dashed houses, shared roofs
shrunken under frost far whiter
than my neighbour's sagging line
of T-shirts, underwear, sheets
windlessly insisting on their
owners being indoors
cooking dinner, or shambling outdoors
over streets the ice-fur
never quite relinquishes;
old men with old dogs
converging by luck or accident
at corner shops or lamp posts,
huddling, stamping,
huffing on blue nails,
their small warm talk
condensed in vapour trails,

I can't help being again
caught up in it, the marvellous
banality of seeing as it is
the on-going act – just exactly what
slips by our whole attempt to grab it,
press it from living into paying,
the sitcom nobody witnesses, that isn't
funny, except as the real thing
can be funny: Chris in our
alleyway of decrepit fences,
carrying his speakers, mike
and recording equipment carefully
from Pat's house to Jenny's,
and the next day,
moving it all back again from
Jenny's into Pat's – okay,
in the end, even Chris
thought it was funny.

And there's, don't forget it,
the unfunny – call it dead,
grinding nothing-to-do
the lads won't tolerate,
gathering in twos, in sixes and sevens,
to slouch in front of Spar,
sharing fags by the memorial's
grey sodden poppies –
you can't say enough in graffiti,
SPAZ, THE CRAZIES, SPUNK, WE HATE PIGS,
the language of hopelessness
has to keep moving.

Arrive with one husband,
skedaddle with another, it won't
go unremarked, but in Langley Park,
where's the accusing finger?
Keeping whispers under wraps –
it's a local folk-art;
the very vicars bicycle in married
and stumble out divorced.
With the century in terminal
spate, a trickle of "life style"
does finally creep
even here, through the coal dust,
lifting a scum of ash
from the lookalike yards,
cats in, cats out, disputing
each other's flowertubs;
each soiled day arriving,
tea-coloured, sulky,
breaking over, sweeping away
thread by blackened thread
from the enduring village
its clinging web of
history, coal
and its abandonment,
three, four generations
survived by rooms
like this one, two
up, two down, the same
continuous roof
on the teeming furrow,
protective of family television
and microwave convenience cooking;
impregnable air-raid cement
converted into bathrooms,

the netties knocked down now,
rebuilt as garages, dark-rooms,
workshops, potting sheds.

Not, of course, affecting these
fine winter mornings, ice locking
puddles into pleasurable pockets,
the estate running out
along the doggy uprooted railway
where Compass Motorhomes & fumes
have colonised the cokeworks –
ribboning through the playground,
the football field, the allotments –
shacks, goats, cabbages, onions,
pigeons, unsavoury ponies –
out into the green, medicinal
half-planted country;
fountains of hawthorn looking
festive with plastic, unravelled
cassette-tapes, sweet-wrappers,
crisp-wrappers, non-reusable hardware
dumped by refurbishing households,
whose high-pitched runabout kids
gun each other down
from the war's dead bunkers.

Why does that flock of jackdaws
lift in a body –
a black knotted old-fashioned veil
floating from an aunt's green hat –
now it settles in a dingier field.

Why settle for it? Why here,
with the walking wounded?
Langley Park. Theme park
on the art of failure
for the left-behind,
the old, the stubborn,
the unlucky, the resentful, the gifted
who don't fit into the times, the shifty
poacher who nails up his catch
in his shed, Jim, for how long
invalided out, shut up in himself,
in his dignity,
while friendly Alice puckers
with gossip, who used to work
in the meat factory, coming home,

bags full of it, to cook and grin
and marry three peony daughters
on a lifetime's savings.

Choose Langley Park and hunch
in the weather of failure,
wind that blows whiningly
as failure, rain that falls
steadily, unforgivingly, the sort of
failure that lets you off towards evening,
telling you plainly that
somebody famous you used to
dream of becoming
never, of course, will become.
Just the same,
the day can be got through,
filthy air, filthy everything,
the sun splashing special effects
behind the pylons, the Ram's Head open,
pumps bowing, Guinness overflowing.
Gary wipes the glasses and plugs in
the organ. The TV streams on.
Linda, in heels, jeans and a sleeveless
plunging neckline, shivers at the bus-stop.
Ray donates mixed grills –
chops and blood-puddings for six –
to the charity raffle,
to which James contributes, framed,
four exquisitely engraved
meditations on landscape.

A place to fall back to, thanks,
when you've paid your youth for
visions in the Himalayas. Or when, at 40,
you fall in love with the cello
and give up theology for Bach; or
after that excruciating marriage; or
after that year when you couldn't
for the life of you stop crying,
they wouldn't let you out,
the rejection-slips accumulating,
the girlfriends not even writing.

Thucydides by Virgil by Juvenal – O
Penguin Classics in modern translation,
where else but in Langley Park
does Hermes slide down on a sunbeam

through a thoroughly dirty window,
bearing contemporary bulletins
in bulging satchels?
The Soviet Empire collapses: *the ropes
are heaved, down come the statues…
the fire roars up in the furnace,
the head of the great Sejanus
crackles and melts.* Or watch
on inter-temporal television
a funeral production from Attica,
Pericles expounding to the Athenians
the virtues of the Langley Parkians:
*We do not feel called upon
to be angry with our neighbour
for doing what he likes –*
a sixties slogan that forewarns, no doubt,
of universal cock-up in the nineties.

So the plague has arrived,
the Spartans will take advantage;
the nations are in revolt,
the Macedonians will take over,
not yet affecting Dickon, next door,
in the act of suspending
a small cage of bought-in-bulk peanuts
from a rowan tree already
snowy with chaffinch droppings; now
he's squatting by his frog pond
breaking the ice with a trowel.
No script, no camera, I think
we do communicate. Suppose
the Latin poet was right
about the greatest happiness being
freedom not to fear;
could he have been right, too,
about choosing what's left
of the country,
avoiding Rome and its channels,
never attending interviews
or stuffing on world-horrors,
but at the same time
sympathetically resisting
security system salesmen,
PVC promotion, Jehovah's
Witnesses, satellite dishes,
free gifts, easy payment catalogues?

And if he was wrong, these
dogs, tadpoles, pigeons,
ferrets, talents, temperaments,
love affairs, hate affairs,
exchanges of trout for tomatoes,
home-brew for expertise in
organic leek growing or
1950s combustion engines –
not to say sexy tattoos,
babies, more babies,
books, batik, what other local,
threatened consolations – all
have, for a time, composed
the substance of something
people call their lives.

Winter Time

Cobalt water
wrinkled under thin ice.
Last day summer time.

Remembering to turn the clock back.
For loving, a precious hour.
For living, no more time.

Mist raining or rain misting?
Woods like an antique tapestry
the cat's got at.

Bright haws, bare snowberries.
Not a leaf to warm them.

Winter jackdaws, widowed harem
quarrelling over small change.

Sikh boy whistling
his *Newcastle Evening Chronicles*
through the beaten leaves.

Two avocados and a red pepper
bought for the joy of colour.

West sky piles up churches on pillars of rain.
East sky accepts the rainbow.

Strong wind
treading the puddle in the wheel rut.

I hold the bonnet steady.
You adjust the headlight.
Hurled air, hurt feelings
threaten this balance.

Swept hills, thinly covered
with sheep and history.
The Tyne in a hurry
to get to the sea.

Salter's Gate

There, in that lost
    corner of the ordnance survey.
Drive through the vanity –
    two pubs and a garage – of Satley,
then right, cross the A68
    past down-at-heel farms and a quarry,

you can't miss it, a 'T' instead of a 'plus'
    where the road meets a wall.
If it's a usual day
    there'll be freezing wind, and you'll
stumble climbing the stile
    (a ladder, really) as you pull

your hat down and zip up your jacket.
    Out on the moor,
thin air may be strong enough to
    knock you over,
but if you head into it
    downhill, you can shelter

in the wide, cindery trench of an old
    leadmine-to-Consett railway.
You may have to share it
    with a crowd of dirty
supercilious-looking ewes, who will baaa
    and cut jerkily away

after posting you blank stares
    from their foreign eyes.
One winter we came across five
    steaming, icicle-hung cows.
But in summer, when the heather's full of nests,
    you'll hear curlews

following you, raking your memory, maybe,
    with their cries;
or, right under your nose,
    a grouse will whirr up surprised,
like a poet startled by a line
    when it comes to her sideways.

No protection is offered by trees –
    Hawthorn the English call May,
a few struggling birches.
    But of wagtails and yellowhammers, plenty,
and peewits who never say *peewit*,
    more a minor, *go'way, go'way*.

Who was he, Salter? Why was this his gate?
    A pedlars' way, they carried
salt to meat. The place gives tang to
    survival, its unstoppable view,
a reservoir, ruins of the lead mines, new
    forestry pushing from the right, the curlew.

Claude Glass

Eyes are too close to Nature to be nice,
So Claude's disciples thought of a device
Through which they could evade the messy world
By catching it in image as it curled
Within a glass held up before its face
To give God's barbarous hills and rivers grace.

His name became an impulse to impart
To Nature all *les belles finesses* of Art;
Taught British tourists for a century
To turn their backs on what they went to see.
Meanwhile the men of coal and iron and steel
Took out of Nature what they knew was real.

Now from the Tyne's black stacks and blacker steam
We drive out to The Lakes and their museum
To seek what never was but always risked
The truth to be the fair, the picturesque –
A landscape cognac that the connoisseur
Will recognise – expensive, sweetened, sure.

Jarrow

(for Fr Aelred Stubbs)

Talis...vita hominum praesens in terris, ad conparationem eius, quod nobis incertum est, temporis, quale cum te residente ad caenam cum ducibus ac ministris tuis tempore brumale...adveniens unus passerum domum citissime pervolaverit; qui cum per unum ostium ingrediens, mox per aliud exierit... Mox de hieme in hiemem regrediens, tuis oculis elabitur —

BEDE, Historia Ecclesiastica Gentis Anglorum

Would want to paint them,
these town bright boys
at the dead end of the track
where it coils down away
from church and mound
leaving almost an island,
as it once must have been
when Bede set his *Lucem Vitae*
lightly on the pages of
these empty mudflats.

One thousand three hundred years
to set that orange apparatus
(for loading coal?) cleanly
in the mouth of the Tyne
and decide to abandon it
there, beneath that regiment
of scarred blue oil drums.
The scene looks set for
a study of bad times
in the lap of old times,

dead machinery teasing the live,
hooting youths who have
nothing to do here in their
circus clothes, their peaked pink
hair like traffic cones.
The more civilised the civilised,
the more barbarian the barbarians.
Such vivid colours, though,
like fresh paint on what
seems to be one more picture of

enough. A passing sparrow would
see it, flying from winter
into winter: the cracked black
skin of the tide between ripples of

couch grass, the blue sheet of river
rusty with ships, the cranes
against the monks' sky, crossed by high
pylons in their chains of power.
Lightbearers. *Lucifera*. Latin would have
named them, as the kneeling church

outlasts them in its green patch of
ruin. I would like to paint
the sparrow's view – the prefabs
(now the monks' cells), the heaps of
sweet timber by the sawmill's warehouse
fenced from an old blind horse
in a field, polished copper lamps
along the walks, a smudge of kids
in the distance. I would, in my painting,
be a brushstroke. *Talis vita in terris...*

North Easter
(April, 1986)

That daffodil trumpets its *gaudia*
straight into the ground, whence
rhubarb arises – red knuckles,
green gleaming rucked sleeves.

But the wind wants everything
to be level with itself:
the crocuses, the washing on the line,
the soiled plastic streamers,
desperate to be blossoms,
impaled on thorns, nailed
to the skeleton trees.

Also rags from the gangrened top-
half of a patched cardboard suitcase;
also bright kelpy tanglements of
orange-tinted baler twine, kinking,
unkinking on the wind's dry littoral;
comb of tarred roofing-felt, rusty cans,
torn carpet, coat, boot, shoe.

What god will arise and slouch
through this realm of rubbish?

The low flower, the coltsfoot,
creeps in its silver scales between
glittering fragments of beer bottle;
the goat willows kneel, fists budding,
among no longer useful speedometers;
rising larks strew nervous hallelujas
in the cooked paths of the Yamaha.

There are no fish now in the river
squamous with air. Which is re-writing,
anyway, its book of revelations in the blood
of old sidings and carburettors.
A glory of oily rainbows stains the stones,
jewels also five drowned black tyres.

Skills

Like threading a needle by computer, to align
the huge metal-plated tracks of the macadam-spreader
with two frail ramps to the plant-carrier.
Working alone on Sunday, overtime,
the driver powers the wheel: forward, reverse, forward
centimetre by centimetre... stop!

He leaps from the cab, a carefree Humphrey Bogart,
to check both sides. The digger sits up front
facing backwards at an angle to the flat,
its diplodocus-neck chained to a steel scaffold.
Its head fits neatly in the macadam-spreader's lap.
Satisfying. All of a piece and tightly wrapped.

Before he slams himself, whistling, into his load,
he eyes all six, twelve, eighteen, twenty-four tyres.
Imagine a plane ascending. Down on the road,
this clever Matchbox toy that takes apart
grows small, now smaller still and more compact,
a crawling speck on the unfolding map.

Night Walking with Shadows

Night walking the dog through the hollow village,
I am followed and preceded by three of me.

The streetlights distribute me between three shamans.
Their huge imaginations hand me, like a trophy,
from the shadow behind me to the shadow before me.

While the full moon gives me a dense
practical shadow, smaller than myself.

I walk, for the dog's sake, out of the lights
up the track by the sportsground, the shacky allotments.

How this white fall of moonlight simplifies the story.
Dog and shadow. Woman and shadow.

Up the V of the valley, a string of brilliants.
In every window, labouring magi.

The chimney pots steam like alembics,
but for every white chain of amazing smoke,
the moon cuts a dead black track.

Spring Again

(Durham, 2004)

A touch of spring
In the look of the air –
That tangy, Mozartian

Unsuspicious colour;
Naïve light rounding a
Steel-scrubbed corner.

Wide-open beech tree,
Bare still,
Pregnant with flower.

Who can believe a
Summer will relieve
This undernourished hour?

'Between Mersh and Averil,
When spray beginneth to spring,
The lutle fowl hath hir wil...'

Though the elm's low bough
That should be in leaf
Is not there now.

The thrush is gone
From the brushwood sheaf,
And the blackened thorn

Is a rack of hooks
To hang wet weather on
In plastic sacks.

For all that's wrong,
'Lenten is come with love to towne.'
New times, old words.

In a light green haze,
Let's try, with the cannibal birds,
To praise love's ways.

17.14 Out of Newcastle
(2004)

Mostly feeling pity,
but sometimes fury
in the press of the crowd,

I scan it for an eye
to talk to, not aloud
but stealthily, quickly,

as one shade
might sign to another
in the queue for Avernus.

Here, we agree,
is where the incurious
or damned unlucky

live on in body
when the spirit dies.
On such a train,

in some murky
siding of a poet's brain,
Limbo was devised

where there's no agony
and no joy, either,
just fleshy emptiness

sweating out the space between
weary I-am-ness
and the unloved pack.

As face retreats from face
to coverts of soft porn,
football, lust in paperback,

the old, waste, token city
(church and castle)
vanishes along the line,

resurrecting in a chain of
rainbows – steel riveted
ribcage for the breathing Tyne.

Put down your book.
Lift up your eyes.
The river's awake and at work

in its leaping bridges.
Electric confetti
zig and zag along its pulse,

celebrating our immense
human smallness
with a carnival.

'Don't rot inside your body,
build your soul.'
Could be its theme song.

We rattle over the rail bridge,
beating along.
Dum diddy, dum diddy...

There are too many of us.
Still, some undeniable voltage
wants to connect us.

*   *   *

American Rhetoric for Scotland

North in the mind, ragged edged, stubborn ribbed,
with your bald soils and scoured hills and cold ruined massacres,
disasters no one is expected to inhabit –
however you ignore them, you are one with your bones.
'Admire,' you implore, 'my redemptory achievements.
my swift roads, my smooth steel, my pylons and high voltages,
my slums reduced to powder, reassembled as skyscrapers,
my lochs relieved of romance, rehabilitated as electrons.'
Nobody believes you. The first mist disposes of them.
You build in your stone ghost.

It takes a man's full arrogance to sing out in your weather,
'I am the creator. Everything is for me!'
Your scraped countryside groups itself around him, without him.
It is over his lighthouse that the gulls swing, buffeted,
wailing, repeating reminiscences, grievances.
Those are his sheep, soft boulders till they move,
cropping expertly, inflexibly along the rainswept ridges,
leaving among thistles and torn matted grasses
nests of round, moist, unhatchable black eggs.

Occasional crofts or byres, or parts of crofts
or half byres, knot the irregular, useless walls
with which the land seems tied. Or is it the land that ties?
Did the houses give way painfully to its tightening,
the lintels sag, the roofs buckle, the beams split
as the ground took it stones back one by one,
with the people rooted to them, or rooted out,
shrugged off into Queensland, Ontario, Birmingham,
or that gaunt crease or angle of yourself spreading east
out of Glasgow?   Some settled for it.
Others borrowed Cleveland, Toronto, made themselves indispensable.
The new world uses them like engines.

And what are they to say to the strangers they come back to?
If they do come back, with their easy ways and smart daughters,
to be chilled in your houses, homesick for Midwestern summers,
too rich for your sun and for the kind, shrewd nephews
who keep, nevertheless, an oblique ascendancy,
who copy or accuse or make fun of what they envy,
who are in turn wistfully envied, since under their
preposterous assertions, their necessary frugality, their greed,
lies that which is forever whispering release:
'No day is property. There is little purpose. Living is enough.'

Living. Its clumsy satisfactions. Its tea and football.
Its women and shows and kids and drams of an evening –
ambitions an honest man attends to if he's lucky,
if the drams are enough and the friends plentiful,
or even if the wife is enough and the tea plentiful.
Though it may be he is evil in his seed,
that the jolt of conceiving him is evil,
that beyond the shimmering coasts and barren islands
Great Doom is readying itself for a descent,
sea that will rise and lash inland, lapping him up,
receding over his tangled, indelible evidences,
quays upended, boats stove in, offices gutted,
cranes caught and petrified in the wince of action,
their bony necks twisted or hurled back or
bent to the swirling water as if to drink it.

But you know better. The two-faced familiar antagonist
still asks for its share of husbands,
still plays fairly or unfairly with the slippery herring,
but clings to you, nevertheless, with its legends in tatters,
its white waters and grey waters repetitious in old age,
old tediums, memories old women live for
as they knit or make trifles for tourists,
new waves that break again and again over your moorlands,
running northwards and outwards out of Clydeside into
Morven and Sutherland and Inverness, and over
Ardnamurchan into Skye and Barra.

Will your mountains be wild enough and strong enough?
Or will you drown, devour whatever feeds you,
melt into the undifferentiated mind that wants you,
with its cameras and appetites and little boredoms,
or even its bewildered fumblings for a simple life,
the better way it half hopes it can pay you for?
You're not for sale, though you give to one or two:
blood-gold sunsets. One white seagull, perhaps,
rising in contradiction to a cataract. Perhaps in sandstone,
a pattern like braided hair. Always the sound of water, Quiet stone.

The raw grey villages subsist on little, settle uneasily
into the shifting hills. Below them, some soft bays open,
or dwindle. Some island vanish. The sun, using the scarce,
undefinable, frail pigments sparingly, moves something like yellow
from one valley to another. This gentleness is moss thin.
Stones don't need nourishment. They break through. They harden.

(1969)

East Coast

Fire and the Tide

Fire struggles in the chimney like an animal.
It's caught in a life.
As when the tide pulls the Tay out,
scarring predictable mudscape –
seawater's knifework
notching quick runnel and channel.

That's how you remember
the alternative lives. You saw them
could never have lived them.
A ribbon of birds is pulled raggedly over November.
You're pulled between now and the way you will not escape.

Summer

Ebb day, full tide.
Yellowhammers whistling in fullblown bushes.
Scent of wet cypresses, lavender, roses.
Dying storm, veiled like a bride.

The Bench

Steep path to where the wheatfields' yellow
Makes a plush gilt frame for the town.
A bench there – no back, but a view –
For lovers, dog-walkers, poets. Tired men
With sensational newspapers climb there, too.

Boating Pool at Night

Enormous, this fragment of July
Stretched between pool and shallow night.
House   house
Light   light
Sky   in the whole sky.

Winter Flowers
(for Kiff and Adele Rathbone)

I don't know why at all
But when, that winter evening,
You brought in fists full of blazing summer flowers,
A brick fell out of the wall enclosing Eden,
Leaving a peephole, just for a moment ours,
Through which we saw the simultaneous seasons,
Breeding, bearing, dying, like the stars;
And the trees – one hoary, dangerous with wisdom,
One green with the impossibility of years.

The Lighthouse

Though I did not intend
On my journey that it should end
At this lighthouse and town
Surrounded by tidewater's flat brown
Halo of muddy sand
Opening and closing like a hand,
Clearly, on looking back, I see
The road led here inevitably.

With its litter of feathers and shells, it bends
On further, blends
With blue water further than I can see.
And is what will be.
The bay – so beautiful.
I – only its animal.
And the lighthouse, ever unsatisfied,
Glutted in the tide.

Night Wind, Dundee

At sundown, a seaforce that gulls rode or fell through.
The small snow is surf. Eddies of strong air
swarm up old tenements. Listen! My window's late
rat-tat-tat guns back at who and whose enemy
milked the sky's agates, polished its ebony.
Warm rooms are lit up in bare blocks of concrete.
Someone's ripped cobwebs from a great vault's rafters,
revealing a moonface, a starfield,
barbarian Orion crucified in God's heaven.

Aberdeen

Old daughter with a rich future,
that's blueveined Aberdeen,
reeking of fish, breathing sea air
like atomised pewter. Her clean
gothic ribs rattle protests
to the spiky gusts. Poor girl.
She's got to marry oil.
Nobody who loves her wants to save her.

The Mudtower

(Tayport, Fife, 1 January 1975)

And again, without snow, a new year.
As for fifty years, thousands of years, the air
returns the child-blue rage of the river.
Six swans rise aloud from the estuary,
ferrying tremendous souls to the pond by the playground.
They're coming for me! No. I'm part of the scenery.
They fly low, taking no interest in migratory ladies.

The stone town stumbles downhill to untidy mudflats –
high square houses shivering in windows, the street of shops,
the church and clocktower, school, the four worn pubs
artfully spaced between dry rows of cottages.
Then council flats, fire station, rusty gasometer,
timber-yard baying its clean smell of pinewood;
grass, swings, mud…the wilted estuary.

You could say that the winter's asleep in the harbour's arm.
Two sloops with their heads on their backs
        are sleeping there peacefully.
Far out in the tide's slum, in the arm of the sand-spit,
the mudtower wades in the giving and taking water.

Its uses – if it ever had uses – have been abandoned.
The low door's a mouth. Slit eyes stab the pinnacle.
Its lovethrust is up from the mud it seems to be made of.
Surely it's alive and hibernating, Pictish or animal.
The sea birds can hear it breathing in its skin or shrine.

How those lighthouses, airing their bones on the coast,
hate the mudtower. They hold their bright messages aloft
like saints bearing scriptures.

As the water withdraws, the mudtower steps out on the land.
Watch the fierce, driven, hot-looking
scuttlings of redshanks, the beaks of the oystercatchers.
Struggle and panic. Struggle and panic.
Mud's rituals resume. The priest-gulls flap to the kill.
Now high flocks of sandpipers, wings made of sunlight,
flicker as snow flickers, blown from those inland hills.

The Fish Are All Sick

The fish are all sick, the great whales dead,
The villages stranded in stone on the coast,
Ornamental, like pearls on the fringe of a coat.
Sea men who knew what the ocean did,
Turned their low houses away from the surf.
But new men, who come to be rural and safe,
Add big glass views and begonia beds.

Water keeps to itself.
White lip after lip
Curls to a close on the littered beach.
Something is sicker and blacker than fish.
And closing its grip, and closing its grip.

The Man in the Wind

The man in the wind
who keeps us awake tonight
is not the black monk of the wind
cowering in corners and crevices,
or the white face under the streetlight
stricken with the guilt of his noise,
or the great slapping hand of the wind
beating and beating the rainy alleyways
while the torturer proceeds with the interrogation

and the prisoner's risen voice
bleeds over cymbals and tympani.

Listen.
His dream of the wind
is the anger that tunes his mind
and wears his skin.
His cry is not what the wind says
but the fear he lives in.
Nor is the wind less human for being wilder,
or being, as now, a roar, a continuous roar
as of waves where there is no shore,
none, and no inland or headland to hinder
the pour of dark water over still more water.

And now it is drowning our polite island,
the little free ports with their spylights alerted,
ships, towerblocks, cranes, steeples, pylons,
the carious skyline gone with his last horizon
to a clean pure end,
to the only end in this night of the uncreated
where the wind's wind, loosened by his sleep
to the force of itself,
moves without meaning or being –
a wave that began before beginning,
that will not end after the end.

Cramond

Then 'twas the Roman, now 'tis I.
HOUSMAN

Remember how in Edinburgh,
on fine spring evenings, the family cars
shook out their dogs and children
to animate the live Scots postcard
at Cramond?

Seaward spread the too blue firth,
patronised by sandpipers.
A far fringe of mountains
framed a classical view.
You could walk to

Cramond Island when the low tide
let you.
But mostly you wanted to
skip in your mind from peak
to concrete peak across the buckling
ship blockade.

Somehow that was simpler
than a free-fall to the Romans,
their mute frontier
devoid of sirens and motorbikes
and slow planes homing over the oil fields
like metal pigeons.

Inverkirkaig

Bloodshed cries *Ai Ai*
in the colour of rowanberries.
Birds will eat wounds all winter.

Flayed hills keep breathing
through the slashing –
waterfall, fighterplane, waterfall.

The salmon leaps and fails.
Drowned to his thigh,
the man praises courage with a hook.

Six men, twelve wings, and the sky cracks
successfully. The squadron
is out of hearing when it falls.

With its gentian eye, the loch
praises gleaming and burnishing.
The salmon leaps and fails.

The man goes on casting and reeling.
A late rain erases in pitiless mercy
home, story, arterial berry.

* * *

Buzzard and Alder

Buzzard that folds itself into and becomes nude
alder; alder that insensibly becomes bird –
one life inside the dazzling tree. Together
they do change everything, and forever.

You think, because no news is said here,
not. But rain's rained weather to a rare
blue, so you can see the thinness of it,
I mean the layer they live in, flying in it,

breaking through it minute by glass minute.
Buzzard, hunched in disuse before it
shatters winter, wheeling after food.
Alder, silently glazing us, the dead.

Cold

Snow. No roofs this morning, alps, ominous message
      for the jackdaws prospecting maps of melt.
Something precipitates an avalanche.

A tablecloth slips off noisily
      pouring heavy laundry into detergent,
a basin of virgin textiles, pocked distinctively

with crystals. Your shovel violates this *blanchissage*
      with useful bustle, urgency
pretends, helpless as the swallowed road on which

the air lets fall again a lacier
organza snow-veil. Winter bridal
the muffled dog fouls briefly. *Don't the cedars*

look beautiful, bent under clouds of fall?
And it's true, time has no pull
on us; we set it aside for another

'very serious and fundamental' briefing:
chaffinches at the birdfeed, a sentinel
jackdaw on exposed slates, worried men

tiptoeing their accelerators, deepening
very carefully each other's ruts.
As if – for how long? – matter had beaten them

and the cold were bowing them back to –
or forward to – a steadier state. Ice
sets in and verifies the snow.

Imagine a hidden rule, escaped from words,
stealing the emergency away from us,
starving the animals eventually; first, the birds.

Path

Aged by rains,
cool under pulsing trees,
the summer path is paved with winter leaves.
Roots lace it like an old man's veins.

And nothing in field, on hill, can so appal
burnt August and its transitory walker
as this which leads a summer
towards its fall.

Now under cover
of the leopard pelt
of that lean way, more heat, more passion's felt
than ever in shimmering field by usual lover.

Fanged with surprising light, the path means harm.
Not calm, not comfort, not release at last.
White innocent motes of dust
rise up and swarm.

Resurrection

Surprised by spring,
by the green light fallen like snow
in a single evening,
by hawthorn, blackthorn, willow,
meadow – everything
woken again, after how many thousand years?

That generous throat
is a blackbird's. Now, a thrush.
And that ribbon flung out,
that silk voice, is a chaffinch's rush
to his grace-note. Birds woo,
or apportion the innocent air they're made for.
Whom do they sing for?

Old man by the river –
spread out like a cross in the sun,
feet bare and stared at
by three grubby children – you've made it again,
and yes we'll inherit a summer.
Always the same green clamouring fells you that wakes you.
And you have to start living again when it wakes you.

Enough of Green

Enough of green,
though to remember childhood
is to stand in uneasy radiance
under those trees.

Enough yellow.
We are looking back
over our shoulders, telling our children
to be happy.

Try to forget about red.
Leave it to the professionals.
But perceive heaven as a density
blue enough to abolish the stars.
As long as the rainbow lasts
the company stays.

Of black there is never enough.

One by one the lights in the house go out.
Step over the threshold. Forget
to take my hand.

In the Weather of Deciduous Souls

Vermont, 2003

(for Jay Parini, and for Laura and Franklin Reeve)

Why don't you Vermonters call October
All Souls' Carnival? Dying and dyed,
The trees dress up in cerements, and here's your
Road show's kinky, country celebration,
Gold leaf and confetti every city Billy
Comes to gawp at, while the scenery collapses
And the lights come down in whooshes of wind
(There's the wind will blow the winter in)
Burying one more year in torn-off days –
Some ashy, some embers,
Some so flushed with going
You want to keep them warm, like happiness,
Like wine that can't be guzzled from the glass,
Like visits from love or sunsets,
Like riotous hours that won't grow stale, but last.
They want so much to be sewn back on the tree.
They want, like you and me, not to be past.

II

Seven Ages

Epigraph
FROM *Reversals (1965)*

Birth.
Impossible to imagine
Not knowing how to expect.

Childbirth.
Impossible to imagine
Years of the tall son.

Death.
Impossible to imagine,
Exactly, *exactly.*

The Spirit Is Too Blunt an Instrument

The spirit is too blunt an instrument
to have made this baby.
Nothing so unskilful as human passions
could have managed the intricate
exacting particulars: the tiny
blind bones with their manipulating tendons,
the knee and the knucklebones, the resilient
fine meshings of ganglia and vertebrae,
the chain of the difficult spine.

Observe the distinct eyelashes and sharp crescent
fingernails, the shell-like complexity
of the ear, with its firm involutions
concentric in miniature to minute
ossicles. Imagine the
infinitesimal capillaries, the flawless connections
of the lungs, the invisible neural filaments
through which the completed body
already answers to the brain.

Then name any passion or sentiment
possessed of the simplest accuracy.
No, no desire or affection could have done
with practice what habit
has done perfectly, indifferently,
through the body's ignorant precision.
It is left to the vagaries of the mind to invent
love and despair and anxiety
and their pain.

The Victory

I thought you were my victory
though you cut me like a knife
when I brought you out of my body
into your life.

Tiny antagonist, gory,
blue as a bruise. The stains
of your cloud of glory
bled from my veins.

How can you dare, blind thing,
blank insect eyes?
You barb the air. You sting
with bladed cries.

Snail. Scary knot of desires.
Hungry snarl. Small son.
Why do I have to love you?
How have you won?

Stabilities

Gull, ballast of its wings.
Word, mind's stone.
Child, love's flesh and bone.

Poem for a Daughter

'I think I'm going to have it,'
I said, joking between pains.
The midwife rolled competent
sleeves over corpulent milky arms.
'Dear, you never have it,
we deliver it.'
A judgement years proved true.
Certainly I've never had you

as you still have me, Caroline.
Why does a mother need a daughter?
Heart's needle, hostage to fortune,
freedom's end. Yet nothing's more perfect
than that bleating, razor-shaped cry
that delivers a mother to her baby.
The bloodcord snaps that held
their sphere together. The child,
tiny and alone, creates the mother.

A woman's life is her own
until it is taken away
by a first particular cry.
Then she is not alone
but part of the premises
of everything there is:
a time, a tribe, a war.
When we belong to the world
we become what we are.

To My Daughter in a Red Coat
(New York, 1959)

Late October. It is afternoon.
My daughter and I walk through the leaf-strewn
Corridors of the park
In the light and the dark
Of the elms' thin arches.

Around us brown leaves fall and spread.
Small winds stir the minor dead.
Dust powders the air.
Those shrivelled women stare
At us from their cold benches.

Child, your mittens tug your sleeves.
They lick your drumming feet, the leaves.
You come so fast, so fast.
You violate the past,
My daughter, as your coat dances.

In March

The snow melts,
exposing what was
buried there all winter:
tricycles and
fire engines and
all sizes of children
waiting in boots and
yellow mackintoshes
for the mud.

With My Sons at Boarhills
(Scotland, 1975)

Gulls think it is for them
that the wormy sand rises,
brooding on its few rights,
losing its war with water.

The mussel flats ooze out,
and now the barnacled, embossed,
stacked rocks are pedestals for strangers,
for my own strange sons
scraping in the pools,
imperilling their pure reflections.

Their bodies are less beautiful than
blue heaven's pleiades of herring gulls,
or gannets, or that sloop's sail
sawtoothing the sea as if its
scenery were out of date, as if its
photographs had all been taken:
two boys left naked in a sloughed off summer,
skins and articulate backbones,
fossils for scrapbook or cluttered mantelpiece.

If you look now, quickly and askance,
you can see how the camera's eye
perfected what was motion and chance before
it clicked on this day and childhood snapshot,
scarcely seen beside hunched football stripes and ugly uniforms.
Shy, familiar grins in a waste of faces.
My knee joints ache and crack
as I kneel to my room's fire, feeding it.
Steam wreathes from my teacup, clouding
the graduate, the lieutenant, the weddings,
the significant man of letters, the politician
smiling from his brief victory.

Faces I washed and scolded, only
watched as my each child laboured from his own womb,
bringing forth, without me, men who must
call me mother, love or reassess me
as their barest needs dictate, return
dreaming, rarely to this saltpool in memory,
naked on a morning full of see-through jellyfish,
with the tide out and the gulls out
grazing on healed beaches,
while sea-thrift blazes by the dry path,
and the sail stops cutting the water to pieces,
heading for some named port inland.

Their voices return like footprints over the sandflats,
permanent, impermanent, salt and sensuous
as the sea is, in its frame, its myth.

In the Nursery

I lift the seven months baby from his crib,
a clump of roots.
Sleep drops off him like soil
in clods that smell sunbaked and rich with urine.
He opens his eyes,
two light blue corollas.
His cheek against mine
is the first soft day in the garden.
His mouth makes a bud, then a petal,
then a leaf.
In less than seven seconds
he's blossoming in a bowl of arms.

To Phoebe
(at five months)

How in this mindless whirl of time and space
Find words to welcome one small human child?
Shakespeare was lucky, art wore Shakespeare's face,
And nature kept the virtues neatly filed.
God's earth was fixed, and round it ran the sun,
A temperamental lantern on a skate.
Our lives by stars were wound up or begun;
The universe was Heaven's unspoiled estate.

But now, lost to the angels, it appears
We share with rats and fleas a murky source.
Our plaited genes mean nothing to the spheres;
Contingency, not prayer, will plot your course.

Yet no small Phoebe *circa* sixteen-three
Was ever free to be what you shall be.

Little Paul and the Sea

Hi yi hee yippee!
It's little Paul
cheering for the sea.

He's so small
the sea won't
look at him at all,

rising up
in a net-white heap,
falling dead
on the sand at his feet.

Such a huge blue reach
to the sky,
and every wave
rolling in to die.

Which is not
what appears to Paul,
for whom
it's a nice big pool.

Hi yi hee yippee!
It's little Paul
stamping on the sea.

Four and a Half Dancing Men

She knows how to fold
and turn the paper,
guiding the scissors with care
to create for her son
five little dancing dolls.
Toe by toe, hand in hand,
ring a ring a roses,
watch them caper

across the plain and up,
up over the mountain,
five happy men
to amuse a small boy in bed.

So cross. So bored. For
all that, a little blond god,
with the shifting realm
of his risen knees to govern.

The fauna buried in his
landslides, the cities
swallowed by his earthquakes
no longer divert him.
He monitors the marching
of five chained men
with silent intensity,
grave as his liquid eyes.

Up and down, up and down,
his to command,
one, two, three, four
manikins spring by.
He tears from the fifth
an arm, and then a thigh.
The troupe trips on,
though sagging at one end.

Four and a half dancing men.
And the half he made
with an act of his hand
seems to please him best.
He smiles. The same
can be done with the rest.
Four blind men, and a half,
unafraid, unafraid.

The Holly and the Ivy

Where have you been? she said.
Not sleeping,
dead, he said.

What did you see?
she said.
Everything. Everything.

There was a wood,
he said,
made of plant-animals.
Berries were eyes,
he said,
roots were noses.
They galloped over highways
and railways
and houses.
No one in the cities could
reach them or catch them.

Were they friendly or angry?

Both angry and friendly.
The holly was a he.
The ivy was a she.
There were plant-children, too,
all leafy and thin.
And they galloped through my window
to my bed – and in!

That's a very bad dream,
she said.
What happened then?

The holly had a knife.
The ivy had a noose.
The toadstools came jumping
on their thick white stumps.

It's a good thing for you,
she said,
dreams aren't true.

How do you know,
he said,
how do you know?

The Doctor

I am the doctor.
It's my joy to make people well.
It's convenient, of course, if they sicken
     in conventional ways.
The mother like a caught moth
     fluttering with bedpan by the bed.
The bigger kids fighting and teasing.
A husband in the cobwebs.
A smell of stale dinner –
     it has to be cooked and not eaten.

To this kind of fireside
I always bring hope and encouragement.
I approach through my smile and display
     my incredible instruments.
I refuse cups of tea and wrapped barley sugar.
Health? Yes, yes,
     you can pick it alive from my lips.
Little boy, little boy.
His eyes open, gushing with confidence.
Little boy, little boy.
He gets well. He decides to grow up.

A Surprise on the First Day of School
(1938)

They give you a desk with a lid, mother.
They let you keep your book.
My desk's next to the window.
I can see the trees.
But you mustn't look out the window
   at light on the leaves.
You must look at the book.

A nice-smelling, shiny book, mother,
With words in it and pictures.
I mostly like the pictures,
   some of them animals and birds.
But you musn't look at the pictures.
You don't *ever* read the pictures.
You read the words!

Innocence and Experience

I laid myself down as a woman
And woke as a child.
Sleep buried me up to my chin,
But my brain cut wild.

Sudden summer lay sticky as tar
Under bare white feet.
Stale, soot-spotted heapings of winter
Shrank in the street.

Black headlines, infolded like napkins,
Crashed like grenades
As war beat its way porch by porch
Up New Haven's façades.

Europe: a brown hive of noises,
Hitler inside.
On the too sunny shelf by the stairs
My tadpoles died.

Big boys had already decided
Who'd lose and who'd score,
Singing one potato, two potato,
Three potato, four.

Singing sticks and stones
May break my bones
(but names hurt more).

Singing step on a crack
Break your mother's back
(her platinum-ringed finger).

Singing who got up your mother
When your daddy wasn't there?
Singing allee allee in free! You're
Dead, you're dead, wherever you are!

At Thirteen

Woodsmoke,

and in those soft legal hollows
nothing but the sanest odours;
even at sundown
nothing but the gentlest scents.

Then the young girl
flows in out of the twilight,
hair streaming, part of her streaming,
breasts held like breath and yet swelling,
arms withheld, aching, yet waiting,
so, like a river,
into the deep light room.

Where now light possesses her.
Eyes harden to reflectors.
Angers stagnate in her throat.
No speech but a cry.
Then a slammed door.

Leaving the mother
who has done so little –
fetched a daysoaked shirt out of the basin,
offered her chicken and rice,
smiled at her vaguely, or kindly,
over some wall of book – who,
pinioned by a small stony shadow,
can be nothing but reproach to her.

Withering slimness.
Closed volume of slimness.
Nothing but reproach to her.
Declaration of fear.

Incident

She must have been about
twelve in 1942.

She stood in front
of the tall hall mirror
and she made a mou.
With her pretty not-
yet-kissed mouth she made an ugly
mou mou
that didn't mean anything
she knew.
So bony, so skinny,
and so very naked.
Little pink belled swellings.
Two.

The mirror did what she did.
Mou mou. Mou mou.

Nowhere to go.
Nothing to do.

Suicide

There was no hole in the universe to fit him.
He felt it as he fooled around. No rim,
no closet, nowhere to hide. The moon
also was fooling. He told
the girl and she giggled. 'As much for you
as for anyone.' But it wasn't true.

Spiders with their eight eyes, snails had more to do.

'When I said I wouldn't kiss him
he said he'd slash his wrists.
He was always saying stupid things like this.'

He saw himself entering women.
Wide open hay-scented barn, transistor on,
heavy rhythm of drums to draw him in.
And then that smallness, tiny loop at the end
where a slipknot tightened over light until a fist
struck. Darkness swelled around him like a breast.

The noose? A way of playing let's pretend.
A dare, a joke, the freedom of the risk.
He was free as air when the girl's father found him,
returning from an evening out with friends.

Transparencies
(A Letter to My Sons, Hay-on-Wye, 1979)

Your time with me ends with August, and now
August is over. Between Oxford and Cambridge –
that English triangle they make with London –
fields must be yellow harvested, as here in Wales.
Little straw-built cities, movable dolmens,
they look solid enough to believe in, stacked in bales.
      I carry my wound back upright in the car
      as if its grief could spill.

But it's a gift, too, this grief-grail, freedom to
love you without you. 'My sons' creates you abstract
as gold fields the windows slide before your faces,
crossing by bus to grandparents whose good sense
still can't splinter to forgiveness, who'll find you,
like your music, alien as energy. And all they have.
      Later you'll look past me and your cleft childhood
      to their calm, whole house

where habit and reason – harvest of half a century's
lesson in upheaval – look solid enough to believe in,
if, by then, abstractions like 'the past' and 'mother'
make you cry – and like to cry. The act of memory's
a film we learn to make and watch so lives
can be performances. Worse than TV,
      to leave your tea mugs and *The Moon of Gomrath*
      plangent on a table

and, as if you were here, set off with the dog
for the river path, where yesterday the sun
struck slantwise, shafted, just as now. I see how
last year's leaves are almost this year's dust.
Papery thorn shapes…maple…alder… stir
in a gust of passing. Molecular squall of gnats
      where the path's still hot. Leaves like syllables
      of light in a text of shadows.

This is a letter I'd never write if I could
send you counsel. Cicero, Polonius – thistles
preaching their beards to their blown seed. Oh,
it's your particular selves I need to hold
to the light as you cross the impossible lens of now
and now. Solid enough to believe… until
      the river ripples over your melting faces
      mouthing at me from its thin windows.

*   *   *

Sous-entendu

Don't think

that I don't know
that as you talk to me
the hand of your mind
is inconspicuously
taking off my stocking,
moving in resourceful blindness
up along my thigh.

Don't think
that I don't know
that you know
everything I say
is a garment.

Love

if not necessary, is essential,
is to its season as a Ferris Wheel
to its fair.
One moment we are standing
whole on the sidewalk, paying,
joking – there
is nothing to it. Then, bang, a bar
cuts off our legs, and we are
hooked out and rocked back and forth,
airsick even before earth pushes us off.

Mov-
ing into orbit is awful. We ride
grimly, hanging on to ourselves inside.
One insect
and three rust spots on the bones
of the box that holds our bones
are what protect
us, until, thank God, we are able to look down
where everything is changing size
but not shape, as the roofs rise
and subside delightfully, and the ground

Breathes
and we breathe too, for the first time. We love
being perpendicular and aloof
while the rest
of the world rolls over and
over and over on the land.
But the best
of it is, we can say just what we please.
'Look out!' we shout to the pigmies
beneath us, 'You are going to go
down!' And they don't understand, and they do.

Of
the end we remember exactly how
helpless we felt, pausing in the air two
or three times,
falling in stages. When we
get off we are so dizzy
we sometimes
wonder if earth can be depended upon.
Later we get used to it.
Flatness, we have to admit,
is fact. And tomorrow the fair will be gone.

Politesse

A memory kissed my mind
    and its courtesy hurt me.
On an ancient immaculate lawn
    in an English county
you declared love, but from *politesse*
    didn't inform me
that the fine hairs shadowing my lip
    were a charge against me.

Your hair was gods' gold, curled,
    and your cricketer's body
tanned – as mine never would tan –
    when we conquered Italy
in an Austin 7 convertible,
    nineteen thirty;
I remember its frangible spokes
    and the way you taught me

to pluck my unsightly moustache
   with a tool you bought me.
I bought us a sapphire, flawed,
   (though you did repay me)
from a thief on the Ponte Vecchio.
   Good breeding made me
share the new tent with Aileen
   while you and Hartley,

in the leaky, unpatchable other,
   were dampened nightly.
If I weren't *virgo intacta*,
   you told me sternly,
you'd take me like a cat in heat
   and never respect me.
That was something I thought about
   constantly, deeply,

in the summer of '54, when I
   fell completely
for a Milanese I only met once
   while tangoing, tipsy,
on an outdoor moon-lit dance-floor.
   I swear you lost me
when he laid light fingers on my lips
   and then, cat-like, kissed me.

Aubade

Intervention of chairs at midnight.
The wall's approach, the quirkish ambivalence
of photographs, today in daylight,
mere pieces of balance. My brown dress
tossed, messed, upheld by the floor.
Rags of ordinary washed light
draped as to dry on the brown furniture.
And the big bed reposed, utterly white,
that ached our darkness, rocked our weight.

Reversals

Clouds – plainmen's mountains –
islands – inlets – flushed archipelagos –
begin at the horizon's illusory conclusion,
build in the curved dusk
more than what is usually imaginary,
less than what is sometimes accessible.
Can you observe them without recognition?

Are there no landscapes at your blurred edges
that change continually away from what they are?
that will not lie solid in your clenched eye?
Or is love in its last metamorphosis arable,
less than what was sometimes imaginary,
more than what was usually accessible –
full furrows harvested, a completed sky?

Two Love Poems

1

You I embrace,
each eye my face,
hold me now
in my first darkness.
Let me stray through you
to the soft shock
of my beginning.
Stay and be witness
to this fluid rock
cooling and stiffening
in repeated rains.
Also to the sloth of hills building,
the gathering of mountains.

2

When we loved
it was as if we created each other.
As if in my body two children,
two embryos,
curled in the well of my sex.

But then you detached yourself,
you receded, transformed into pure sound –
a bell sharpening itself on its distance,
a blade honing itself to tremulous thinness.

While the mirror held me dumbly – my woman's face,
my body like a globe
nourishing its stray curl of flesh,
my huge breasts and body bound,
bound to the shape of this world.

Wanted

'I want you forever and ever,' I want to say.
Meaning that no night passes, and no day
Without your being wished for, thought of,
Abstract as age to youth, or war in peace.
Will the ache of your always absence ever cease?
Or will we be someday, somewhere, together enough
For you to keep turning pages till night is grey?
For me to want you away?

Posted

Instead of your letter
a late train out of the north
plunges towards London, bringing me down
to myself.

Instead of your words
this scribble inside my skin
is literature your hand, my hand
sealed in.

It's all we could never say
but only do.

I dare not read for fear of
losing you,

but fold myself
unopened – though I wrote
as much of it as you – into
this note

which I'll receive
once I come back to me,
tear open, study, scarcely believe
I see.

Drought

After the exhilaration of the peaks,
look on, look back:
infatuations, screes parched as their rocks.
A river of dry water scours dry land,
those twisted, black, alluvial obsessions.
Memory is a river without rain.

Restore the flood of simple speech again,
affectionate plash of word thrown over pain,
the brown of perpetual flowing where your hand
thrusts white beneath the cool of sliding waters,
invites, invents, forgives its own distortion,
gripping the green of live and rooted matters.

After the End of It

You gave and gave,
and now you say you're poor.
I'm in your debt, you say,
and there's no way to repay you
but by my giving more.

Your pound of flesh is what you must have?
Here's what I've saved.

This sip of wine is yours,
this sieve of laughter. Yours,
too, these broken haloes
from my cigarette, these coals
that flicker when the salt wind howls
and the letter slot blinks
like a loud eyelid over the empty floor.

I'll send this, too, this gale between rains,
this wild day. Its cold is so cold
I want to break it into panes
like new ice on a pond; then pay it
pain by pain to your account.
Let it freeze us both into some numb country.
Giving and taking might be the same there.
A future of measurement and blame
gone in a few bitter minutes.

An Impenitent Ghost
(USA, 2004)

The sumptuous tackiness of the motel
Told me its tale before my plastic key
Triggered the wink that worked its magic spell.
Behold! A stage set for adultery.
I hardly had to look, I knew it well,
The stained, upholstered suite, the huge TV,
The wine, the mattress big enough for three.
Nothing amiss as far as I could tell,
Except a face I wasn't looking for,
Watchful beneath her wrinkles in a gleam
Thrown from the looking glass that faced the door.
Drawn curtains chasing mirrors with a beam?
Or love's impenitent ghost that to ignore
Would mean I knew it was myself I'd seen?

'All Canal Boat Cruises Start Here'

(Regent's Park, 1987)

A musk of kittening
snuffed out her morning dream:
the childhood tabby whelping on her mother's shoes.
Still no one could find those
x-ray photographs of embryos.

'I didn't know I could dream smells,'
she said at breakfast.
'You're pregnant,' he said. 'You're a miracle.'
'I'm guilty where there's too much evil.'

Later they walked by the canal:
the Sunday crush, the peacefulness,
a crowd of sleepy explosives spoiling the waterfowl,
exclusive wagging dogs, the lovers' binary excuse,
the straggling families.

'They don't see us,
they're all wound up in themselves,' as she
looked understanding at one impervious mamma,
the daughter's pale silk hair shining,
a sulky boy scuffing behind.

Was that it? That look flashing (was he?)
furtive, from a second-hand suit?
Scary, the shabby solitary, hating you
and apologising.

In the fenced off zoo, an elephant
took a tiny white keeper for a trot.
And, crikey! that barge cat
leaping three feet of slime to the quay.

But in painful labour
it was blue sky and fishermen she remembered,
each hopeful alone
in his nest of a basket and stool.

'They didn't catch fish,
but love, what a guard of honour,'
as the waving drawbridge of rods
bowed the pleasure boats through.

This

isn't 'making' love,
This is feeding off the substance of
what was made when we were made.

This is the body unafraid
of the soul. This is Abelardian glut
in a starved school.

This is negation of adulthood's rule
that talks by rote.
This is travelling out to where

a curved adventure
splashes on planes of sunlight to become
one perfectly remembered room:

white walls, white wings of curtain, window
screened but open
wide to cricket chirr in a field where no

discovery is new.
This is the always has been. What we do
is home. And this is I and you.

*   *   *

In the House

Among others it is the same. It is repeated.
A box not solid but with apertures
showing it to be, to the eye, hollow,
a container for light and noise,
not necessarily in three dimensions.

It might be the third in a series of mirrors.
It might be the real thing.

Whatever it is, it has claims on me.
Its surface establishes itself
outside and around me,
drawing me through or into
what I take to be my proper dominion.

These keys are my keys, this door my door.
The interior is entirely familiar.

At the same time, nowhere is my choice
evident as a force for arrangement.
What meaning has this long white
chain of machinery, even as teeth,
extended, or painted, to the point of its disappearance?

It waits in the silence of concealed energy.
It grins with the jaws of a piano.

Again, these interminable stairs bristling with children.
'Mother, mother,' they wail. They bleat with desire.
They quarrel and hold up their wounds to be kissed.
And yet when I bend to them
I'm kissing a photograph. I taste chemicals.
My lips meet unexpectedly a flatness.

And here are vases and reflections of vases
on the tables; gardens, and reflections
in the windows of the gardens.
Delphiniums and poppies, veins and arteries,
they compose an expensive anatomy.

The sunlight is apparently generated indoors.
The season is synthetic but permanent.

Look, I am free, free to go anywhere.

There is nowhere to go but on and on
through soft contradictory perspectives,
corridors increasingly smoothed by carpets,
incandescent, metallic, immaculate, sweetened.

Nothing has happened. Nothing will happen.
There is neither an exit nor a reason for getting out.

Night Thoughts and False Confessions

He:

How uneasily I live
in the house of imagination.
True beams drive cleanly, rising,
sliding from hissing traffic, only to
slip or miss on your chancy ceiling.
We lie in your bed's lewd negative.
I smell you not sleeping.
I can feel you being human and woman.
On the slopes of the absolute
absolutely nothing would happen.
The world would revolve and evolve,
pure white, stone white and blue,
the beautiful figure of the desert,
musical and mathematical, its deep throat
blameless, immaculate, swallowing you.

She:

With wary brutality,
the thrush cracks the house of the snail.
When you said you were leaving me
your face flashed beaky and cruel.
My shell disintegrated completely.
You beat me and beat me
on the slab of your mind's concrete.
I was sweetness in your kitchen,
obedience in your word-stall.
I was softness overflowing in your garden
scented deep at nightfall.
I cry for lost days, for youth,
for love questioned too late,
as the cooked trout weeps white eyes
on the gourmet's plate.

The Suburb

No time, no time,
and with so many in line to be
born or fed or made love to, there is no
excuse for staring at it, though it's spring again
and the leaves have come out looking
limp and wet like little green new born babies.

The girls have come out in their new bought dresses,
carefully, carefully. They know they're in danger.
Already there are couples crumpled under the chestnuts.
The houses crowd closer, listening to each other's radios.
Weeds have got into the window boxes. Washing hangs helpless.
Children are lusting for ice cream.

It's my lot each May to be hot and pregnant,
a long way away from the years when I slept by myself –
the white bed by the dressing-table pious with cherry blossom,
the flattery and punishment of photographs and mirrors.

We walked home by starlight and he touched my breasts.
'Please, please!' Then I let him anyway. Cars
droned and flashed, sucking the cow parsley. Later
there were teas and the engagement party. The wedding
in the rain. The hotel where I slept in the bathroom.
The night when he slept on the floor.

The ache of remembering, bitter as a birth. Better
to lie still and let the babies run through me.
To let them possess me. They will spare me
spring after spring. Their hungers deliver me.
I grow fat as they devour me. I give them my sleep
and they absolve me from waking. Who can accuse me?
I am beyond blame.

The Takeover

What am I to do? Where am I to go?
The house has been entirely taken over by women.
To every corner they have brought their respectable destruction.
Listen and you can hear them bustling in my lost rooms,
sorting the dust into piles, embracing the furniture,
polishing, pummelling, scurrying, complaining;
pulling up the papers like weeds.

Impossible to know how not to enrage them.
Their rules are exuded inaudibly – vapours
that congeal into speech only when misunderstood.
They are like music. Every woman is an orchestra.
Or an explorer, a discoverer of uninhabitable moods.
If they love me,
it may be because I divest them of boredom.
I am useful as a conductor of superfluous energies.
But how through their wire-like waists and wrists
do their quick lusts slip unresisted into my lap?
Why do I allow them to litter my mind?

They moved in politely, not knowing who I was.
How pretty they were, flitting from mirror to mirror
in their gauze dresses. How delightful and thoughtful.
I should have known when they said they liked me
they liked tidying up messes,
they needed rooms to have taste in.
Their little red pulses beat I, I, I,
under the most delicate skin.

Silence is what they're afraid of.
They take precautions always to move in a pack.
Knowing also that loneliness never attacks an argument,
all the mothers and sisters and daughters
glare suspiciously at each other over the tall
generations, even when they appear to be writing letters
or playing the piano.

Not one of them forgets for a moment
I am able to escape. They make it my fault
they have locked themselves up in my house.
They hate my free tempers and private indulgences.
But only the saint or the reprobate need not let
affection affect him.

If I were a good man or a bad man,
I think I might make them behave.
As it is, they have made me believe in their attentions.
I don't know what I would want to replace them
if they should leave.

The Mother

Of course I love them, they are my children.
That is my daughter and this my son.
And this is my life I give them to please them.
It has never been used. Keep it safe, pass it on.

Generations

Know this mother by her three smiles:
A grey one drawn over her mouth by frail hooks,
A hurt smile under each eye.

Know this mother by the frames she makes.
By the silence in which she suffers each child
To scratch out the aquatints in her mind.

Know this mother by the way she says
'Darling' with her teeth clenched,
By the fabulous lies she cooks.

Five Poems of Innocence and Experience

The Crush

Handsome as D'Artagnan,
inaccessible as Mr Darcy.
She observes him in the bulge of her
mother's teapot... once.
There are other views. Church.
He, robed in the choir, she
behind hats, among pews.
Her eyes grope towards him,
swerve, avoid the impossible
terror of his attention.
Weekdays she wanders near his house.
He pounds the piano.
The *Fantasiestüke* weigh within her
like a dangerous possession

The Marriage

They will fit, she thinks,
but only if her backbone
cuts exactly into his rib cage,
and only if his knees
dock exactly under her knees,
and all four
agree on a common angle.

All would be well
if only
they could face each other.

Even as it is,
there are compensations
for having to meet
nose to neck
chest to scapula
groin to rump
when they sleep.

They look, at least,
as if they were going
in the same direction.

The Affair

He moves off at dawn,
away from the swollen sheets,
the room like a stage, its hooded light
extravagant with gestures and features,
its revelations already hurrying away from them
as they stand and dress.

Only a door between himself
and the widening greyness. The houses
flatten themselves a little into their limbo.
A blackbird, tentatively. The first car.
A light on, yellow, in an upstairs window.

These things as they are,
on the scaffolding just as they are,
of the night beneath them.

The Demolition

They have lived in each other so long
There is little to do there.
They have taken to patching the floor
While the roof tears.

The rot in her feeds on his woodwork.
He batters her cellar.
He camps in the ruin of her carpet.
She cries on his stairs.

Old Scholars

They have written it
all in their minds a thousand times,
so neither believes that
the wound behind his lips can be
healed by her lips, or that
he could come out of the storm
from the leaves of October
to find in her lap
what her eyes give him
easily and lazily.
All the same, here they are,
two thumbed manuscripts,
remembering mainly
the work of it, mainly
the work of it.

The Other House

In the house of childhood
I looked up to my mother's face.
The sturdy roofbeam of her smile
Buckled the rooms in place.
A shape of the unchangeable
        taught me the word 'gone'.

In the house of growing up
I lined my prison wall
With lives I worshipped as I read.
If I chose one, I chose all,
Such paper clothes I coveted
        and ached to try on.

The house of youth has a grand door,
A ruin the other side
Where death watch & company
Compete with groom and bride.
Nothing was what seemed to be
        in that charged dawn.

They advertised the house of love,
I bought the house of pain,
With shabby little wrongs and rights
Where beams should have been.
How could those twisted, splintered nights
      stand up alone?

My angry house was a word house,
A city of the brain,
Where buried heads and salt gods
Struggled to breathe again.
Into those echoing, sealed arcades
      I hurled a song.

It glowed with an electric pulse,
Firing the sacred halls.
Bright reproductions of itself
Travelled the glassy walls.
Ignis fatuus, cried my voice,
      and I moved on.

I drove my mind to a strange house,
Infinitely huge and small:
The cone to which this dew-drop earth
Leeches, invisible.
Infinite steps of death and birth
      lead up and down.

Beneath me, infinitely deep,
Solidity dissolves.
Above me, infinitely wide,
Galactic winter sprawls.
That house of the utterly outside,
      became my home.

In it, the house of childhood
Safeguards my mother's face.
A lifted eyebrow's 'Yes, and so?'
Latches the rooms in place.
I tell my children all I know
      of the word 'gone'.

Old Wife's Tale

'Well then, goodbye,' she said coldly,
'hot men must mate.'

But the energy of injury –
oh, it hurts like hate.

Eros

I call for love
But help me, who arrives?
This thug with broken nose
And squinty eyes.
'Eros, my bully boy,
Can this be you,
With boxer lips
And patchy wings askew?'

'Madam,' cries Eros,
'Know the brute you see
Is what long overuse
Has made of me.
My face that so offends you
Is the sum
Of blows your lust delivered
One by one.

We slaves who are immortal
Gloss your fate
And are the archetypes
That you create.
Better my battered visage,
Bruised but hot,
Than love dissolved in loss
Or left to rot.'

(1990)

155

Questionable

When she laid a light hand on his elbow saying
'I seem to be hungry,' she knew she meant
Oh, to be thirty years younger,
lying with his head in my lap
tracing with one feather finger
the beautiful bowline of his upper lip.

But when he replied in his charming accent,
'Let's go find something to eat,' it wasn't evident –
no? – he meant more than that.
So Nudeln mit Pfifferling had to do.
Maybe what his eyes said was innocent.
Maybe it was not. She never knew.

False Flowers

(for Caroline Ireland)

They were to have been a love gift,
but when she slit the paper funnel,
they both saw they were fake; false flowers
he'd picked in haste from the store's display,
handmade coloured stuff, stiff as crinoline.

Instantly she thought of women's hands
cutting in grimy light by a sweatshop window;
rough plank tables strewn with cut-out
flower heads: lily, iris, primula, scentless
chrysanthemums, pistils rigged on wire
in crowns of sponge-tipped stamens,
sepals and petals perfect, perfectly
immune to menaces from the garden.

Why so wrong, so...flattening? Why not instead
symbols of unchanging love?
                              Yet pretty enough,
she considered, arranging them in a vase
with dry grass and last summer's hydrangeas
whose deadness was still (how to put it?)
alive, or maybe the other side of life.
Two sides, really, of the same thing?

She laughed a little, such ideas were embarrassing
even when kept to oneself,
but her train of thought
carried her in its private tunnel through supper,
and at bedtime, brushing her teeth,
she happened to look up at the moon.
Its sunlit face was turned, as always, in her direction.
The full moon, she couldn't help thinking,
though we see only half of it.

It was an insight she decided she could
share with him, but when he joined her
and together they lay in the dark,
there seemed no reason to say anything.
The words, in any case, would be wrong,
would escape or disfigure her meaning.
Good was the syllable she murmured to him,
fading into sleep. And just for a split second,
teetering on the verge of it, she believed
everything that had to be was understood.

On Watching a Cold Woman Wade into a Cold Sea

The way that wintry woman
Walked into the sea
Was as if, in adultery,
She strode to her leman.

Something in the way she
Shrugged off her daughters,
Moping by the sea's hem
As if they were human

But she of the pedigree
And breed of Poseidon,
Slicing through the breakers
With her gold plated knees,
Twisting up her hair
With a Medusan gesture;

Something in the augury
She shook from her nature
Made women look at women
Over stiff cups of tea,
And husbands in their season
Sign suburbanly to see her.

Oh go dally with your children
Or your dogs, naked sirs!
The venom of the ocean
Is as kindness to hers.

* * *

Musician's Widow

Plants she loved, all growing things.
Soil was nourishment richer than food for her,
richer than sex as she grew older. But she
hated death, hated his unjust death in particular.
The music of him tunnelled through her mind to pursue her.

For a time she remembered to return to him.
She left the upholstery of the new home, the ferns,
the fuchsias, the piano-furnished living-room,
and followed her spade into the cold warmth
his absence had hollowed out for her in earth.

Desire for him she burned with his body, though.
Detritus of nostalgia was a waste of good.
And she had to come back as woman to the world,
a green branched seedling of her purpose, need,
the life behind her gaping like a seed.

The Professor's Tale

(New England)

It's best, if you can, to love your children,
but adjusting to their strange dispositions
in a nasty world means discipline.

I knew a widow, a PhD, steady and musical,
whose daughter, at ten, suddenly
without warning or reason, stamped on her violin.

I think she had a funny son, too –
made a habit of knifing the piano,
or throwing hi fi's and typewriters out the window.

Naturally, with such children, she
came to me for advice. It was not I,
however, who told her to tip them off her life.

She was someone I admired for her agenda.
Not a day slipped by without improving itself
culturally or horticulturally under her eye.

I used to stop by on Sundays – Lapsang, langoustes,
a discourse on *Rosa semperflorens*. Beautiful house,
cool and feathery like her flowers, even in August.

One day, her eyes wet stars, she laughed and confessed,
'All I want is appreciation. When I put myself into a project
I'd like something back in return.' Well, of course.

Practising in life what in theory she knew to be
practical. Or maybe subtle. Her garden embodied
espressivo what (*pianissimo*) she needed to tell me.

'Not that not to do well is wrong.
But that not to be seen to do well
is inexcusable.' I remember her pretty Sèvres,

quaint little antique cups with pink roses.
And those charming photographs of her children
smiling from the grand piano, at appealing ages.

Stone Fig

The young fig tree feels with its hands
along the white sunny wall
and at the end of August
produces seven fruits,
seven royal fists that will be
runny with seed, ripe
with a musky honey that rarefies sweetness.

For the sick woman in the bedroom
behind the all-day-drawn curtains
I set the fruit in the sun
by the kitchen window.
Seven brimming wineskins
and a flint from the garden
she must have collected with a smile,
for it looks exactly like a fig.

A stone fig,
a hard, smooth, comfort-in-the-hand
Platonic Idea of Fig.
I watch the others daily for readiness;
this one, and now that one.

As if they were the last of her feelings
the old lady gobbles the figs.
Quickly, quickly, such greediness.
She eats them like anaesthetic.
Here's pith in her pale fingernails,
purple on the stubble of her chin.

Her legs are dry twigs. She can't
trust them to take her to the toilet,
then back again. Her skin is mottled
with overripeness I look away from.

She wants, she smiles, to sleep
and sleep and sleep. And then
to sleep again.

Hadrian's

Animula, vagula blandula,   Little soul, gentle and fickle,
Hospes comesque corporis,   Guest and friend of my flesh,
Quae nunc abibis in loca   Where will you spend your exile,
Pallidula rigida nudula,   Cold, annulled, colourless
Nec ut soles dabis iocos.   Who used to give me happiness.

Emperor Hadrian, AD 76-138

A Sepia Garden

Though you won't look at it,
a flat, generous lawn;
two rows of cypresses, ragged
(these days such places can't afford
a full-time gardener); kitchen plot
with stakes for runner beans;
brambles along a brick wall;
and beyond the washing lines,
a wild place with bearded trees
that must have been an orchard.

You can still pick plums there,
and grey apricots, but today,
pulping the windfalls,
an all-purpose handy man
is driving a tractor-mower.
Preceding us, he makes it easier
to push you in your chair.

He burrs off, cutting a pale corridor
between old-fashioned beds: sage,
potentilla, buddleia attended still
by peacock butterflies; and now in August,
fringed with misty thickets. Ordinary
lavender, but we have to stop.
Even you, hunched like stone,
your eyes slammed shut, feel it
begging, ordering you: re-collect yourself.

Pick a stalk. Crush it in your fingers.
A scent so strong it stings.
Your eyes water. Who is it
lifting... from a drawer, is it?
something you ache to touch
and don't dare. A fire opal.
Gold shoes in tissue paper.
A black lace Spanish shawl
scaly with sequins.
A torn cloth doll; its too-blue
porcelain eyes stare at you
as the album, bound in rust,
cracks open wavy pages.
You wrinkle your nose.
A childhood that was yours, and still is,
rushes out like a nursery rhyme,

disintegrates, a handful of
grey-blue ash, lost in the grass

over which we creep,
the present 'me'
listening with head bowed
to the present 'you',
rehearsing complaints,
canvassing chances
(*I won't last the night*)
for painless, everlasting
release from rotting nails
and puffy, useless ankles,
tussles with the nurses,
hours on the commode,
indignities of shaving, balding,
balancing leaden breasts on a bird's chest –
awful little mucks that make your life.

Did you ever worry as a child
about dying and coming back a ghost?
What age would you dress up in?
Would they give you a choice?
The problem would arise in heaven, too,
though you never subscribed to it.
Is it really you?
I thought I'd never see you again.

You raise it every time, that question of
'really being', its Dorian refrain
an echo trembling in your sepia garden,
drifting through the corridors of tableaux.

I can't help supposing that
it never really fitted, your long life –
those dreary, loose-cut, madam
hand-me-down roles: 'rich man's daughter'
followed by 'don's frightened wife'.
Far too baggy for you,
who would have made a devout botanist;
a happy stone mason; possibly an artist...

In America, we assume there's a self
like a spine in us. Whatever we achieve,
we construct, let's say out of selfishness.
But imagine someone lecturing *you* on
Establishing Identity through the
Acculturation Process. *Absolute rubbish!*

I can hear the tuba in your voice
dismissing *all that rot about identity*
to the lowest ditch of the ridiculous.
So for you, there's been daily irritation,
the cramped frustration of attempting
the jigsaw with pieces missing. My dear,
I promised to love you, and I do.
But no good woman ever lived harder
to stitch a spirit to! As true:
no one could possess more – surely, it's
still called – 'character' – than you.

The wind's up. I see the handy-man
has put away his mower. Time to take you in.
So kind of you to come. Now all the fuss
of blundering to the lift, those awkward doors,
corridor smells, efficient-looking nurses.

Under my cheery words and hasty kiss,
the pressure of your uncathartic tears.
I avert my eyes from other humps in chairs.

Something has to feel, connect, suffer.
Something must be...

Think of it as new-mown grass, or picked lavender,
about as much 'self' as they'll save of us
in a gauze pouch, or a rubbed leather book
between pages of mottled photographs
when they throw us away with our clothes.

Bloody Bloody

Who I am? You tell me
first who you are,
that's manners. And don't shout.
I can hear perfectly well.

Oh. A psychologist.
So you think I'm mad.

Ah, just unhappy.

You must be stupid if you
think it's mad to be unhappy.
Is that what they teach you
at university these days?

I'm sure you're bloody clever.

Bloody? A useful word.
What would *you* say, jolly?

It's bloody bloody,
I assure you,
having to sit up
for a psychiatrist –
sorry, *behavioural psychologist*,
I know there's a difference –
when I want to
lie down and sleep.

The only sensible thing,
at my age, is to be
as you well know
dead, but since they
can't or won't manage
anything like that here,
I consider my right to sleep
to be bloody sacred.

I can't hear you,
I'm closing my eyes.

Please don't open the curtains.

I said *keep the curtains shut!*

Thank you.
       Hate you?
Of course I hate you,
but I can't, in honesty,
say I blame you.
You have to do your job.

There.
That's my telephone.
How fortunate.
You'll avail yourself
of this opportunity, won't you,
to slip tactfully away.

Hello? Yes,
two pieces of good news.
One,
you've just interrupted a most
unnecessary visit,
a young psychological person
is seeing herself out.
Two,
you'll be relieved
to hear I'm worse, much worse.

Black Hole

I have grown small
inside my house of words,
empty and hard,
pebble rattling in a shell.

People around me, people.
Maybe I know them.
All so young
and cloudy, not... not real.

I can't help being the hole
I've fallen into.
Wish I could tell you
how I feel.

Heavy as mud, bowels
sucking at my head.
I'm being digested.
Remember those moles,

lawn full of them in April,
piles of earth they threw
out of their tunnels. Me, too.
Me, too. That's how I'll

be remembered. Piles
of words, sure, to show
where I was. But nothing true
about me left, child.

Lost

Stone-age, stone-grey eyes
clear in her glove-like skin;
a look of having been ironed
before she shuffled in.

Cradling a pink blonde doll
in a quilted bag, pink satin,
she lifts it out a while,
she puts it back again.

Her dead child? Poor, poor lady.
We burn to know... *what reason?*
No sign, from mouth or body.
She stuns our pity, even.

A Tricksy June

I'm an old woman who wants to die.
    They make me live.
I know a woman who wants to live
    She's going to die.
Why? Why? It's tricksy, June.
    Grass looks greener for never sighting the sun.
Nights shrink, days stretch.
    The nurses have to smile. The dinners come.
Is a Mind
    turning down on us or up on us its slate thumb?
Who do you think orders
    these ugly salvia-trimmed gardens to bloom?
Up north, my home,
    pear-blossom's snow on the grass. Must be
the martin's back.
    I'm missing those old-fashioned yellow roses
hugging my gate,
    already losing their frowsy, blowsy furbelows.
Who lets them yawn
    and disintegrate, petal by lazy petal
without complaint?

Granny Scarecrow

Tears flowed at the chapel funeral,
more beside the grave on the hill. Nevertheless,
after the last autumn ploughing,
they crucified her old flowered print housedress
live, on a pole.

Marjorie and Emily, shortcutting to school,
used to pass and wave; mostly Gran would wave back.
Two white Sunday gloves
flapped good luck from the crossbar; her head's plastic sack
would nod, as a rule.

But when winter arrived, her ghost thinned.
The dress began to look starved in its field of snowcorn.
One glove blew off and was lost.
The other hung blotchy with mould from the hedgerow, torn
by the wind.

Emily and Marjorie noticed this.
Without saying why, they started to avoid the country way
through the cornfield. Instead they walked
from the farm up the road to the stop where they
caught the bus.

And it caught them. So in time they married.
Marjorie, divorced, rose high in the catering profession.
Emily had children and grandchildren, though,
with the farm sold, none found a cross to fit their clothes when
Emily and Marjorie died.

To witness pain is a different form of pain

The worm in the spine,
the word on the tongue –
not the same.
We speak of 'pain'.
The sufferer won't suffer it
to be tamed.

There's a shyness, no,
a privacy,
a pride in us. Don't divide us
into best and lesser.

Some of us, 'brave'? 'clever'?
watch at the mouth of it.
A woman vanishes,
eyes full of it, into it,
the grey cave of pain;
an animal drills
unspeakable growth for cover.

Outside, we pace in guilt
Ah, 'guilt', another name.

Not to reproach
is tact she learns to suffer.
And not to relax her speechless
grip on power.

Who's Joking with the Photographer?
(Photographs of myself approaching seventy)

(for Ernestine Ruben)

Not my final face, a map of how to get there.
Seven ages, seven irreversible layers, each
subtler and more supple than a snake's skin.
Nobody looks surprised when we slough off one
and begin to inhabit another.

Do we exchange them whole in our sleep, or
are they washed away in pieces, cheek by brow by chin,
in the steady abrasions of the solar shower?
Draw first breath, and time turns on its taps.
No wonder the newborn's tiny face crinkles and cries:
chill, then a sharp collision with light,
the mouth's desperation for the foreign nipple,
all the uses of eyes, ears, hands still to be learned
before the self pulls away in its skin-tight sphere
to endure on its own the tectonic geology of childhood.

Imagine in space-time irretrievable mothers viewing
the pensioners their babies have become.
'Well, that's life, nothing we can do about it now.'
They don't love us as much as they did, and
why should they? We have replaced them. Just as we're
being replaced by big sassy kids in school blazers.
Meanwhile, Federal Express has delivered my sixth face –
grandmother's, scraps of me grafted to her bones.
I don't believe it. Who made this mess,
this developer's sprawl of roads that can't be retaken,
high tension wires that run dangerously under the skin?
What is it the sceptical eyes are saying to the twisted lips:
ambition is a cliché, beauty a banality? In any case,
this face has given them up – old friends whose obituaries
it reads in the mirror with scarcely a regret.

So, who's joking with the photographer?
And what did she think she was doing,
taking pictures of the impossible? Was a radioscope
attached to her lens? Something teasing under the skull
has infiltrated the surface, something you can't see
until you look away, then it shoots out and tickles you.
You could call it soul or spirit, but that would be serious.
Look for a word that mixes affection with insurrection,
frivolity, child's play, rude curiosity,
a willingness to lift the seventh veil and welcome Yorick.
That's partly what the photo says. The rest is private,
guilt that rouses memory at four in the morning,
truths such as Hamlet used, torturing his mother,
all the dark half-tones of the sensuous unsayable
finding a whole woman there, in her one face.

* * *

After Her Death

In the unbelievable days
when death was coming and going
in his only city,
his mind lived apart in the country
where chairs and dishes were asleep
in familiar positions,
where geometric faces in the wallpaper
waited without change of expression,
where the book he had meant to come back to
lay open on a bedside table,
oblivious to the deepening snow,
absorbed in its one story.

Apology

Mother, I have taken your boots,
your good black gloves, your coat
from the closet in the hall, your prettiest things.
But the way you disposed of your life gives me leave,
the way you gave it away.
Even as I pillage your bedroom,
make off with your expensive, wonderful books,
your voice streams after me, level with sensible urgency.
And near to the margin of tears as I used to be,
I do what you say.

The Loss

Alive in the slippery moonlight,
how easily you managed
to hold yourself upright
on your small heels.
You emerged from your image
on the smooth fields
as if held back from flight by a hinge.

I used to find you
balanced on your visible ghost
holding it down by a corner. The blind
stain crawled, fawning, about you.
Your body staked its shadow like a post.
Gone, you leave nothing behind,
not a toe to hold steady or true
your image which lives in my mind.

Hands

Made up in death as never in life,
mother's face was a mask
set in museum satin.

But her hands. In her hands,
resting, not crossing, on her Paisley dress
(deep combs of her pores,

her windfall palms, familiar routes
on maps not entirely hers
in those stifling flowers)

lay a great many shards of lost hours
with her growing children. As when
tossing my bike

on the greypainted backyard stairs,
I pitched myself up, through the screened door,
arguing with my sister. 'Me, marry?

Never! Unless I can marry a genius.'
I was in love with Mr Wullover,
a pianist.

Mother's hands moved *staccato* on a fat ham
she was pricking with cloves.
'You'll be lucky, I'd say, to marry a kind man.'

I was aghast.
If you couldn't be a genius, at least
you could marry one. How else would you last?

My sister was conspiring to marry her violin teacher.
Why shouldn't I marry a piano
in Mr Wullover?

As it turned out, Mr Wullover died
ten years before my mother.
Suicide on the eve of his wedding, O, to another.

No one said much about why at home. At school
Jennie told me in her Frankenstein whisper,
'He was gay!'

Gay? And wasn't it a good loving thing
to be gay? As good as to be kind,
I thought then.

And said as much to my silent mother
as she wrung out a cloth until her knuckles shone,
white bone under raw thin skin.

The Minister

We're going to need the minister
to help this heavy body into the ground.

But he won't dig the hole;
others who are stronger and weaker will have to do that.
And he won't wipe his nose and his eyes;
others who are weaker and stronger will have to do that.
And he won't bake cakes or take care of the kids –
women's work. Anyway,
what would they do at a time like this
if they didn't do that?

No, we'll get the minister to come
and take care of the words.

He doesn't have to make them up,
he doesn't have to say them well,
he doesn't have to like them
so long as they agree to obey him.

We have to have the minister
so the words will know where to go.

Imagine them circling and circling
the confusing cemetery.
Imagine them roving the earth
without anywhere to rest.

Siskin

(Glasgow, 1967)

Small bird with green plumage,
yellow to green to white
on the underparts, yes, a siskin
alive on my own cedar,
winter visitor, resident in Scotland,
wholly himself.

I saw him, and you, too,
alive again,
thin but expert, seated
with your bird-glasses, bird book
and concentrated expression,
hoping for siskins in Vermont.

He pleased me for your sake –
not so much as he would have pleased you.
Unless it was you he came for,
and I something you inhabited
from the second his green flame
flickered in that black tree
to the next second when he was gone.

The White Room

Long summer shadows calm the grass,
each figure a finger.
Which ones are pointing to the past,
which to the future?

The tiny grey grandmother
loosens an immense shadow.
We shiver in it, but for her
it's a pontoon to the handsome fellow

she married – when was it
they honeymooned in the Philippines?
Teddy Roosevelt was President,
and he'd sent the marines

to educate the Filipinos; God
advancing with his stick.
And grandfather was Christian-good,
but he came home sick,

and the baby died; then money troubles,
syphilis and silence as he sank
into the brass-locked, tissue-papered culls
of her steamer trunk.

How it hunches there, anchored hulk
in the surf of her candlewick bedcover
in the bride-white room we had to visit
with its incense of Bible-leather,
mothballs and sweet unappeasable hurt.

Elegy

Whenever my father was left with nothing to do –
    waiting for someone to 'get ready',
or facing the gap between graduate seminars
    and dull after-suppers in his study
grading papers or writing a review –
    he played the piano.

I think of him packing his lifespan
    carefully, like a good leather briefcase,
each irritating chore wrapped in floating passages
    for the left hand and right hand
by Chopin or difficult Schumann;
    nothing inside it ever rattled loose.

Not rationalism, though you could cut your tongue
    on the blade of his reasonable logic.
Only at the piano did he become
    the bowed, reverent, wholly absorbed Romantic.
The theme of his heroic, unfinished piano sonata
    could have been Brahms.

Boredom, or what he disapproved of as
    'sitting around with your mouth open'
oddly pursued him. He had small stamina.
    Whenever he succumbed to bouts of winter bronchitis,
the house sank a little into its snowed-up garden,
    missing its musical swim-bladder.

None of this suggests how natural he was.
    For years I thought fathers played the piano
just as dogs barked and babies grew.
    We children ran in and out of the house,
taking for granted that the 'Trout' or E flat Major Impromptu
    would be rippling around us.

For him, I think, playing was solo flying, a bliss
    of removal, of being alone.
Not happily always; never an escape,
    for he was affectionate, and the household hum
he pretended to find trivial or ridiculous
    daily sustained him.

When he talked about music, it was never
        of the *lachrimae rerum*
that trembled from his drawn-out phrasing
        as raindrops phrase themselves along a wire;
no, he defended movable doh or explained the amazing
        physics of the octave.

We'd come in from school and find him
        crossed-legged on the jungle of the floor,
guts from one of his Steinways strewn about him.
        He always got the pieces back in place.
I remember the yellow covers of Schirmer's Editions
        and the bound Peters Editions in the bookcase.

When he defected to the cello in later years
        Grandmother, *in excrucio*, mildly exclaimed,
'Wasn't it lovely when Steve liked to play the piano.'
        Now I'm the grandmother listening to Steve at the piano.
Lightly, in strains from the Brahms-Haydn variations,
        his audible image returns to my humming ears.

When the camel is dust it goes through the needle's eye

This hot summer wind
is tiring my mother.
It tires her to watch it
buffeting the poppies.
Down they bow
in their fluttering kimonos,
a suppressed populace,
an unpredictable dictator.

The silver-haired reeds
are also supplicants.
Stripped of its petals,
clematis looks grey
on the wall. My mother,
who never came here,
suggests it's too hot
to cook supper.

Her tiredness gets everywhere
like blown topsoil,
teasing my eyes and tongue,
wrinkling my skin.
Summer after summer, silt
becomes landfill between us,
level and walkable,
level, eventually, and simple.

A Marriage

When my mother knew why her treatment wasn't working,
She said to my father, trying not to detonate her news,
'Steve, you must marry again. When I'm gone, who's going
To tell you to put your trousers on before your shoes?'

My father opened his mouth to – couldn't – refuse.
Instead, he threw her a look; a man just shot
Gazing at the arm or leg he was about to lose.
His cigarette burned him, but he didn't stub it out.

Later, on the porch, alive in the dark together,
How solid the house must have felt, how sanely familiar
The night-lit leaves, their shadows patterning the street.
The house is still there. The elms and the people, not.

It was now, and it never was now. Like every experience
Of being entirely here, yet really not being.
They couldn't imagine the future that I am seeing,
For all his philosophy and all her common sense.

III

Haunted

It's not when you walk through my sleep
That I'm haunted most.
I am also alive where you were.
And my own ghost.

Green Mountain, Black Mountain

I

White pine, sifter of sunlight,
Wintering host in New England woods.
Cold scent, icicle to the nostril,
Path without echo, unmarked page.

> I formed you, you forgot me,
> I keep you like a fossil.
> The air is full of footprints.
> Rings of the sycamore spell you.
> Your name spills out on April ground
>   with October leafmould...

Beech bole, cheekbone of the interior,
Sugaring maple, tap of sour soil.
Woody sweetness, wine of the honeybark,
Mountain trickle, bitter to the tongue.

> You acquired me out of wilderness,
> Grey maples streaked with birches,
> With your black-shuttered
> White wooden houses flanked with porches,
> Your black-painted peeling front doors.

Pairs of shuttered windows,
Sheltered lives.
Child's work, the symmetry,
Thin graves for narrow souls.

> Terra there was before *Terra Nova*.
> You brought to my furred hills
> Axes, steeples; your race split
> Hugely on the heave of the Atlantic...

In April the earth serves patiently its purpose.
Trees unclench their closed crimson fists against return.
How many weeks before ease will annul these
Dark, matted, snow-beaten scraps of mowin?

> Dry wind-eaten beechleaves
> Flutter under their birth arch.
> Steeplebush and blackberry
> Stoop to beginnings.

Green mountain with its shadow future,
Unwritten days in the buried stone.
Black mountain, colour of roots,
Clay in the roof, gag to the mouth.

II

In Border Powys, a Land Rover
stalls on a hill track.
Dai Morgan climbs out with a halter,
plods to a sodden field where
a mare and her colt have mauled
the wet soil of Welsh weather
all a mud-lashed winter.

Unlatching the gate, he
forces the halter on the caked,
anxious head of the mare,
then leads her away to where
a plan of his own makes fast
to some spindle purpose
the fate of the three of them.

The inscrutable movements of the man
puzzle the horses, who
follow him, nevertheless,
up the piebald track,
snowdeep in drift in places,
tyre-churned with red mud.

These are the Black Mountains
where the drenched sleep of Wales
troubles King Arthur in his cave,
where invisible hankerings of the dead
trouble the farms spilled over them –
the heaped fields, graves and tales.

And Dai, with his brace of horses,
nervous of strangers, inbreeder of races,
is Teyrnon still, or Pryderi the colt-child,
fixed without shape or time
between the ghost-pull of Annwfyn,
that other world, underworld, feathering
green Wales in its word-mist,
and the animal pull of his green dunged boots.

III

Rain in the wind
     and the green need of again
          opening in this Welsh wood.

'Vermont' I want to call it.
     Green Mountain, rafter
          over sleepers in the black

hill of returnings, shadows
     in the dry cave
          of the happened.

At peal of memory
     they rise in tatters, imperatives,
          the word fossils,

webs of thready handwriting,
     typewritten strata, uncut stones
          culled for the typesetters' cemeteries

*

If you, mother, had survived
     you would have written...?
          As when we were children

and everything was going on
     forever in New Haven,
          you scratched in your journal,

     It is a strange reaction but suddenly the war
     has made it imperative to spend time at home
     reading and being with my children.

The pen drew its meaning
     through vacancy,
          threading a history.

*

So what shall I do
     with this touchable page that has
          closed over doubt in her voice these forty years?

I set the words up on the table,
     feeling for continuities,
          tap them with my quick nail. Listen.

But her shell has buried her echo in them.
    It is small, hard, a milk tooth
        a guilt pebble, time preserved like an ammonite.

Then maybe on the second
    or the third day of March
        you overhear a blackbird in a dead elm,

or a thrush singing almost before you wake,
    or you walk unexpectedly into the calm
        ravage of a riverbank

where a broken branch
    kneels into rising water to remake
        predictable green tips,

and I know that it matters
    and does not matter...
        It is you in me who lives these things.

*

We thought she'd want us, knowing it was cancer,
But when we went to her she winced.
Her hand became a supplicating blur
That winter, and we didn't see her much.
There was a kind of wilting away in her
As if she couldn't bear the human touch
Of voices. Or it was something more
Unkind in us... resentful helplessness,
A guilty anger. She was dying
At us.   Dying was accusing.

IV

After April snow, such a green thaw.
A chiff-chaff chips a warmer home in that cloud-cliff.
The river bulges, flexing brown Japanese muscles,
moving its smooth planes in multitudes.
Threads of white melt stitch
the slashed flanks of the hill fields.

Soon the animal will be well again,
hunting and breeding in grass-covered bones.
It peers from these clinical windows,
apprehensive but healing.
To be whole will be enough.
To be whole and well and warm,
content with a kill.

V

Crossing the Atlantic. That child-pure
    impulse of away, retreating
        to our God-forgetting present

from the God-rot of old Boston and Leyden.
    To remove to some other place
        for sundry weighty and solid reasons.

And then to be the letter of the place,
    the page of the Lord's approval,
        within the raw green misery of the risk.

For there they should be liable to
    famine and nakedness
        and the want, in a manner, of all things.

Without things, then, the thing was to be done,
    the mountain renamed, the chance
        regiven. Taken again.

*

Crossing the Atlantic, Passport,
    briefcase, two trays of cellophane food
        and a B grade film.

No, I mean
    across to the America
        that lives in the film of my mind.

You would have to be
    alive there, reeled out
        from the spool of your life.

Not as a photograph,
    unhappiness or happiness staring
        from the onceness of a time,

but as the living practice of a now
    rehearsed as certain habits and expressions:
        your shoulders' loosened stoop to the piano,

the length of you decanted on a chair,
    animate in argument, ash scattered
        from your cigarette like punctuation.

And there, among the muses of your house,
    a breeding pack of violins, and cellos
        punished in the corners,

gleaming with the naked backs of girls
    smug in the enslavement of one lover
        or another since the eighteenth century

made its music bread and solace
    for the likes of us who,
        having no other faith,

still kept our covenant with
    German Bach, with Schubert,
        after-dinner Mozart string quartets.

*

The Polish ghettos drained
    into the cattle cars.
        Murdered Vienna bled us violins.

*

Chestnut blossom with its crimson stigmata,
Stamen-thrust from confused hands,
Five white petals, multiple in competing order
So that each candlelabrum stands
As a tree of defeats around a *pietà*.

To be as one mother in a storm of sons,
The charred faces and cracked skulls of a
Comfortable century. Petal-white sands
Made of tiny shellfish. The crashed motorcycle
Where the sea withdraws with no grief at all.

VI

In dread of the black mountain,
Gratitude for the green mountain.
In dread of the green mountain,
Gratitude for the black mountain.

In dread of the fallen lintel and the ghosted hearth,
    gratitude for the green mountain.
In dread of the crying missile and the jet's chalk,
    gratitude for the black mountain.

In dread of the titled thief, thigh-deep in his name,
   gratitude for the green mountain.
In dread of the neon street to the armed moon,
   gratitude for the black mountain.

In dread of the gilded Bible and the rod-cut hand,
   gratitude for the green mountain.
In dread of the falling towers behind the blazing man,
   gratitude for the black mountain.

In dread of my shadow on the Green Mountain,
Gratitude for this April of the Black Mountain,
As the grass fountains out of its packed roots
And a thrush repeats the repertoire of his threats:

> *I hate it, I hate it, I hate it.*
>   *Go away. Go away.*
> *I will not, I will not, I will not.*
>   *Come again. Come again.*

Swifts twist on the syllables of the wind currents.

Blackbirds are the cellos of the deep farms.

Mowin (184) is the Vermonters' term for a hayfield or mowing field.

King Arthur in his cave (185) refers to the Welsh legend regarding Arthur and his warriors who are said not to be dead but asleep in a cave (sometimes Craig-y-Ddinas near Carmarthen). At the peal of a bell they will rise to rescue Wales from her oppressors when her need is greatest. Teyrnon and Pryderi are characters associated with horses in the First Branch of the *Mabinogion*. Annwfyn or Annwn is the Welsh otherworld, comparable to the Irish Sidh. The colours of things and creatures belonging to Annwfyn are red and white.

The quotations in V are from William Bradford's *History of Plymouth Plantation* as quoted in Perry Miller's *The American Puritans* (New York, 1956).

Correspondences

A Family History in Letters

To Philip Hobsbaum,
and in memory of my mother,
Louise Destler Stevenson

CHRONOLOGY

INTRODUCTION: THE FAMILY

Genealogy: The Chandler Family   *192*

1968   An Obituary: Mrs Neil F. Arbeiter   *193*

1968   Eden Ann Whitelaw to her sister Kay Boyd in London   *194*

1968   from *The Clearfield Enquirer:* Clearfield's New Public   *198*
Monument and Museum

PART ONE: IN THE HAND OF THE LORD, 1829-1929

1829   Condolences of a minister to his bereaved daughter   *200*
after the death of her young husband in a Shipwreck
off Halifax, N.S.

1830   The Minister's wife, in confidence, to a beloved sister   *202*
during a January storm

1830   *An Obituary:* The Minister's Wife   *203*

1832   A prodigal son: Reuben Chandler is stricken with guilt   *205*
in New Orleans, having run away from restricting
regimes at home and at Harvard College

1838   A family blunder: Elizabeth Chandler Boyd writes to   *208*
her brother Reuben on the occasion of his engagement
to a Southerner

1840   A daughter's difficulties as a wife: Mrs Reuben   *211*
Chandler to her mother in New Orleans

1849   Fragments: Mrs Reuben Chandler writes to her husband   *214*
during a cholera epidemic

1855   A blunder rectified: A final word from Cincinnati   *215*
businessman, Reuben Chandler, to his runaway wife

1859   A successful American advises his sons studying   *216*
abroad: Reuben Chandler to his sons in Geneva

1864   Letter to a mother from a Confederate soldier: Matthew   *218*
Chandler to Marianne Lavalle Chandler

1867   Notes to a father from a young man gone west: Jacob   *219*
Chandler to his father Reuben Chandler

1895   Maxims of a Christian businessman: From the journal   *221*
of Jacob M. Chandler, Cincinnati's Citizen of the Year

1896   A worried father writes to his daughter at Oberlin   *222*
College: Jacob Chandler to his daughter Maura

1900   A New Year's Message to myself: From the journal of   *224*
Maura Chandler on the eve of her marriage to Ethan
Amos Boyd

1910   A vigorous letter from a salesman of the Lord: Ethan   *226*
Amos Boyd to his wife Maura

1929   from *The Clearfield Enquirer:* A Notice of Insolvency   *227*

1929   A letter to God on hotel notepaper from Ethan Amos   *228*
Boyd

PART TWO: WOMEN IN MARRIAGE, 1930-1968

1968   A London letter: The poet, Kay Boyd, replies ambig-   *229*
uously to her sister in Clearfield

1930   Two Cambridges: A letter from Maura Chandler Boyd   *231*
to her daughter Ruth Arbeiter in England

1936   A letter from an English novelist: Paul Maxwell, author   *233*
of *A Second Eve*, writes to Ruth Arbeiter in Vermont

1936   Two Poems and a Rejection Slip: From the notebooks   *235*
of Ruth Arbeiter

1945   A Love Letter: Ruth Arbeiter to Major Paul Maxwell   *237*

1954   From an Asylum: Kathy Chattle to her mother, Ruth   *239*
Arbeiter

1954   Mrs Lillian Culick, divorcée, to Dr Frank Chattle   *244*

1968   End of a summer's day: From the journal of Ruth   *247*
Arbeiter

PART THREE: LIVING FOR NOW

1968   Professor Arbeiter to his dead wife   *250*

1968   Nick Arbeiter writes poems on the road to Wyoming   *252*
after a funeral in Vermont

1972   Epilogue: Kay Boyd to her father, Professor Arbeiter   *257*

The Chandler Family *

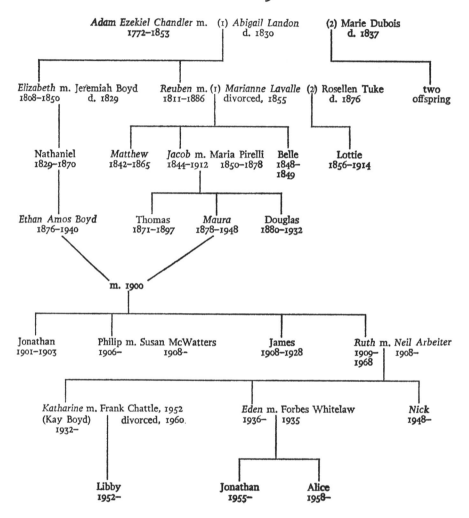

* The names in italic are represented by letters in this book

THE CLEARFIELD ENQUIRER

JULY 5, 1968

Obituary

On the 4th of July, Mrs Neil F. Arbeiter, née Ruth Chandler Boyd, died peacefully in the Vermont State Hospital in Bennington. Mrs Arbeiter was a descendant of the Chandler family whose history is intimately connected with the town of Clearfield. She was fifty-nine years of age.

Mrs Arbeiter was the only daughter of the lay preacher and social reformer, Ethan Amos Boyd. She was born in Clearfield in 1909, when the Chandler House was the center of an experiment in Community and Christian Living conducted by her father. From 1926 until 1930 she attended Oberlin College in Ohio where she graduated *Phi Beta Kappa, Magna Cum Laude*. She was married in 1930 to Neil Freisingham Arbeiter, the Harvard historian, and is survived by him and her three children: Mrs Katharine Ann Chattle, now domiciled in London, England, Mrs Eden Whitelaw of Clearfield, and an only son, Nicholas, who is about to enter his Senior year at Dartmouth College in New Hampshire.

During the painful years preceding her death, Mrs Arbeiter courageously persevered in those works for the public welfare which distinguished her all her life as a New Englander and a patriot. A founding member of the Halifax County League of Women Voters, she was three times elected to the State Board. She was an active supporter of Planned Parenthood, a member of the State Committee for the Preservation of Wild Life, and the author of four pamphlets in the *This is your United Nations* series.

She will be lovingly remembered for her selfless dedication to her country, to her church, to her family and friends. Funeral services will be conducted in the First Presbyterian Church tomorrow, July 6th, at 4.15 p.m. The family requests that no flowers be sent but that donations be made instead to the American Cancer Society.

Eden Ann Whitelaw to her sister Kay Boyd in London

NOVEMBER 5, 1968   MOSSY HOUSE, CLEARFIELD, VERMONT

Dear Kay. So…a summer.
   Four months since she died.
      And your decision not to return,
wise, I wonder?
         Because of course you're missed.
           Poor father!
He's in no mood for anger.
   Tries to live normally:
      office hours, meals, long walks.
Sundays, his string quartet.

You know what's become of the house.
   He asked me to clear it.
      Mother's desk, books, correspondences,
piles of old stuff, mostly letters.
      'Too busy' his excuse.
         Meaning that the dear couldn't face it,
the uselessness, pain of a return
      to a place she's still alive in.
For if she's a ghost, she's here,
          is this house.

Now every day I'm like my own ghost
   moving within hers.
      I blow off the usual mouse droppings
         (packing the stoneware).
I swat late wasps.
   I air out the stale rugs, blankets.
      Then sit up nights.
In the silence.
   The children are asleep
      upstairs in our childstained bedrooms.

Only I in her room,
   her blue wall paper.
      It ought to keep her out!
It ought to keep her dead to what it's come to!
   A stump with its root in her grave.
      An Amen to us.

Yes, and I'd like to save everything,
    have it again.
        Our summers for our children.
Picnicking, haying, those
    purple-mouthed banquets after berry-picking,
        dawdling days, naked in the brook;
or just the naming of places:
    The Star Rock, The Bear Pits, The Druids,
        the view from the hill.

It all seemed interminable in those days.

And now I'm over thirty,
    looking back, looking on.
        Hunched on the spindly pink sofa under the lithographs,
reading and sorting, rereading...
    dead evidences, grievances, a
        yellowing litter of scraps scratched over with lives.

So I cry and cry and then
    wish there were some way to justify
        the release of it.
For it's not for her particular death,
    but for what dies with her.
            Something that calls
for our abduction
    out of things. Nostalgia
        for expended generations.

Yet never more lovely,
    this North-East, this November.
        Maples, barren as wires... like
seas of spun wire
    between the swell of the cloudbanks
        and the black shelving continents of pine.
The hills turn silver in the sun,
    a kind of necessary silver,
        until the seasons converge there,
meeting in confusion,
    the blown leaves and snowflakes
        fountaining together.

Then night after night
    I dream the same nightmare.

On the last warm day
        We all go down to the lake.
        We all drive down to the beach
at the edge of the lake.
    But the lake's shrunk away from its lips
            and lies small as a river,
and the beach is the lake's wrecked floor,
        wrack and litter.
                    And the children,
they tear off their shoes,
        steal ahead of us, beachcombing.
We adults stalk behind,
        parents,
                two of us, loitering.

And the sky is very blue
    and the slick mud, silver, and the
        bare posts are like nails
pulled up out of their shadows.
        Oh, you'd say summer,
                but the woods are grey.
Then a jeep jolts down to the quay
        and two men get out. They
            shuffle a flat-bottomed boat
to the edge of the water,
        climb in and pull themselves, float by
            float by float along a rope
lying slack on the harbor.
        We watch them reel it in,
doubled, always, by water.

And then the children,
        who have rounded the shore,
            cluster opposite, jeering.

Their arms are full of driftwood,
        and their faces so clear
            we seem to share them with some
menace or fascination
        as the boat crawls nearer.
            Then I know they will be gone.
I never will be able to retrieve them.
        I cry out.
            Stumble forward.

Come back! Come back!
> They seem not to hear.
>> And then the children are not our children,
but us.
> Not Jonathan, Libby, Alice, but
>> you, me, Nicholas.

That's when I wake,
> usually as now, with the dawn
>> grey and cold in the empty window.

Kay, please come home.
> Please won't you come home?
>> Come help me keep her alive a little longer.

Clearfield's New Public Monument and Museum

An Historical Note on the Chandler Home

According to Mrs Eden Whitelaw, a daughter of the late Mrs Neil F. Arbeiter who died last July, the Chandler Home is to be opened to the public next summer. Professor Arbeiter has agreed to its being used as a museum and library, and Mrs Whitelaw, who will continue to reside with her family in 'The Old Red Barn' next door, assures us that the original furniture will be preserved, and that a selection of family letters will be made available to the public.

The Chandler family was established in New England when Reverend Adam Ezekiel Chandler emigrated from Yorkshire in 1789. In 1800 he married a daughter of the Landon family in New Haven, after which he settled in what was then called 'Mossy House' in Clearfield. Until his death in 1853 he preached Hellfire and abolition from the pulpit of the First Presbyterian Church. He was famous throughout New England for his uncompromising Calvinism and for his devotion to the cause of Negro emancipation in the South.

During the 1830s and 40s, the Chandler home was a station in the 'underground railway' which aided escaped slaves to flee north into Canada. After the Civil War, the house passed into an era of austere elegance under the ownership of Dr Chandler's grandson, the wealthy and pious Jacob M. Chandler of Chandler Stores, Inc., Cincinnati and Boston. In 1902 the property descended to Jacob's daughter, Maura, who had married the social reformer, Ethan A. Boyd in 1900. Boyd converted the house into a dormitory and retreat for city factory workers. In 1909 it became the center of an experiment in cooperative socialist living, the 'Eden' of English novelist Paul W. Maxwell's *A Second Eve*. In 1929 Ethan Boyd went bankrupt. He ended his days in 1940, a broken and tragic figure, in a mental institution in New York State.

Despite the Great Depression, the Cincinnati Insurance magnate, Herman Arbeiter, was able to save the Chandler estate when his son, Neil, married Ethan and Maura Boyd's only daughter, Ruth, in 1930. The house has passed on through the Arbeiters to the descendants of the original Chandlers who have generously made provisions for their home to be a community monument.

There is no doubt that the Chandler Home remains today a link with our town's great past. We hope it will stand as a monument to Yankee common sense and idealism at this time when the oldest American institutions are in jeopardy. In the teeth of subversion and doubt, let us keep one corner of our dear New England bright and unspoiled. Let us honor our traditions and the dedicated spirit of our ancestors – honest, hardworking, decent Christian Americans – for the sake of whom and whose children Ruth Arbeiter did not live and die in vain.

PART ONE

In the Hand of the Lord

Letters and documents selected from the Chandler Family Archives of the Chandler Memorial Library, Clearfield, Vermont... being a partial record of members of the family descended from Adam Ezekiel Chandler who was, from 1800 until 1843, Minister of the First Presbyterian Church of Clearfield, in the County of Halifax.

Condolences of a minister to his bereaved daughter after the death of her young husband in a shipwreck off Halifax, N.S.

SEPTEMBER 3, 1829   CLEARFIELD, VERMONT

My wretched daughter,

I have studied your letter with exacting and impartial attention.
What shall I say?
Except that I suffer, as you, too, must suffer
increasingly from a sense of the justice of your bereavement.

What did you expect, Elizabeth,
from your childhood preferring, despite my prognostications,
the precarious apartments of the world
to the safer premises of the spirit.
Have I not heard you declare, and on more than one occasion,
that only if your earthly aspirations should be cut down
would you cast yourself upon the Mercy of God?

What your conduct has been your conscience will teach you.
What God in his Justice has performed is plain enough.

Is is possible you imagine you have claims on his Infinite Mercy?
Even presupposing that God has summoned you this sacrifice,
do you deem it in the interest of The Lord to secure your favor?
Is not sacrifice punishment of Sin?
Is it not through God's Will that we all do not perish
instantly? Instantaneously consumed!

Avoid, my child, those rocks on which multitudes have been wrecked!
Think not to gain peace with The Lord by measuring
Immutable Requirements with the petty inch rule of ability!

His requirements of you are but three:
Repentance. Faith. Love. Only these.
How often in my life has some Act of the Almighty
opened vast caverns of tempestuous night and vicissitude!
Yet never before have I felt so keenly, so intimately,
the power of His Unfathomable Choice.

Such a talent cut off!
Scholarship. Humility. Devotion to
Truth and Duty. All in a twinkling rendered useless by that
Hand of Mysterious Providence which plunges like lightning
into the heart of us, scooping, as it were,
but a single drop from the tainted well, swelling,
could we but see it, with the waters of human iniquity
the Eternal River of Heaven which flows from the Throne!

How can I give you the comfort you desire?
Turn rather to that Shepherd you have rejected.
Let him bear you to His Glorious Pastures
where in company with the Chosen of His Flock
you may content your soul with the reflection that
what is loss to you is gain immeasurable to that
dear one now with God.
                         For
fine as was his spirit upon this earth,
drawn down by the body which confined it –
what now must it be, washed white in the Blood of the Lamb,
drenched daily in that Inexhaustible Spring
which is the source of our Everlasting Joy?

My blessing upon you and upon your little one.
May you find in the Love of Jesus hope you had abandoned.
May the Light of His Countenance shine upon you and
give you peace, now and in the Life Everlasting.

                From your loving father on earth who lives in
                The Lord,

                        Adam Chandler

The Minister's wife, in confidence, to a beloved sister during a January storm

JANUARY 14, 1830   CLEARFIELD, VERMONT

My dear Eliza,

Your letter came to hand in good time.
Would answer it at length were it not
for vexations: weather like the Arctic,
violent storms, no wood cut. Dr Chandler
gone to Boston. Youth from Harvard
in exchange here, sprawled by the one fire,
bawling for malmsey, concocting us morsels
for tomorrow's theological banquet while we
shiver on his polar side, hungry for the supper
our wet coals smoke but won't cook!

Anne's in bed. Grippe. And Elizabeth
frantic lest her Nathan, who has weak lungs,
contract it. Black Beck's in the pantry.
I can hear her, poor woman, screaming through
four closed doors. A finger. She crushed it
in the clothes mangle. Doubt she'll save it.

So, with one thing and another,
my reading flags. I average, perhaps,
a page a week. Must content myself,
I fancy, with the learning I possess, or
glean what I can from the backs of newspapers.
I've learned this: Alkalis are thought to be
metal oxides. How I rejoice in this fact.

But the children all ail, and not noiselessly.
Each day's a struggle. Scant food. Stacked drifts.
The horses, sheep, sickly, and poor Bob,
the Labrador, dead in the hayloft, forgotten
after last week's rat-catching!
Alas, I must stop.
My hand's gone numb.
The stove's gone out.
I pray you,
        keep well and God bless you.

From your everloving sister,

Abigail Chandler

202

Obituary
The Minister's Wife

On September 3rd, in the thirty-ninth year of her life in the Lord, Mrs Abigail Landon Chandler, dearly beloved wife of our pastor and brother in Christ, Reverend Dr Adam E. Chandler of the First Presbyterian Church of Clearfield in the County of Halifax, Vermont. She leaves desolate a husband and five children.

In the time of earthly sorrows let us remember that for this pious woman Death was not a termination but a transition.

In its infinite peace, her soul is even now amongst us.

***A prodigal son: Reuben Chandler is stricken with guilt
in New Orleans, having run away from restricting regimes
at home and at Harvard College***

My dear father,
       That I write, sick,
             from a convent in New Orleans

may distress you less
       than that I write at all.
             Pray for my soul.

No.
       Satan has not tempted me with Popery.
             Likewise I turn from the Anti-Christ, Reason, with revulsion.

Yet I have been ill,
       disturbed in my mind,
             found unconscious on the road

by some pupils from this convent,
       struck down, nearly blind,
             from the power of a sun which,

to those bred in our blue Yankee climate,
       is a weapon of fire
             in the hand of the Adversary.

Yet I do not attribute my state
       to the heat or to illness.
             A dream has troubled me night after

night in this place.
       A vision so vivid,
             so beyond my powers of exorcism,

that I lay it in repentance at your feet.
       I regret my past wilfulness and wickedness.
             I beg you regard me as your son.

I dream I am walking on one of these
       high southern levees,
             a baked and dusty road,

pitted with human footprints,
      scarred deeply with cart tracks,
           and also with the tracks of cattle,

horses and sheep and other animals.
      This road I follow with my eyes, head
           lowered, afraid to look up or to the

right or left, though I feel,
      like a palpitating veil,
           the thick vegetation of the Bayou

looming from its moss;
      the fierce, silent pulse of the
           Mississippi; and the sun,

close above me,
      burning through its perishable,
           imagined membrane,

burning, enlarging,
      descending until I needs must,
           from the pressure of it,

kneel down forcibly in the dust,
      raising my hands to God for
           succor and mercy.

I look up.
      And lo, the dome of the Heavens
           is filled with the sun,

and its circle of horizon
      is lashed with the sun's fiery tongues.

To my left,
      an unbounded ocean
           breathes in and exhales.

To my right,
      not a jungle
           but a desert!

Then I look upon the ocean
      and see that it is made not of water
           but of human bodies, hideous and naked;

men, women and children are being
    swept up and dashed down,
        yea, again and again and again

into vast eddies of one another.
    And I see these are living beings,
        some of our country and county.

There is Mad Mistress Beaton,
    shorn of her rags, wig and spectacles.
        And poor, harmless postmaster Brown,

hollow, like a sheep's skull,
    but grey and elongated
        like a tangle of weatherbeaten driftwood.

Always I seem to see my sister Elizabeth,
    but when I cry out, she
        throws back black strands of turbulently

heaving hair and stares horribly through me.
    The next morning she is flung from my sight
        and where she was… is now a coal black

negro, streaked with his blood,
    writhing and shaking his fists and wailing
        even as he vanishes,

'Follow me,
    and I will make you fishers of men!'

I turn then, in terror,
    to my right…to the desert
        where it spills out in miles and miles of

nothing at all.
    And I pray, as Christ prayed,
        for salvation through rejection of Evil.

And then I'm running
    mad with unquenchable thirst,
        between boulders and craters and

dry mountains, starved of vegetation.
    And then I am falling,
        and I fall

thus to wake in the sweat of my sheets,
    weeping like a child,
        stared at by some puzzled black-coiffed

hag who, roused from her sleep and
    doubtful of my sanity, stands beside me,
        uncertain of what to do.

What I am to think, father?
    What is Our Heavenly Father if
        such dreams are of his making?

What is His Love? His Omnipotence?
    His Challenge? His Forgiveness?
        Even His Retribution?

Meaningless as the flesh of that ocean?
    As the stones in that desert of sand?
        Does God, mocking, squat in detachment

behind a great mangle of sun,
    prescribing to the saved as to the damned,
        my own Hell on earth?

My pain... the ache of existence?

    I remain your undeserving and most unhappy son,

    Reuben Chandler

A family blunder: Elizabeth Chandler Boyd writes to
her brother Reuben on the occasion of his engagement to a Southerner

In truth, beloved brother,
> this news of your 'heart's arrangement'
>> martyrs the best affections of my own.

Engaged!
> And to a Southerner!
>> And how, pray, tell father?

If only you could see him...all but
> nailed to *The Emancipator*,
>> racked by the Judas-justice of this land!

Four of our 'midnight Quakers'
> passed amongst us in a month
>> and with precious, brave Marie so near her time,

the burden, as usual,
> devolved absolutely on me!
>> I suppose there must be some good Southerners.

Well, Nathan and I are as
> calm as can be expected.
>> I had (with reference to marriage)

put aside all mementoes of mine.
> I had thought the hurt healed
>> and the scar strong.

But now the utter carelessness
> of your happiness (and selfishness)
>> breaks through my aching wound like a vengeful worm

Lost, lost, dearest friend!
> All his tokens I cherish
>> (corpses in my little gilt box),

his ring,
> his portrait,
>> the fine, silken flame of his hair...

they rise from the dead to me now
        like neglected ghosts
                and publish my blame from their shrine.

It happened one day
        as I sat (in tears) with his likeness,
                dear Nathaniel crept up to my knee.

'Who is this?' I asked smiling,
        (he saw I was weeping).
                'God,' he (so innocent) replied.

'My dear!' I reproved him.
        'Christ, then.'
                'No, *Papa*.'

'Yes, Papa, the same,' the child cried.
        'Is not Papa my Father,
                And Father is God,

And God changed to Jesus
        who died!'
                Just imagine my feelings!

I took him in my lap
        in a thunder-shower of kisses,
                saying 'Papa is *with* Jesus

because Jesus died *for* Papa.
        But we all will be with Papa
                when we die.'

And he cried... and even father –
        in a little while he joined us –
                cried, imploring us to pray!

And so we prayed
        and as we did, I felt
                a sunbeam spread about me

bearing in tender armfuls
        wondrous hope.
                And I saw my beloved husband

at rest in the bosom of Eternity,
        and my own soul, like your own,
                asleep on the Breast of the Lord.

209

So, now, my dear brother,
 may His light shine upon you,
  and give you His Peace and His Wisdom even now.

And may you be forgiven
 for the pain you have brought to others,

  from your loving and Christian sister,

Elizabeth B

A daughter's difficulties as a wife: Mrs Reuben Chandler
to her mother in New Orleans

SEPTEMBER 3, 1840   CINCINNATI, OHIO

Now that I've been married for almost four weeks, Mama,
    I'd better drop you and Papa dear a line.
        I guess I'm fine.

Ruby has promised to take me to the Lexington
    buggy races Tuesday, if the weather cools.
        So far we've not been out much.

Just stayed here stifling in hot Cincinnati.
    Clothes almost melt me, Mama, so I've not got out
        my lovely red velvet-and-silk pelisse yet,

or that sweet little lambskin coat with the fur hood.
    The sheets look elegant!
        I adore the pink monogram on the turnover

with exactly the same pattern on the pillowcases!
    Darlings!
        How I wish you could breeze in and admire them!

And the table linen,
    and the bone china,
        and the grand silver candlesticks,

and especially those
    long-stemmed Venetian wine glasses
        with the silver rims.

My, didn't your little daughter
    play the queen the other day
        serving dinner to a whole bevy of bachelors!

To tell the truth, Mama,
    Reuben was a silly to ask them,
        just imagine me, tiny wee me,

hostess to fourteen dragons
    and famished monsters,
        doing battle with fuming pipes and flying plugs.

Poor Rube!
    He doesn't chew and hardly ever smokes.
        He must have felt out of place.

I was frantic, naturally,
    for fear of wine stains and
        tobacco juice on the table cloth,

so I set Agatha to dart in and dab with a towel,
    and told Sue in the kitchen, to brew up some coffee
        quick, before they began speechmaking.

But it was no use.
    They would put me up on a chair after the ices,
        and one of them – Big Tom they call him –

(runs a sizable drygoods business here)
    well, this Tom pulled off my shoe,
        tried to drink wine out of it while

I was dying of laughter,
    and Tom was laughing too, when suddenly
        I slipped, and fell on the Flemish decanter!

It broke.
    Such a terrible pity.
        And so funny at the same time.

I must admit the boys were bricks,
    carrying the tablecloth out to the kitchen,
        holding it out while I

poured hot water from a height,
    just as you always said to.
        Everything would have been all right.

The party could have gone on.
    Then Reuben had to nose in and spoil things,
        sending me to bed!

So the boys went off, kind of sheepish.

Later Reuben said I had disgraced us
    and where was I brought up anyway,
        to behave like a bar maid!

But it wasn't my fault, Mama,
    They were his friends. He invited them.
        I like to give men a good time!

I'm writing this in bed because
    my head thumps and drums every time I move
        and I'm so dog tired!

The only time I sleep is in the morning
> when Reuben has left for the office.
>> Which brings up a delicate subject, Mama.

I've been thinking and thinking,
> wondering whether I'll ever succeed in being
>> the tender, devoted little wife you wanted me to be.

Because...oh, Mama,
> why didn't you tell me or warn me before I was married
>> that a wife is expected to do it every night!

But how could we have guessed?
> Ruby came courting so cool and fine and polite,
>> while beneath that gentlemanly, educated exterior...

well! I don't like to worry you, Mama.
> You know what men are like!
>> I remember you said once the dears couldn't help it.

I try to be brave.
> But if you did have a chance to speak to Papa,
>> mightn't you ask him to slip a word,

sort of man to man to Reuben...
> about how delicate I am
>> and how sick I am every month,

not one of those cows
> who can be used and used!
>> Someone's at the door.

I forgot,
> I asked Fanny Daniels to come up this morning
>> to help fix a trim for my hat.

I'll have to hustle!
> Give all my love to dear Spooky and Cookie.
>> How I miss them, the doggy darlings!

Oceans of hugs and kisses for you, too,
> and for precious Papa,

From your suffering and loving daughter,

Marianne

Fragments: Mrs Reuben Chandler writes to her husband during a cholera epidemic

NOTE: *Most of this journal, written on shipboard, seems to have been destroyed, probably by fire. What remains suggests that Mrs Chandler journeyed to New Orleans without her husband's permission, thus becoming indirectly the cause of her baby's death.*

AUGUST, 1849   EN ROUTE FROM NEW YORK TO NEW ORLEANS
                               ABOARD THE 'GENERAL WAYNE'

Two weeks aboard the 'General Wayne'
is little more than a floating hospital
        vomiting spells. I attribute them to
            is truly ill. For two days he has
                in his bunk.
                    Belle seems to recover. At least
                        fretful which indicates improvement.
                    struck by a nervous disorder.
I sleep very little and take no solid food.
                                    (*page torn*)

(*Second page*)
Yesterday evening poor little Cookie died.
She was seized suddenly with spasms, poor thing,
and died in an hour. You will accuse me of
                    but it was truly frightful.
            I have not slept for weeping.
                only a dog!
                                    (*page torn*)

(*Third page*)
            arrived safely in New Orleans but
            embark. We are all in quarantine
                might be better, but Belle is
                    all day by her bedside. Doctor
                        plague and gives me no hope
                            pray for survival.
                                    (*page torn*)

(*Fourth page*)
            have not been able to put pen to
                all over. Our dear little girl
                    among the blessed, my beautiful
                        authorities let no one near.
                        darkies. I am full of
                one who was without fault and so
                        lies shrouded in my sister's
                            blame God and myself, dear
                    why you have left me without support?
                                    (*page torn*)

214

A blunder rectified: A final word from Cincinnati businessman, Reuben Chandler, to his runaway wife

APRIL 4, 1855   CINCINNATI, OHIO

Nor do I wish to prolong this tired debate.
I will be brief therefore.
I arrived back from New York late
to find your letter.
So be it.
It was never in the book of my mind
to hold you by force
if I could not restrain you
by the bonds of wifely affection.
Consider yourself free.
On one condition.
That you send both boys to me
entrusting, by law,
their future to my direction.

Of the causes of strife between us –
your selfishness, your vanity, your whims, wife,
your insistent and querulous disobedience,
no more.
It is enough for you to live with your naked conscience
upon which must lie the death of our infant daughter
as her innocent body lies, unfulfilled, in its grave.
Farewell.
Find peace if you can with your sister,
her friends and fashions.
Frivolity is an armor of lace
against the mind's inner vengeance and poisons.

I shall send the boys abroad for their education
as soon as I am advised of a suitable school.
Respect my will with regard to the bills of divorce.
Direct all correspondence to my lawyer, Mr Duval
(you have his address).
Now amen to this farce.

                                        R.C.

A successful American advises his sons studying abroad:
Reuben Chandler to his sons in Geneva

NOVEMBER 5, 1859   CINCINNATI, OHIO

My dear sons,

I have just received Monsieur R's term report
and am much pleased.
He says you work diligently and faithfully
Such work, my sons, prepares you for the time
when you will be men in this our own rich country
where labor is the standard of nobility,
idleness, wretchedness,
and careless indolence, a sin
against the Creator whom we worship.
For here we are judged and respected
according to the work we accomplish.

Summer has passed away
and the beautiful fall,
and now we have winter with its
bitter snows and winds.
Yet, on careful inspection do we find
that nothing is evil or ugly in God's Universe,
but all is for His good and wise purpose.

When you were young
you put to me many questions which,
when I could not answer,
made you cry.
Now you are wiser and older
and know as I
that religion to the mind
is as nourishing food to the body.
Little need, therefore, to urge
or admonish you.
Read your Bible with attention
and the Great Book of Nature with understanding
and you will find in both revealed
Our Good Deity,
His World in all its glory.
His just laws under which we live.

Business is good.
We number one hundred fifteen persons, store and factory.
All have more to do than they can accomplish.
It will be a busy, pleasant place when you return...
to follow with humble spirits and pure hearts
the peaceful ways of commerce and just economy.
Nanna sends her love. Dear little Lottie
begs you come and admire her frocks and pets.
She is a bright spirit, and if we live,
will be a source of joy to us continually.
And now, my dear boys, trusting you to continue well
and to work honorably, I remain your affectionate father,

R.C.

Letter to a mother from a Confederate soldier:
Matthew Chandler (aged 18) to Marianne Lavalle Chandler,
divorced by Reuben Chandler in 1855
Directed to an address in New Orleans

FEBRUARY, 1864   A CAMP IN TENNESSEE

Beloved Mother,

You have left me too long, all alone,
in the land of the despot.
God grant that I soon may be able to set us free.
From this day forward I hate every Yank, as my father.
From him I scorn to take quarter, as
to him I refuse my surrender.

I arrived in Tennessee, quite safe, without any hindrance,
though I shook in a fever of vengeance all the way.
I begin this day in earnest my work of murder.
With God's help I'll shed a whole river of
Union blood. Then Hell be my portion
if I don't make my sweaty horse swim in it!

     Yours from your loving son,

          Matthew Chandler

NOTE: *Matthew died of wounds in a Washington hospital in 1865.*
Marianne died, the rumor is of drink, in New Orleans in 1872.

Notes to a father from a young man gone West: Jacob Chandler to his father Reuben Chandler

NOTE: *These few pages were written, presumably to his father, by the young Jacob M. Chandler in 1867. Although much of this letter has been lost, there is reason to believe it was written as a sort of journal on a voluntary expedition to Colorado, and was posted in excerpts en route whenever possible. Jacob M. Chandler spent two years in the West gaining experience as a surveyor, a miner and a sheep rancher before he returned (poorer than when he set out) to take over the family clothing business in Cincinnati.*

SUMMER, 1867   COLORADO

So we struck across the mountains, travelling for two days without sight of a human being. At dusk on the second evening, we drew rein on the summit of one of those lofty hills which form the spurs of the Rocky Mountains. The solitude was awful. As far as the eye could see stretched an unbroken succession of peaks, bare of forest – a wilderness of rocks with stunted trees at their base, and deep ravines where no streams were running.

A gleam of light at the bottom of the gorge caught our Indian's eye. Descending the declivity we reached a cabin rudely built of dead wood brought down, probably, by spring rains from the hills. We knocked at the door. It was opened by a woman holding a child of about six months. She was scrawny and lined, I would have guessed fifty, but she said later she was thirty. She gazed at us searchingly for several minutes, and then asked us in and provided us with milk and corn-bread, a welcome meal.

The cabin was divided into two apartments, a kitchen which served also as store-room, dining room and sitting room; the other chamber was the bunk room where the family slept. Five children of all sizes tumbled out of this latter apartment and stood gawking at us from the rough-adzed doorway while we ate.

The women said her husband was a miner. Four years before he had come with the family from the East. Pushing on in advance of the main movement of immigrants in the territory, he had discovered a rich gold placer in this gorge. While he spent his days working it, his wife, with her own hands, turned up the soil in the nearby valley, raised all the corn and potatoes required for support of the family and made all the clothes.

We asked if she had ever been attacked by Indians. 'Only twice,' she replied. 'Once three prowlers came to the door and asked for food. My husband handed them a loaf from the window, but they lurked in the bushes all night. Another time a large war-party encamped a mile below us. A dozen surrounded the house. We thought we were lost. We could hear their bullets rattle against the

219

rafters, and you can see the holes they made in the door. We should have all been scalped if a company of soldiers had not come up the valley that day and burned the red-skins out.

'There is no end of bears and wolves. We hear them howling all night. Last winter the wolves came and drummed on the door with their paws and whined piteously, like big dogs begging for their dinners. My husband shot ten and I six of them. After that we were troubled no more.'

When we asked her if she were not lonely, she gave a little cry, whether in laughter or anguish I could not tell. 'I'm too busy to think,' she exclaimed, 'in the daytime. I must wash and boil and bake and look after the cows who wander off in search of pasture. I must hoe the corn and potatoes and cut wood. We have no schools here, as you can see, but I have taught the oldest children how to read. Every Sunday we have family prayers. We each read a verse of the Bible (except the baby) and then the children repeat it until they know it by heart.'

We finished our meal and thanked her and gave pennies to the children, who took them without looking at us and then scuttled off into the pitch darkness of the bedroom. She said she would have liked to ask us to pass the night there, but she and her husband were hard pressed to find beds for their own brood. 'One day,' she confided to us, 'we shall have a fine house with two storeys and a carpet and some proper English china and I shall want for nothing. We are saving for a saw mill, and by next spring should have our own lumber business and maybe a dray-horse or two.'

After we had watered and rubbed down our horses we said good-bye. For a long time after we left I saw her standing by her unpainted door every time I looked back. She stood in the sun, frowning as though it dazzled her. I could not help hoping she would at last have her fine house and her saw mill. As we were obliged to reach Denver by the next day to pick up a mining party, we pressed on through most of the night. We camped, finally, in the shelter of a boulder, and I went to sleep praying for that strange, brave couple who had chosen to risk their lives for the sake of a little gold, a saw mill and perhaps a set of proper English china.

Maxims of a Christian businessman: From the journal of
Jacob M. Chandler, Cincinnati's citizen of the year 1895

The Foundations of Belief
1. Christ demands full surrender
2. Give Sunday to the Lord
3. Alcohol is Satan's most powerful weapon
4. No man is beyond redemption

A Guide to American Home and Business Ethics

Work is next to Godliness; a man should keep books when dealing with the Deity.

The Golden Rule of the New Testament is the Golden Rule of Business.

Religion is the only investment that pays dividends in the life everlasting.

By doing good with his money a man, as it were, stamps the Image of God upon it and makes it pass current for the merchandise of heaven.

Advertising makes Business articulate. It is a language of faith between buyer and seller.

'Labor is life! 'Tis the still water faileth.
Idleness ever despaireth, bewaileth.
Keep the watch wound or the dark rust assaileth.'

Have faith. Only believe that you can lick a man and you can lick him!

No day seems long enough to those who love work.

We have no one to fear except ourselves.

To have no aim in life is next door to committing a crime.

Let a boy's first duty be to his conscience, his second to his home because there is a mother there, his third to the welfare of his country.

Everything can be determined by the three little words, 'Is it right?'

Money has feet and walks away, but right habits are abiding.

Economy, like charity, begins at home.

The path of virtue leads through the valley of sacrifice.

Body and soul must go hand in hand to reach the goal.

Smiles are roses along the way.

A worried father writes to his daughter at Oberlin College:
Jacob Milton Chandler to his daughter Maura

MAY 5, 1896   CINCINNATI, OHIO

Though not altogether unsuitable, my daughter – your letters abounding in girlish merriment – allow me to suggest that accounts of such frivolous and literary pastimes as you and your fellow scholars (or should I say scholaresses?) choose to indulge could be significantly improved by some small attentions to spelling and the principles of grammar. A sterner critic, or one less fond, might find in your latest scribble (you correctly term it) intimations of carelessness unbecoming in a woman of grace and intuitive decorum.

Yet, my dear, I am willing to concede that a person of your temperament, torn from the bosom of her loving family, must (if she does not weep out her days in melancholy remembrances) stride into the rough world more than a little giddy with the ebullience of youth and the lighthearted gaiety of irresponsibility.

I do not reproach you for your laudable, if unfeminine, desire for a share of the world's knowledge. My advice is to delight while you may in the manifest abundance of God's world, provided that while you rejoice in this life you remain sensible, always, of that which is to come.

I am distressed, however (and make no attempt to dissemble my feelings) that you chose and deliberately chose to pass so few hours with your brothers, your mother and myself this past Easter. Your excuses (your studies, your scribblings, your acquaintances) make few amends for your sudden and inexplicable withdrawal from the family circle. Rather they augment the pain you have caused us.

Did I speak for myself alone, I could not in conscience complain. A father must provide for his own. Your debt to me is not one deserving of acknowledgement. That I have worked, yea toiled, for your health and wellbeing full seventeen years of your life has been an unbegrudged sacrifice. Yet once, in his days of poverty and misfortune (days you will not remember, you were but a babe) your father vowed never to darken the familial hearth or diminish by a shade the brightness of your mother's eyes through the slightest reference to his burdens in private business. This vow he has kept! To this day, as you know, no shadow from the world has darkened the glow of my household.

Yet your mother suffers! Suffers, I believe, through the thoughtlessness of that being who should now be her greatest comfort. For it is you, my child, who have occasioned the loss of her beauty, health and good cheer which, throughout your childhood, so encouraged and nourished your own. Next time you are at home, Maura, notice her careworn face. Her hands once whiter than yours. Her fine strong shoulders, stooped with the years of childbearing. Think, my daughter, of who it was by your bedside when, swollen with fever, you lay in your tainted sheets, poisoning the air with your breath. Who was it who comforted you, embraced you, was at all times ready to cure, with the magic of a kiss, the bruised knee or cut finger of the plaintive child who ran weeping to her?

Maura! Maura! Those kisses were never gifts! Bestowed as they were with the charity of Our Lord Himself, those kisses were loans! Loans upon interest these many long years! Now it is time to repay them, graciously, selflessly, with little acts of kindness and understanding. For think, my dear, if you were ill, how that face would appear like an angel's hovering above you, its every wrinkle a wavelet of sunshine. Hers. Who will leave us one of these days! Yes, burdens, increased by your burdens, unless lifted, will break her down. Those hands that have done so much for you will lie crossed on a lifeless breast, and those lips, those neglected lips, will be closed forever.

This admonition I send in the spirit of Love. Its purpose is not to rebuke but to touch, to remind you of duties which ambition, it may be, has obscured. With it I send my blessing, in the hope... nay, in the belief and knowledge that you will return to us a New Woman. Gentle. High hearted. Self-forgetful, with a sweet and winning interest in all the little things of the home, to shed upon us all and upon your mother in particular, the divine luster of Christian Peace which alone can illuminate and make radiant forever
The Kingdom of Home.

From your loving and affectionate Father,
J.M. Chandler

A New Year's message to myself: From the journal
of Maura Chandler on the eve of her marriage
to Ethan Amos Boyd

Without false pride.
Without true faith.
With little hope
and with no glad energy,
but still, thank God,
steeled firm in belief
that there is a right way
and a wrong
through our human loneliness,
I begin this New Year's
Day of my life in marriage.

Cold. Midnight-morning.
Candlelight out in the cold.
Oval on the near side
and the far of the
mimicking window.
My face on the far side
and the near. My life.
This room that I know,
doubled also, hung
there in the snow.

So the unknown begins as
reflections of the known.

Perhaps it was never meant
that I work as I intended.
Perhaps it was never meant
that I write, learn, elevate
myself as I intended.
My vocation. My mission.
What does Nature
ask of Woman?
Give to him that needeth.
Employ the hour that passeth.
Be resolute in submission.
Love thy husband.
Bear children.

For now it behoves me to
crush out all personal sorrow,
forsake the whole ground of
self interest, ask not,
'Do I love him?' but affirm!
'It is good! It is right!'

If I keep every moral commandment,
fulfil every physical requirement,
feed mind into heart,
proffer heart to humanity –
stands it not then to reason
a woman will be happy
in her season?

I do not believe it. How
can I believe it
when the darkness comes?
When there, out
there in the snow
hangs a mockery, room
through which those huge,
slow ghost-flakes amble and fall!
Failure and suffering,
tedium, childbearing,
disease, deaths, days –
burying us all!

Yet without false pride,
without true faith,
with little hope
and with no glad energy,
I am, dear God, firm,
firm in belief
that there is a right way
and a wrong
through our human wilderness.

I begin, in this room,
this year of my life and marriage.
I begin, in this room,
this New Year. My life in marriage.

A vigorous letter from a salesman of the Lord:
Ethan Amos Boyd to his wife Maura

Blessed One,

I think of you hundreds of miles away, and of our dear green innocent Vermont and reconcile myself with difficulty to these torrid streets. If it were not for Faith, for my earnest Belief that Spirit is All and the ALL THINGS REAL proceed from it, I think I should find Business unbearable. My love, I am alone among the Sadducees!

It is to preserve my ideals in this Egypt that I've taken to playing Moses and have drawn up a set of Tablets which, my dearest wife, I am eager to share with you that you may be better instructed in my simple ways.

Eschew	*Engage in*
Late Hours	Early Bed
	(Never After 9.00 p.m.)
Stuffy Rooms	Daily Exercise
White Bread	Brown Bread
Animal Food (Flesh and Fowl)	Raw Vegetables
Alcohol	An Occasional Pipe (for me)
Gossip	Philosophy
Novels	Mercy
Expense	Baths

I am pleased to say I have been successful in keeping to this regime, and feel the better for having eaten nothing but vegetable food this past week.

I have had time to make one or two public addresses; on Sunday to the Ethical-Social League and yesterday to the Women's Trade Union Association. The Unions face a shortage of money which your father, among others, could do much to remedy were he Christian and highminded as he pretends. He is not *positively averse* to our turning Mossy House into a workers' retreat, but only skeptical as to our making a profit from it. I tell him that is not of account!

Whatever his opinion, I shall rise up from this city with my flock within a month. If he distrusts my means, tell him purposes like mine have for centuries fed the hungry and clothed the naked. Yea, even as a Salesman of the Lord shall I succeed.

I exist, my angel, in the invisible radiance of your trust. When I ponder on your loveliness, on the womanliness of females and on the sleeping allegory within that veils their Sphinx-like secret, I marvel that Man has deserved propagation in this wicked world.

> Until we meet I survive on your letters,
> Your devoted husband,
> Ethan Boyd

THE CLEARFIELD ENQUIRER

JUNE 2, 1929

The State of Vermont, County of Clearfield in Insolvency

Notice is hereby given that the Honorable Wm. A. Shapley, Judge of the Court of Insolvency and for the said county of Clearfield has issued a warrant against the estate of ETHAN AMOS BOYD of Mossy House, Clearfield Town in the Said County, an insolvent debtor; and the payments of any debts and the delivery of any property belonging to the said insolvent debtor to him and for his use, and the transfer of any property by him, are forbidden by law.

A meeting of his creditors will be held at the Court of Insolvency in Burlington on the 10th day of June next, at 9.00 o'clock in the prenoon, for the proof of debts and the choice of an assignee or assigness.

Horace Coleman, *June 2, 1929*
Deputy Sheriff

A Letter to God on hotel notepaper from Ethan Amos Boyd

Dear Lord,
I am ill, I know,
from my own earnestness.
I am stumbling-foolish.
Everything I have wished to do, to be...
No. I have not done. Not been.

I have no learning or acquaintance
with learned colleges or degrees.
I have no profession or any patter
the world calls manly or
gentlemanly. I have no money.
Except as I sell Thy word
I am rot in my family...mine,
my daughter's center.
My home – happier without me.
My wife – silent.
For long periods, completely silent.

One baby we lost.
He was one or thereabouts.
His mother even yesterday,
after twenty years, in tears for him.
And now this turbulent, gifted,
unfinished nearlygrown son.
Unnecessarily,
the doctors agree.
(Curious, Lord, that both should be
taken unnecessarily.)
Fifty. Fifty-three.
And only these fumbling hands
with which to continue fighting.
This sick mind and bad eyesight
quivering between Thy Love and my fear.
To keep one from the strength of the other.

PART TWO

Women in Marriage

A London letter: The poet, Kay Boyd, replies
ambiguously to her sister in Clearfield

NOVEMBER 11, 1968   HAMPSTEAD, LONDON

Your letter arrived with its letters
   lunging at my conscience.

      Alone in wet London

with the wind trailing rain
   around these ugly brick villas,
      and the four o'clock night

arriving with my late lunch,
   I ask myself often
      why it is impossible to go home?

Why is it impossible,
   even here,
      to be peaceful and ordinary?

The ordinary offers itself up,
   can be eaten, breathed in.
      It counts on being dependable.

This is a window.
   This is an apple.
      This is a girl.

And there is a cyclamen –
   blood climbing out of the ground.
      And there is a blind of rain.

And now between the girl
   and the flower-flame on the window sill
      the window is a blur of rainwater.

I wonder how she felt, Persephone,
    when she bit for ever into the half-moon pomegranate?
        Did she miss ordinary things?

She could have lived
    without risking the real fruit.
        There were only six seeds.

She willed to eat nothing else.
    It was hunger.
        Without nourishment how could she live?

Eating, she lived on through
    winter after winter,
        the long year perfected,

the cold, waking rain
    raising a few seeds to green
        from her creative darkness.

But the mother smiled and smiled.
    She was brilliantly consumed, a sacrifice
        sufficient for each summer.

Should any daughter blame her?
    The mother made her choice.
        She said her 'no' smiling.

She burned the kissed letters.
    She spat out the aching seeds.
        She chose to live in the light.

Would you wake her again from the ground
    where at last she sleeps
        plentifully?

Two Cambridges: A letter from Maura Chandler Boyd
to her daughter Ruth Arbeiter in England

Dear Ruth,
    With the wedding six weeks behind,
       and the whole country, so it seems,

tilted sideways and ready to
    slide right off the world
       like a plate of oysters,

there you are in the one Cambridge,
    and here I am
       in the other.

As father used to say,
    'The true life of the intellect
       secretes an impregnable cocoon.'

Guess what? I've bought you an ice box.
    Also a huge bed, big enough for four.
       At a charity sale for the unemployed.

Everybody says I'm crazy,
    but suppose you two come back
       without a job or a house or

a bean to buy a beefsteak?
    Everything you own these days
       is an investment.

Now for your wonderful letter!
    To think of your getting to Cambridge
       in time for that ball!

What did they give you to eat?
    Was the food fresh? They tell me
       the English don't know how to cook vegetables.

I'm grateful for the snap of Kings' Chapel.
    It brought tears to my eyes.
       To think how poor father would have loved it!

I meant to warn you, Ruth,
   before you left. I've heard the English
      take a light view of drink.

Greta's nephew, Fred,
   came back thoroughly *amazed*!
      He said he saw Christian women in public saloons!

But then Greta says that Fred
   came back with all sorts of notions.
      He said – since you're our poet –

there's a young man from Harvard –
   you ought to know about him. Eliott?
      Something like Lawrence Eliott.

I don't suppose it matters.
   These new-fangled writers don't go deep.
      Not like my beloved Dickens.

Now I must catch a train and hustle up to Clearfield
   before Philip and Sue, who are
      driving there all that way!

Give my best love to Neil
   and tell him to keep an eye on you.
      Who, dear, is Bloomsbury?

Don't be too impressed by those aristocrats.
   Hold up that pretty head
      and be proud you're a free American!

             As ever,
                your loving Mother,
                M.B.

A letter from an English novelist: Paul Maxwell,
author of 'A Second Eve', writes to Ruth Arbeiter in Vermont

21 OCTOBER, 1936   SOUTH KENSINGTON, LONDON

Two years ago. Only two years, and the terrible chasm between that autumn afternoon in a Vermont pasture and that unknown spring or autumn morning when we will meet again grows wider and wider. So you have two daughters now! Kathy and Eden. Eden and Kathy. Two American girls.

The impact of your letter was such that I almost see you. You and your baby in that big shabby kitchen with the broken floorboards hidden under the patchwork rug, and the clay mugs marching along the high shelf over the hearth. There. I *can* see you clearly. You are holding the baby in the crook of your left arm while with your right you are pouring water from a jug into a large stoneware basin set solidly on the scrubbed table. The water is just the right temperature. You question it with an elbow to make sure. Gently, you are laying the poor naked scrap in the womb-like basin.

She howls immediately, but you are serious and firm. You rouse the soap to lather and you wash the head (the black mane you describe). Then you carefully wash limbs and belly, taking care not wet the navel which is not yet healed after its brutal severing from the placenta.

The baby is perfectly clean and perfectly frantic. You remove her, red-faced and howling to a salvational towel. Tenderly (but again, seriously, thoroughly) you dry the thicket of hair, miraculous hands and feet, the little runnels and pleats of the fleshier thighs. Vigorously you powder each inch. You snow sweet powder into the delicate rift of the buttocks. Finally, you pin on the nappy (you, of course, call it a diaper) and slip a fresh muslin nightdress – gently, so gently – over the baby's head, taking care not to damage the life-giving palpitation of the fontanelle.

When you sit down it is in one of those plain unpainted rocking-chairs, polished by generations of your grandmothers. You unbutton your blouse. Not Leonardo, not Raphael, not Bellini has on canvas depicted such dazzling, inflammatory white breasts. But you, of course, are unaware of their beauty. For you, they are not lilies, nor succulent apples of honey; nor are they two 'breasts dim and mysterious, with the glamorous kindness of twilight between them'. No. They are practical technical instruments for nourishing your child. The greedy thing pummels and sucks. The milk flows too swiftly. The child splutters, chokes, has to be balanced over your shoulder for a painful winding.

But now at last she has settled into a rhythm of felicitous satisfaction. She is happier, perhaps than she ever will be again in her life.

You? Are you opening a book? Yes. You take a book everywhere even now. (You keep a book, still, in your handbag when you wait for a bus or go to the dentist.) So you open what is lying on the table...is it *The Rainbow*? Is it my collection of War Poets?

The baby has stopped sucking. It is asleep. You hardly notice. Ruth, you are not reading at all. Instead you are staring out of the window where a simple frill of muslin frames (I remember precisely) a harvest of red and orange hollyhocks.

Dearest, I am dreary in London where everyone bores me with German politics. I'm so vehement in my campaign to get back to the States, my friends have ceased drinking with me. I bore them to distraction with encomia.

Nourish me with a long letter. *Eve* progresses slowly (tell me if what I have written here about your baby seems suitable for the novel). I return two poems of yours, unfortunately rejected, but redolent as always of

my own dear Ruth,
your Paul

Two Poems and a Rejection Slip:
From the notebooks of Ruth B. Arbeiter
1936

VERMONT AUTUMN

We have come to the end of a summer in this gold season.
        The year trembles.
I stare down these vistas of light, emblazoned with leaves,
as into the future of the past – its silence and memory.
        The empires are asleep there.
        Egypt and Europe.
They are locked in each other's stone arms
        legible as geology.

Oh, pharaohs and princes buried in the dust of dead legends!
Are you resentful of Time that has stripped you of meaning?
Did you, like these leaves, burn away in gold rust into rest?
        Or did you, like trees, only counterfeit
        wanings and deaths?

Can you feel in old roots the new energy coiled in this continent?
Can you fructify as it reels out in wave after wave after
        wave of imperious shimmering?
        Look!
It surrounds you with a halo, now golden,
        now pulsing and green!

THE SHORT AND THE LONG DAYS

All in the spell of the short days
We passed as it were through a mine or maze
Which was Time's interminably coiled cave.
No help nor any hope he gave,
Nor miracle of answered prayer;
Nor would he for our asking send
The slightest pin-point candle there
To light our end.

Groping along the hours, we clung
To them like ledges. Minutes hung
From our necks in leaden spheres
As, pendulum-like, they counted days as years.

Then change of sun made Time our friend.
Look how he lights with sky our ways!
How short the distance to the end
Of these long days.

THE POETRY REVIEW

The Editor regrets that he is
unable to make use of your
MSS. He is grateful for the
opportunity of considering
your work, and is sorry that
pressure of time makes it
impossible for him to write a
personal letter.

A Love Letter:
Ruth Arbeiter to Major Paul Maxwell

SEPTEMBER 3, 1945   CLEARFIELD, VERMONT

Dearest,

You must know that I think of you continually,
often entering unexpectedly
that brighter isolate planet where we two live.
Which resembles this earth – its air,
grass, houses, beds, laundry, things to eat –
except that it is articulate,
the accessory, understanding, speaking of
where we are born and love and
move together continually.

Departures are dreams of home,
returns to bodies and minds we're in the habit of.
And what are these terrible things
they are taking for granted? Air and grass,
houses and beds, laundry and things to eat –
so little clarity, so little space between them;
a crowd of distractions to be
bought and done and arranged for,
drugs for the surely incurable pain of
living misunderstood among many who love you.

One evening not long ago
I walked to the high flat stone where,
as children, we used to lie in wait
for the constellations. It was dusk and hazy,
the hills, soft layers of differentiated shadow
thick with the scraping of crickets, or katydids,
or whatever you call those shrill unquenchable insects,
sawing their way through night after summer night.
Seated on the stone,
straining into the distance,
it was strangely as if I were
seeing through sound. As if an intensity,
a nagging around me, somehow became the mist –
the hills, too, breathing quietly, the sun
quietly falling, disappearing through gauze.

Such seeings have occurred frequently
since we were together. Your quality of perceiving,
a way through, perhaps, or out of, this
damaging anguish. As when we looked down –
you remember that day – into the grassy horse pool
where one bull frog and one crimson maple leaf
quietly brought our hands together.

Dearest, what more can I say?
Here, among my chores and my children.
Mine and my husband's children. So many friends.
And in between, these incredible perspectives,
openings entirely ours in the eddying numbness
where, as you know, I am waiting for you
continually.

                                                    Ruth

From an Asylum:
Kathy Chattle to her mother, Ruth Arbeiter

MAY 2, 1954   THE GOOD SAMARITAN HOSPITAL, NEW YORK

Mother,

If I am *where* I am
because I am *what* I am
will you forgive me?

God knows I have fought you long enough...
soft puppet on the knuckles of your conscience, or
dangling puritanical doll made of duty and habit
and terror and self-revulsion.
At what cost
keeping balance on invisible threads?
At what price
dancing in a sweater set and pearls
on the stage sets of your expectations?

Yes she was a nice girl!
Yes she was good!
Got married. Had a baby.
Just as she should.

Her head was made of walnut
His body of wood.
Then they had a little baby
made of flesh and blood.

Oh mother, poor mother!
Daddy thinks I'm wicked.
Here they think I'm crazy.
Please think I'm dead.

Dead, yes, and watching
from that safe, safe distance.
There. Your stubborn shoulders.
Tight smile
Head in relief, tilted a little,
tense with controlling intelligence.
How can I make you believe
I am myself – a self –
only when dying alive?

Without some interior self-murder
I am blank, void.
The face which I know must be watching
but is never there.
To the flow, you might say, of my experience
what a screen is to the flow of a film.

When I had little Libby, yes,
I was almost real.
But used. Used up.
Almost killed, being able to feel.
'Motherhood will settle her nerves,'
Daddy said, who was never a mother.
I knew in the coil of my head
how I hated her! Hated her!

Christ, how she howled!
And nothing I could feed her...
my milk, canned milk, powdered milk, goat's milk...
nothing would soothe her.
The doctor? Sympathetic but busy
And I, pouring breastmilk and blood...
uncontainable tears...
Once, in a quiet hour, I wrote to you.
Frank burned the letter.

He had begun to be gnawed.
Fine unseen teeth were
gnawing him...whittling him.
Wife
forcing him into the prison of a family
Baby
shaping him into the
middle class, money-earning
ulcered American Dad
Frank's maleness, idealism...
self-flattering, easy conceit
never could admit.

Remember when he bought us that
crazy red, ramshackle farmhouse?
Miles out in the used-to-be country?
Well, his sports car, his sideburns,
his scotch tweeds and 2 a.m. barbecues
gave our wife-swapping, beef-eating neighbors
some unthreatening entertainments!

But by that time we were enemies.
By day hardly speaking.
At night, mutual and experienced torturers.
Libby, our principal weapon,
spun helplessly between us.

'Don't take your venom out on the child!'
Frank would yell at me.
Then whisk her out in his MG
To the zoo. To the park.
One day he brought her back
bloodied by a swing.
It was late. Dark.
I didn't say anything.
Called the doctor. Made bandages.
Filled up on whisky.
Later on, both drunk,
he threw me down the cellar stairs
'Slut!' he kept shouting.
'Slovenly, drunken bitch!'
Which was close to the truth.
I never could live with my life
unless I was drunk.
I never could sleep or cry
until I was drunk.
I drank all day.

One week Frank went away...
just one of his conferences...
and Libby came down with 'flu. A fever.
But she wasn't that sick.
Just sick enough to slash nerves into strips.
Moaning and vomiting
whining and bullying...
Panic like a hornet in my brain.
Even my diet of whisky couldn't keep me sane.
No. Don't you tell me she's only a baby.
You know as well as I do, dear,
that babies have selfish grown
bitch personalities curled up in them...
like molars or hair.
When she screamed
she knew she made me scream.
And when I screamed,
she knew I screamed guilt.
Mother! Can't you feel what I felt?
I had to get out of there.

For her sake. For her sake. I...
Mother, I wished she would die.

So I slept myself sober.
Installed my crone baby-sitter.
Drove to the station.
Took the first train.

It was one of those days when
April is like October. Rain
through a wind full of
knife-edged, excitable sunlight.

Walking from Central Station
feeling slenderer, blonder...
familiar shiver of pleasure when
men stopped to stare.
Sky again! Younger.
Too scared to go to bars...
wandering like a schoolgirl from
museum to museum...

The Modern Art. The Guggenheim.
The Frick. The Metropolitan.
At the end, in the end
to the Cloisters.
You took me there often as a child,
you remember? Your small puzzled
prudish fat daughter!

But weirdly, mother, weirdly,
this time it was just as before.
Just as hallowed and hushed and mysterious.
Just as drenched in its greyness and gentleness.
As if I'd been waiting there somewhere...
some part of me waiting in childhood,
expecting myself to come back.

There was one chapel...
could I have dreamed it?
Crouched, resigned, half-caryatids,
shouldering the arches like sins...
on the altar, stiff, under a baldachin,
a statue, a crude wooden Mary
dangling her homunculus son.

She was worn, wormeaten,
hunched in the vestiges of drapery.
Her features? Weary.
Weary and purposeless with suffering.
Her face? Void. A wound of
perpetual suffering.

And she stared at me, down at me,
suffering, out of one
glazed terrible eye.
I took in that gaze like a blade!
What was it? A threat or a lie?
Or did she know?
Her thin Christ had no head!
But did she know?
I don't know what I did,
or why. It blurs now, but I
woke up to find myself here
where they've taken my belt and my
wedding ring, where they
specialise in keeping me weeping.

Come when you can, or when
the whitecoats let you.
But they may not let you, of course.
They think you're to blame.
Good God, mother, I'm not insane!
How can I get out of here?
Can't you get me out of here?

I'll try, I'll try, really,
I'll try again. The marriage.
The baby. The house. The whole damn bore!

Because for me, what the hell else is there?
Mother, what more? What more?

Mrs Lilliam Culick, divorcée, to Dr Frank Chattle

MAY 21, 1954   THE CENTER FOR RESEARCH IN URBANIZED HUMAN BEHAVIOR,
DEPARTMENT OF SOCIAL PSYCHOLOGY,
BLYTHNESS COLLEGE, NEW YORK

Darling,
Or may I still Frank?
Or should I kneel?
'Sir.' 'Dr Chattle'
so... salutations from your patient
patient. Anyway, be
decent, dear, and don't destroy me
yet, although you're livid,
I just know it,
at the lie of this
departmental envelope.
But I've tried to write, to
phone so often, Frank, each
empty, echoing evening.
Even if we're through
it's unmanly not to
meet me, not to discuss
us, not to confess.

Does this purposeful burying of
reasons mean you're
banking on a bust-up Frank?
Won't you take a share
of the blame? Well,
I don't know what game
you were playing, but I swear
Kathy's hangups were never
sparked off by *me*!

Ruth phoned and jabbered on
hours about your kid.
She can't know anything.
She'd forget I was
Pollyanna Sunshine
if she walked in and
found us in bed!
                Oh,
let's skip the shit
honey!
I've been in a mood.

Be nice.
I need you.
To be with.
To talk to.
My depression's come back
and I'm living on Valium.
I can't eat.
I can't talk.
I don't know what I want.

Could it be the cut we've
made in our sex life?
I've got some queer shakes.
I can't chew. I
can't sleep. I'm always so
dizzy with Seconal.

Can't you guess what I want?

Well, it may not be you,
Frank. Yes, damn it, I'm
not sure you'd do
in the long run. Oh, you
talk too much and you
kid around too much. You
let yourself down. You know
I never wanted us to be
lovers in the first place!

But I think you understand me.
Won't you make me happy?
Remember what you wrote
about my bones?
I love your little poem
about my bones and my
muscles like dolphins,
and the sea life in the
tides of my skin.

I'll not whet your appetite because
I *don't* know what I want.
So don't come.
Not tonight, anyhow.
Perhaps I'll drop in
at your office tomorrow.
I could do with a
prescription.

I'm all nerves
and I can't swallow.
I've lost five
pounds out of guilt!
(I wish there were some
safe pills for guilt.)

Oh Frank.
Have you felt what
I've felt?
Will you forgive me?
For this letter?
For this agony?
Don't be angry.
I've been lonely.
Let's try to meet soon.
                    OK?

End of a summer's day: From the journal of Ruth Arbeiter

Dreaming or dying? The room as usual.
Ceiling and woodwork, whites of a calm grey eye.
Curtains in motion. Membranes between myself and the
screaming of the locust. Bed-cage. Locker.
Aluminum pitcher and tray. Neil in the guest chair,
his bought flowers like blood spots.
Why carnations in rose season? Habit.
No, kindness. No, habit of kindness.
An artificial smell all the same.

As when I was waiting for father in that hot
hellish hospital in Cambridge after Jimmy died.
Jimmy. Would be now fifty...nine. At twenty
a comedian. Grotesque, all nose and glasses, fuzz for hair.
Poor mother's two-hundred-brush-stroke Sundays...
still it would never lie down. 'Ruthie,' he whispered,
'run back and fetch me my specs, there's a sister,
and a morning paper.' That between the night's operation
and at noon being dead. Mother at her best brave, praying.
Phil gone for Dad. I, bulky, alone, eighteen,
in the aseptic corridor, hating that I was hungry.
'I am selfish,' I thought, crying about that.
'I can't be unhappy enough.'

College days. Ohio in the nineteen-twenties.
It might just as well have been the nineteenth century.
Our philosophy reconciling Christ and Darwin.
Our Modern Lit embarrassed by Wilde. In those days...
those sandwich days before the Crash I hardly noticed,
before Belgium and Pearl Harbor and Auschwitz –
senseless un-American disasters which destroyed, but
never touched me. Left me a litter of conveniences.
My life. Our double life, poor Neil's and mine,
in Boston, in Cambridge...Harvard's Cambridge...
so many brilliant, miserable, significant people.

They would have frightened you, Dad, who followed,
stumbling, in the footsteps of your Maker...
His footprints too deep for you. Your hurt face peering over.
Dear Dad, dear failure, dear
specialist in injured feelings!
Did you guess how we lived on our tip toes,

towards the end of it, Mother and I?
Every purchase a crisis. Every meal a negotiation.
While you waded away in the swamp of your complaints,
telling everyone that everyone was against you until
everyone *was* against you, and they took you away,
blind, sick and mad, a disquieting absence at my wedding.

Amazing. It is amazing.
Your face. Very clear.
Can you see me? Can you hear me?
I know that, like me, you intended to live a long time.
You admired old age and its accumulation of understanding.
You looked forward to seeing me, half mother,
half Virgin, surrounded by the halo of your grandchildren.
Borne aloft, perhaps, by hundreds of little children!

There. That locust again.
Insect anguish stretched past the limits of restraint.
Jet scream through the blue above the lake.
June and July.
The Children in the rock pits, bristling with tin spades.
They called it 'The Fortress' that crevice in the boulder
where Kathy – in her red striped jersey – and Eden – always
skinny, bony, shivering – played and played.

The wind up suddenly.
                    'Time to pack up now.'
                                    'Oooooh!'
a wail in chorus. 'Please, Mommy, one last swim, Mommy!'
'One. Then we go.'
Nicholas, his sunburned body curled hot on my thigh,
is asleep still, in his blind skin.
But the girls splash in carelessly as frogs.
The waves flutter.
The little moored boats, each doubled by the lake,
loosen their masts across the querulous water.

Of course, this is the loss that you prepared me to
prepare for, Paul. That June and July.
Waking beside you at no hour...leaning for love over
rare wine gone sour in the glasses...ashtrays spilling over
into books we were never able to get to the end of...
nights we were never able to get to the end of...
love into sleep and sleep into love again,
telling time by a laughable hunger or the
slow spreading path of the sun in the dust, on the wallpaper.

Dearest Paul. Suppose we had gone back...or on.
Would it have been different?
Would you have changed us all?

The question ceases to matter before the question is resolved.

I think I must have thought too often of your thoughts.
Whether of me, or, more likely of your new book...
unfinished. Like your life, unfinished.
Never begun, really, never committed to anything so
self-defining as a name, a place, a family...anything
that might twist the eddying possibilities
into a frame around you. Not a failure, like Father.
Not a liar like myself...who finds, not you, but this
usual earth strange to take leave of.

PART THREE

Living for Now

Professor Arbeiter to his dead wife

AUGUST, 1968   CLEARFIELD, VERMONT

The worst time is waking
                              as if every nerve were working
scalpels in the running wound, knives in the gash.
For in life, love, nothing begins or ends with a clean crash.
The brain knows, but habit is like cash or clothes.
It continues its momentum like a blind weight through glass.

I can't lie down in the dark with your severed voice, Ruth.
In this room full of trivial attentions I am still your guest.
'You're cold, dear. Let me fetch you your rug.'
'You're tired, I know. I'll tell them you need to rest.'
Here. Again. On the phone. Overheard in the hall,
'I'm sorry. My husband is working. At seven? I'll tell him you called.'

Ruth, in our thirty-six years lost to eye-strain and bad temper
you never spoke to me once of what I know.
I neither dared nor dared not to speak to you, though
sometimes your inattentions drove black words like swarming insects
swimming in held-back tears through my desperate paragraphs.

I was proud of you, Ruth. My girl.
My critic. My helpmate. Hostess to a pack of fools
you could always smile at. Confidante of students
too shy to seek me out. Friend of all milkmen and maids.
One day. One June, you gave tea to Isaiah Berlin.
And invited our Clearfield carpenter.

These last years have been…what, Ruth?

Living with someone who's dying. Not letting her know.
And she, although not told, knowing.
As though the courtesy of our mutual lie
were drawing us together under its canopy.
I read to you. Henry Adams. You had so much to say.
You asked for a handkerchief the last day. Impatiently.
          As if death were a head cold.

I dream most nights of a garden. Formal. Like Versailles.
Laid out in terraces, box hedges, sculptured old
gods and goddesses.
                We are walking together on a gravel path
when suddenly the vista changes. Frames of ash
are descending in geometrical patterns
                        to a dry fountain.

But the worst is waking.
Reaching for the radio through the strings of your voice.
Listening to the whining of hillbillies, over and over.
        Closing my eyes
    as if the night could never be over.

Nick Arbeiter writes poems on the road to Wyoming after a funeral in Vermont

JULY-AUGUST, 1968

I

(*Albany*)
West, man, West.
            I'm being fed to my own bogged veins!
Know yourself. Your inheritance.
Self-hating. Self-abasing.
            How we eat of ourselves!
'Just the family,' father said.
                        Death was real.

Then the crows flocked in
                        trained for crises,
to deck out a flesh corpse like waxwork,
to croak hoarse Amens to a long box,
to peck out old photographs.

Christ thought he could sell us the straight gate
                        if we paid him in sacrifice,
if we gave up the apple of knowledge
                        for his extraordinary wine.

But Christ's Presbyterian blood for her was grapejuice.
His narrow gates opened to the total wind.

I remember they made her smile
for the earth seeping in
            through the aisles of her abandoned body,
      eroding it,   book and pew.

II

(*Akron*)
Waking up every morning in a different city
which is always the same city in a different place
with always the same woman sprawled adrift in the sheets
as if lost in the confusing surfaces of her names…

how soft it feels floating up through the old gauze places.
Hollyhocks and blue wallpaper,   stones,   resonances,
            window-glass watery as a lake.

252

Two little girls and a woman reflected among the bright leaves.
They shimmer there inverted in a glaze crimson as sumac.
They are beautiful,   they smile at me,   they invite me to drown.

Now an air conditioner bores me with monotonous stories.
A window, flowered with curtains, frames me a Greek façade.
That strip of red neon must have been left on all night.
It flashes mechanically   VACANCIES   VACANCIES.

My last night's girl shrouds her breasts,   moans for coffee.
Doors slam in the dew-drenched cars.
Their engines start up.

III

(Scotts Bluff)
In Nebraska it's the moon.
Mario's Steakhouse and Bar in the middle of the moon.
Ramshackle leftover, left over U.S. 20.   102 Fahrenheit.
                    Clay   wind   and sand.
The dry waves in rings around the wrecks of meteorites.
Slabs of eroded igneous. Tongues out at the stars.

Tonight there is empty thunder over the white bandage of the highway.
Occasional cars are missiles,   are implorers…
voices wailing to rain gods locked in the dry horizons.
Walking in crimson dusk or in scalding wind.
Wading through the sediment of ages cleft for no one…
these are the world's negations. This is the wilderness.

Scotts Bluff. Bleaching like a relic in the North Platte's
wandering incision in the dead sheet of the Plains.
Pleistocene valleys rucked up in raw clay, claws
reaching to root out and tear up all inhabitants and habitations.
Jaws, incisors unappeased by city names…
Jail Rock and *Smokestack Roundhouse* and *Twin Sisters*.
They will not be made flesh. They will not accept parables.

At one time, in the ice age, there would have been a glacier here.
Bedded in alluvium the teeth of Tithanotherium.
Bones of Merycoidodon,   Poebrotherium in fleshy clay.

The dry creeks are shot thick with millennial flints,
with the dust of the dog-sized horses of the dust of Pawnees.

IV

They say to you
    whatever is in your mind.
        The white sands.

V

(*Laramie*)
At every motel the formica boys
        swagger in with their chromium girlfriends.
The restaurant rocks as the juke box slings out
        hits from a two-years-stale menu.

I smoke in a corner booth, take in the floor show.
The girls with their leathery eyelashes and fringed thighs.
The boys with their low-slung belts, their sharpened shoes.

'Let it be, let it be' and rock-a-bye-baby, Daddy.
You taught us discretion in a woman
        was worth all the dollars in Hollywood.
No one could have bought you equipment to play your own wife.

We knew her moods like the roads in our New England county.
You knew her like a map
        you could depend on to get to your destination.

VI

Palms up cupping the globe of his twelve-year-old cognac,
Father reminisced and accused himself.
Neighbors called on tiptoe, bearing jam and casseroles.
Bald Maxwell quoted Keats and got drunk.

'When I think of the waste, the sheer waste,' Father maundered.
'And with so much to give and to live for...'

'She gave us her light,' agreed Maxwell.
'She burned out her love for more of us than she could afford to.'

VII

It's dangerous to live in a noose of 'I want' and 'I ought'.
Antaeus, held too high by Hercules, broke his root to the soil.
Our race thins. We're second growths
        fighting for what's left of the sky.

VII

We accuse you, fathers,
                    we accuse you of lies.
of pouring out a smoke screen
                    of high-minded fervor,
and then setting off to murder
                    under twin banners, Profit and Compromise.
We accuse you of signing on
                    with Corporation Hypocrisy,
of willing us a money machine
                    that feeds us by consuming us like fuel,
of letting cities rule
                    while the grass withers and the
rivers pullulate with acids,
                    of setting up houses like music boxes where
love is only wound up once
                    and then allowed to run down.
We accuse you of using reason
                    to sanction massacre,
of making freedom
                    a one way street with barbed wire.
We accuse you of not understanding
                    even now why you are what you are,
though under the asphalt
                    there rises a burning savage
and over his ashes
                    you glide in a soft mirage.
Will you have time to hear us
                    who go easy and barefoot?
who are earthbound in airports?
                    who are flesh among cars?
will you give us your deserts
                    and let us bring life there?
Will you watch us making love
                    between your carports and skyscrapers?

We are weak.
          We are human.
                    We are unsure.
We train our few possessions
                    to stand under us like ankles.
We like dreams.
      We like trips.
                    We've got a Hell you've never been to.
Black or white,
                    men are miracles to us.

Sick or poor,
          truth is sustenance to us.
Waking or dreaming
          they're the same thing to us.
So that there be peace among the animals.

Epilogue: Kay Boyd to her father, Professor Arbeiter

HAVERSTOCK HILL, LONDON, N.W.3.

Dearest Father,

This is the anniversary of our loss.
I write to the shushing of trees outside my window
(London planes, sycamores in Massachusetts)
Watching them sift light restlessly on a tiny garden.
The leaves are palm-shaped, like New England maples,
but the wind drags them aside like a loose drapery
as if trying to expose some savage or gipsy origin.

Our maples never stooped to be voluptuous.
They were prim New England. Trim domes. Upright clouds.

Yes, leaves sweep away from the trunks of these English trees
the way mist lifts from her farms.
The bark is like topographical shading
Or the shadings of accent and stone in this wrinkled country.

'Come back,' Eden wrote, after mother died.
'Come help me to keep her alive a little longer.'

But I didn't go back because I couldn't see what to come back to.
I couldn't think who to go back as.
That Kathy my name was, that Mrs Frank Chattle
died in New York of divorce.
Kay Boyd, the woman, the writer, has survived.
She lives a long way from Eden. The tug back
is allegiance to innocence which is not there.

'In the floodtides of *Civitas Mundi*
New England is dissolving like a green chemical.
Old England bleeds out to meet it in mid-ocean.
          Nowhere is safe.'

It is a poem I can't continue.
It is America I can't contain.

Dear Father, I love but can't know you.
          I've given you all that I can.
          Can these pages make amends for what was not said?
          Do justice to the living, to the dead?

IV

Problematica

The Garden

She feels it like a shoulder of hair,
the garden, shrugging off the steamed, squeezed
eye of her kitchen window. Self-engendered chaos.
milky convolvulus, huge comet daisies. Tear
open the stocking of the leek pod and it frees
mathematically its globe, its light radiants.

But still she feels it hateful. August in its sweat,
the children filthy and barefoot... angry woman
in a stained striped apron, sipping juice off a knife –
thick syrups of pounded rose hip and pulped fruit.
In bright air, between briar roses and a viney drain,
Arenea diadema sips the silk-spindled fly.

Her pet cat's a killer, a fur muff
curled fatly now in a catnest of hot
grass and goutweed. Of this morning's robin
too much was left – feathers, fluff,
feet, beak, the gorgeous throat, caught
in the gored, delicate, perfectly balanced skeleton.

The Unhappened

Clasped in its rigid head of bone,
The sea tosses,
Sleepless with tides.

Woman without body to the one moon.
Woman without shape.
Unborn faces.

Time in conception done and undone.
Unknown losses
Made and unmade.

The Grey Land

I must have been there,
and you – and you,
for we were the stippled landscape
we walked through.

Our curious eyes,
our hands and lips and ears
were flickering paths we took
through flickering years.

And we were the rooms,
the houses, voices, faces,
colours and lights, our own
familiar places.

Your way and mine
we chose, or thought we chose.
We passed and the swaying foliage
withered and froze.

Touching, talking,
exchanging our breath for wind –
lovers and friends, look back
at the land behind,

at all that remains
of the green delirious way,
the orderly rows of grey
and shades of grey

where you and you
and I, as in a cage,
stand motionless, formal, names
stained on a page,

while, without odour,
lifeless, colourless air
thickens with mist as if something
were rotting there,

and shadowy actions
vanish before we know
what to regret or forgive
in what they show.

On Not Being Able to Look at the Moon

There may be a moon.
Look at the masklike complexion of the roof,
recognisable but relieved of familiarity.
The street, too. How weakened, unstable.
Shadows have more substance than the walls
they lean from. Thick phosphorescence
gathers in the spaces between window
and black window. Something subtle, like a moon,
has been creeping under surfaces,
giving them queer powers of illumination.

In this centreless light
my life might really have happened.
It rises, showing its wounds, longing for
abrasive penances. It touches me with a mania for
stealing moonlight and transforming it into my own pain.
I can feel myself closing like an eye.
I'm unable to look at the moon
or at anything pitted and white that is up there
painted on the sky.

About Crying

There is crying about crying.
Ignore it.
This is what we all do.

There is crying about
What has to be said
But wants to be cried.

Ignore it.
This is what we all do.

There is crying about
What won't be said,
What has to be cried.

Well, there is that.

Ignore it. Ignore it.

We would like
Not to have to ignore it.

The Three

Clotho

In this picture I preside. I usher in
River and bathers, the green garden.
This tall white birch is my lively cocoon.
Out of it I spin chervils – marriages, babies.
All my blown hair is seed, is a tide in bloom,
Furious as history, indifferent as it is.

Lachesis

In this picture I persuade. I lead men in,
Conduct them through the garden.
Composed, smooth-headed in my spidery greys,
I drop their lines precisely, deploy them
Precisely. These are the criers out in my displays.
Their outrage burns in words as I destroy them.

Atropos

In this last picture I work alone.
I kill roots to plant stone.
I bring to hard soil no fruit, no hurt.
No cry issues from my burnt hillside.
Green burden and echo wait under my foot
For the igneous reaches, the granite tide.

The Sirens Are Virtuous

They are not what you think.
The sirens are virtuous.
Very smart. Very dedicated.
In their true form,
ladies, not women, not fish.
They abhor boring islands.
But wherever a human vortex is,
there they are at the centre.

'Come unto me, all ye who labour
and are weary without reason
and I will give you
fresh causes of feverish concern,'
sings one, penetrating the plugged ears
of the never-at-rest.

Looking guiltily inward
from under the O, slowly swinging,
of Ought, these men are terrified –
its noose lowering –
so they witness with relief
its transformation into a mouth.
Lips. Warmth. Breath.
What is it to them
that it's shouting, not kissing?

The ladies are professionals.
They divide and devour
professionally.
Helmsman from the helm.
Herdsman from the herd.
Though always there is one
who will not peel off and die joyfully,
in a good season
thousands can be loved, sucked,
drained, disposed of.

'There, our laps are full,'
cry the ladies at intervals,
shaking out their skirts,
shaking the bones from their aprons.
'And how we adored them, the drab cockatoos,
the serious darlings, the nearly salvational
whey-faced fellows of feverish concern.'

Icon

The scene they play
is the midwife's
without the midwife.

Blood, groans
have drained into the gold,
and all her pain

is inward and to be.

The child
is like a prophet
on her knee.

A Doctor of Science.

In joy
his forehead
flexes in its sphere.

His hand
that claws her face
catches her tear.

Respectable House

Worth keeping your foot in the door.
Worth letting the lamplight stripe your shoe
and escape in the dark behind you.

Worth the candle-width of a velvet floor,
the swell of a stair, a tinkle of glasses,
and overheard – rising and flaring – those fortunate voices.

Push open the door. More. And a little more.
You seem to be welcome. You can't help stepping inside.
You see how light and its residents have lied.

You see what the gun on the table has to be used for.

Meniscus

The moon at its two extremes,
promise and reminiscence,
future and past succeeding each other,
the rim of a continuous event.

These eyes which contain the moon
in the suspect lens of an existence,
guiding it from crescent to crescent
as from mirror to distorting mirror.

The good bones sheathed in my skin,
the remarkable knees and elbows
working without audible complaint
in the salty caves of their fitting.

My cup overfilled at the brim
and beyond the belief of the brim,
absolved by the power of the lip
from the necessity of falling.

*   *   *

Thales and Li Po

Thales, out scanning the stars for truth,
walked into a well.
Li Po fell in love
with the moon's reflection
in the Yellow River.

Which was the right way to die?
It doesn't matter.
Try an analysis of sky.
Or passionate, ignorant,
embrace a lie.

Cain

Lord, have mercy upon the angry.
The anguished can take care of each other.
The angels take care of themselves.
But the angry have no daughters or mothers,
only brute brothers, *I, I.*

Hearing that faint *Abel, Abel,* they stop their ears.
Watching that approved flame snake to the sky,
they beat stubby blades out of ploughshares,
cut the sun out of the air,
stamp on small fires they might have seen by.

He and It

(A Pathetic Fantasy)

This world is not *it*, he felt.
Something is missing.
Impatiently as day pressed into the west,
he waited for it to be embers.
Swans churning water in the ordinary river
he wanted to be women or gods,
and when boughs of the competent willows
lost their pure neuter droop and
he saw they were miserably weeping,
he couldn't prevent himself thinking,
'What is missing is me.'

Nothing complained
when he drew the world
gently through the narrows of his need
till it cradled his head.

How comfortably it fits its creator
is what he describes.
From his helmet of globe
he declares that sky burns,
wind bites, swans hound him with meaning.

Nevertheless, his voice
sounds a little faint now.
He knows he can't be losing.
He relies on his friend the sun
to beam him messages of light.

He allows the stars to be hopeful
when he winks them at night.
He likes their cyes.

And even then,

There may be a language in which
memory will be called 'letting in the sorrow'.
It would be a black language.
The sorrow would be a rainbow
after the storm, at its beginning.

Music in this language would mean
'measuring the rhythms', and poetry
'translating the dreams'.
Power? A hush in which to honour
wind's work, and the sun's.

A long litany of astonishment
would be, in this language,
a hymn of thankgiving: 'Even as it died,
the sea made power out of its own pulse,
pounding to salt the poisoned cities
of the suicides.'

Inquit Deus

The world is the world
but you ask it the wrong questions:
　　What can I make of it?
　　When will it pay me?

Its full stop weighs in your palm
like a pitted moon.
　　Why do I suffer?
　　When will you save me?

Here's your life line, vertical,
your head line, horizontal,
your fingers off in space
with that galaxy, your mind.

But this sea-bitten pebble
you're so perilously keeping
is all you have to live for,
and its love is blind.

Clovenhoof's-bane

Nucleic crystals, pursed in the invisible,
Drift between pyres through pastures emptied of stock.
If myths were mortal, panic would cull the devil.
The season's immersed in slaughter and roiled muck.
What's learned how to fly, propagate, strike
               and hoard its luck?

Herd's-bane, heart's-bane, clovenhoof's-bane,
Wandering to and fro among the animals,
Choosing – to stoke its fires – the human brain
So that Virus the Small at last shall inherit the earth,
Outlasting love, the ordeal of it, grief,
               and the love of gain.

The Garden of Intellect

It's too big to begin with.
There are too many windless gardens
Walled to protect eccentric vegetation
From a crude climate.
Rare shoots, reared in glass until
Old enough to reproduce themselves,
Wholly preoccupy the gardeners
Who deliberately find it difficult
To watch each other, having planted themselves
Head downward with their glasses
In danger of falling off over their thumbs.

Some beds bear nearly a thousand petunias;
Others labour to produce one rose.
Making sense of the landscape, marking distinctions,
Neat paths criss-cross politely,
Shaping mauve, indigo and orange hexagons,
Composing triangles and circles
To make the terrain seem beautiful.

But to most of the inhabitants
These calculated arrangements are
Not only beautiful but necessary.
What they cultivate protects, is protected from
The man-eating weeds of the wilderness,
Roses of imaginary deserts,
Watered by mirage, embellished
By brilliant illusory foliage, more real
For having neither name nor substance.

*　*　*

Trinity at Low Tide

Sole to sole with your reflection
   on the glassy beach,
your shadow gliding beside you,
   you stride in triplicate across the sand.
Waves, withdrawn to limits on their leash,
   are distant, repetitious whisperings,
while doubling you, the rippling tideland
        deepens you.

Under you, transparent yet exact,
   your downward ghost keeps pace –
pure image, cleansed of human overtones:
   a travelling sun, your face;
your breast, a field of sparkling shells and stones.
   All blame is packed into that black, featureless
third trick of light that copies you
        and cancels you.

Negatives

1

Condensed stillness lit meanly
   at four in the morning.
Streetlights a broth of murk,
   amber, unhuman...
As I start to describe them,
horror begins to trust me.

2

A cheap gold-plated wristwatch,
the weakest hand counting seconds
between one quartz minute and another.
One Two Three Four Five.
Spastic stroll without sound.
Count five to put these words on paper.
Or detonate the eclipse of someone.

3

Smoke is my neighbour's crop, His plot
is one of eight clay pots sharing a chimney.
Sixteen chimneys grow smoke along the terrace.

Look. The wind makes a cat of the smoke;
a scuttling black cat, poured velvetly on slate,
filters through the rooks' aerial look-out posts

to where my sad-eyed neighbour stares heavily
at my fence over his fence. He won't watch me
watching him toss crumbs to the clever rooks.

4

Television's virtuous wiles.
    The immortal sheen
of the lovely presenter. She
    wraps up an African massacre.
Now a panel of benign
    communicators...

The waxen head on the pillow
    no longer sees. She
keeps the set on for company,
    but can't press
the digits on her other friend
    the telephone,
silent mostly, on the bedside table.

5

What appeared to be another
    filthy rag in the moist alleyway
was underfoot slime, cold
    nucleic porridge, though
one webbed foot protruded
        and came away
    spelling 'frog's leg'.

6

Two whole scrubbed pigs hanging
    hock to hock
from hooks in the ceiling: art
    in a butcher's display,
two evolutionary masterpieces
    minus identity.
Pieces of nature, not yet part
    of the economy.

7

This dream that names itself 'Landsend Beckoning'
   is windless, unwooded, surrounded by ashy beaches.
A raw spit of land severs us from the sea.
   A white-haired black girl invites me to explore.
We have been warned of snakes, but see none –
   only a cave's thready breath and bituminous odour.
Long waves wash sideways over the sand,
   ribbed and intersecting. 'They are like leaves,'
she says. 'Do you remember leaves?
   Now we must learn to swim in their oily rainbows.'

'Love Stories and a Bed of Sand'
(after a photograph of graffiti by Jamie Ross)

In flood, familiar footpaths and
childhood cycle ways, heel-trodden mud
packed firm between arthritic roots;
anglers, picnickers, comforting as woodcuts.
The way things used to be,
should be, should have been?
Sensibility is a strange sandbag.
The picture book
lies down in level water as I look.

Persons, those personal *I*s.
Suppose they're crying from their *e*s and *o*s.
No one. No one.
Here's a stone with a severed name.
Anyone at home?
Did DP or VB spraypaint that heart?
Who crept in alone to smear it out?
Mind whispers, *sadist, masochist, rapist.*
Rust-stains on a blanched wall only exist.

Hold your hand over a flashlight
or up to strong sunlight,
and there's your blood and you
red as coals perishing.
A piece of star that feels, a meteor that sees,
loves, labels as it looks.
But what's that furnace in those drowning books?
By flood, by fire, by straining human hand,
love stories and a bed of sand.

A Love Sequence

1

All day, all night,
white passion.
Are you love or snow?
All homes are estranged,
sealed in this fallen sky.

2

Making love we call it,
but all we make
is sacred oil for the only present.
Pool of ourselves. Wash of our tidal innocence.
The future stands by for libation
but is not blessed.

3

Love oozes its creams.
lays sugars on naked branches.
So frail, permanent,
this ancient time between us.

4

Tall scalloped peaks
embellish the fence around us.
The fluted edge of our shell
or a torn letter?

5

In new-fallen love
we are everything we notice:
forked prints – crows' or rooks';
night rabbits' hobbled morse;
saffron calligraphy of the dog's piss.

6

In the drag of the sledge,
a sound of children whispering.
What are they trying to tell us
about thaw?

Calendar

The blank days
are heaped up ahead of me,
a sierra I have to cross
in order to get there. Where?

The marked days
are a slag of words.
In the course of crossing
I must have upturned them. How?

The days for crossing
have a solid, permanent appearance –
mountains of sandstone and sun
between shadowy valleys of conifers.

The days I have crossed?
Every one of them misty rubble.
A penline suggests
there is hardness there. Or art.

And this day I am crossing,
crossing in sun and rain?

Seems perfectly flat.

The sun celebrates my defeat
as I struggle towards it.
The rain lays a wreath on each drop
as it dies in its puddle.

Washing the Clocks

Time to go to school, cried
the magnifying lens of the alarm clock.
Time to go home now, the school's
Latin numerals decided.

Days into weeks, months into years.

It's time now thoroughly to wash
the outsides and insides of the clocks.

The broken clocks line up along the dresser,
worn out, submitting patiently.
An old woman in a yellow head-square
prepares to take them apart.

First she pries the glass off a black clock.
The glow-painted arabics fade as she scrubs.

Next, with a little lead key, she
applies herself to a school clock.

Tears must have rusted the hinge.
She has to force the case open.
Two pointed swords and a needle
clatter to the tessellated floor.

Where have they gone? Look for them.
Feel for the hands in the dust,
in the blowing sand. Finger by finger
the numerals break off and drop down.

How competently she's removing
the scarred blank face of my old school clock.

Behind it, the whirring machine,
gleaming brass rods and revolving cogs
making up time by themselves,
rinsing the mesh of their wheels in mysterious oil.

An Angel

After a long drive west into Wales,
as I lay on my bed, waiting
for my mind to seep back through my body,
I watched two gothic panels draw apart.
Between them loomed an angel,
tall as a caryatid, wingless,
draped like Michelangelo's sibyl.
Never have I felt so profoundly looked into.

She was bracing on her hip an immense book
that at first I took for a Bible. Then
prickling consciousness seemed to apprehend
The Recording Angel.
The pen she wielded writhed like a caduceus,
and on the book
ECCE LIBER MORI had been branded.

This book she held out towards me,
arm-muscles tensing, but even as I reached
I knew it was too heavy to hold.
Its gravity, she made me feel, would crush me,
a black hole of infinitely compressed time.
Each page weighed as much as the world.

Drawing my attention to a flaw in the book's crust –
a glazed porthole, a lens of alizarin –
she focused it (it must have been a microscope)
and silently motioned me to look.
Fire folding fire was all I saw. Then the red glass
cleared and a blizzard of swimming cells
swept underneath it, lashing their whip-like tails,
clashing, fusing, consuming each other greedily,
fountaining into polyps and underwater flowers.
Soon – fast-forward – forests were shooting up.
Seasons tamed lagoons of bubbling mud
where, hatching from the scum, animalculae
crawled, swarmed, multiplied, disbanded,
swarmed again, raised cities out of dust,
destroyed them, died. I turned to the angel,
'Save these species,' I cried.
And brought my face right down on her book,
my cheek on the lens like a lid.

Instantly I knew I had put out a light
that had never been generated by a book.
That vision-furnace, that blink into genesis?
Nothing but a passing reflection of the angel.

Rising, for the first time afraid,
I confronted her immortality
circling like a bracelet of phosphorus
just outside the windscreen of the car.
For it seems I was still driving.
Solidity and substance disappeared.
A noose of frenzied, shimmering electrons,
motes of an approaching migraine,
closed around me.
And through that fluorescent manacle,
the road flowed on through Wales.

Washing My Hair

Contending against a restless shower-head,
    I lather my own.
The hot tap, without a mind, decides
    to scald me;
The cold, without a will, would rather
    freeze me.
Turning them to suit me is an act of flesh
    I know as mine.
Here I am: scalp, neck, back, breasts,
    armpits, spine,
Parts I've long been part of, never
    treasured much,
Since I absorb them not *by* touch, more
    because of touch.
It's my mind, with its hoard of horribles,
    that's me.
Or is it really? I fantasise it bodiless,
    set free:
No bones, no skin, no hair, no nerves,
    just memory,
Untouchable, unwashable, and not, I guess,
    my own.
Still, none will know me better when I'm
    words on stone
Than I, these creased familiar hands
    and clumsy feet.
My soul, how will I recognise you
    if we meet?

Naming the Flowers

makes no difference to the flowers.
These inside-out parasols,
orbwebs on crooked needles,
grey filmy cups in the clockwork
of summer 'goatsbeard'

are to themselves not 'seeds',
not 'systems of distribution',
never the beards of goats,

though for us they anticipate
bare patches, old age, winter time.
They tell us to pronounce now
all that we wish to keep.

My fields of recollection
already are fancy with toadflax.
Wheels of sky-blue chicory
purl into purple angelica;
hogweed is taller than my sons.

The path I will follow?
Shocking with unfinished steeples.
'Foxglove', I'll say, then 'balsam',
'rose bay willow herb', 'red campion'.

I'll note particularly
the pinched liquorice temper of my fingers,
pods of sweet cecily. Scabious
will be last into my grey-blue coma,
reminding me of heaven,
the shell-frail colour of harebells.

In winter time my bare patch
will be heavy with names.
I am only a namer.
Names, all alone, are seeds.

V

The Art of Making

Morning

You lie in sleep
as liquid lies in the spoon
and sounds trouble a surface
which trembles without breaking.
The images flow and reverse:

> The whistler, the walker,
> the man worrying his accelerator,
> a parabola of motors
> in which the milkman moves.

Just so, daily,
dissolving chromatics
of the commonplace
absorbed by the listening eye.

> Just so, rarely,
> the language, the salvage,
> the poem
> not made but discovered.

Theme with Variations

Distractions, considerations.
There are so many.
There is money.
There are possessions.
There are the professions and inventions.
And there are the men alone,
and forever those
soft thighs thought of and thought of
in empty rooms.
For there only is one love –
which is never enough.

Evasions, sophistications.
They have a use.
There is booze.
There is titivation.
There's the fox on the flesh
where the breast
pushes up to the throat.
There's the flash in the groin,
and the long meal's anecdote,
but only the one love
that is ever real.

Ovations. O deprivations!
Such semen has crept
into blonde violins,
rich horns, shy string quartets
out of Beethoven's furious genitals,
and Schubert's,
and Mozart's,
that ladies who bend to their cellos,
their velvet knees apart
know well there can only be one love,
which is never Art.

To Write It

You must always be alone.
But don't beg a soupscrap of charity
or birdcrumb of tolerance.
Shift for yourself.
As furniture heaves off your life
you'll love your deliverance.

Until loneliness slips in, scrawny
and hungry, Miss Loneliness, over the
barrenness, bribing with company.
Restlessness, one of her attendants.
And the drunk twins, of course,
Memory and Remorse.

Refuse them. Stay faithful to Silence, just
Silence, sliding between that breath
and now this breath, severing the tick
from the tock on the alarm clock,
measuring the absence of else.
And the presence, the privilege.

The Price

The fear of loneliness, the wish
to be alone;
love grown rank as seeding grass
in every room,
and anger at it raging at it,
storming it down.

Also that four-walled chrysalis
and impediment, home;
that lamp and hearth, that easy fit
of bed to bone;
those children, too, sharp witnesses
of all I've done.

My dear, the ropes that bind us
are safe to hold;
the walls that crush us
keep us from the cold.
I know the price, and still
I pay it, pay it:

Words, their furtive kiss,
illicit gold.

In Passing

Suppose I had paused a few seconds
clattering down those public stairs,
and you (by chance?) had met me.
Would a look or a brush of hands have swept away
or thickened the cloud between us?

Say I had found you on the phone
and not clicked off so quickly.
Would you have heard the heartdrum
beating, beating where my tongue should be?
Nothing's happened; nothing's to confess.

You asked how experience becomes a poem
in the weightless hour that makes poetry.
Look, it's happening now in a country,
not home, not foreign,
in language that puts its clothes on carefully

after unpaid, love-making labour in that
dark, erotic mill, the imagination.
Imagine believing that a cloud can be
talked into becoming a mountain long after
it has lost itself in common day.

Ah Babel

your tower allures me –
its lettered battlements,
sounds, words,
but the high forehead unfinished.

I would desert my eyes
for the windows that are you.

Your multiple stones
despise clouds.
Your country's bleached sand
and black scars

lead to a sky
as clean as meaning.

Nameless
in mist and silence,
grey against grey,
I exist in your promise,

praise you for this present
of a vast home,
pronounced ruin,
all that is known.

From the Men of Letters

How lucky we are
to have a room in language. We
who are known take pride in our hotel.

Naturally
the unknown want to be us, but
they are crippled.

All of us are crippled, but
they are most crippled whose
disasters encourage our art.

They live
swarming and unnamed
in the rubble of a moment.

We live
decently rehoused
in the storeys of a time.

When they throw their arms
around our words
and weep

we are horribly embarrassed.
How will their experience
forgive our tall books?

The Figure in the Carpet

Might be human,
might be design:
a diamond face, half mouth,
half upright hair;
two square-rimmed eyes
that stare
in a sad direction.
He – or is it she? –
wipes the clear
left eye
with a wrist
more paw than hand.

The other arm,
crippled, perhaps,
(it will not bend)
holds a cross
which is part
of the interlocking risk
of pattern
or of art.

'Usually
I am man or woman.
I do not ask.
I feel happiest
when I melt into the plan
without description.'

A Riddle for Peter Scupham

on his 70th birthday

Creeping close and closer as it falls away,
Haunted in its unprotected garden by
Its own enchanted lanterns, dead by day, but
Lively when goodnight revolves its pictures in the
Dark, and moth-white shadows repossess their
Home – upstairs and down, the fitful ghosts,
Outside and in, the stuff that dreams are made
On, finding in airy nothing, forms
Despaired of, habitations through the poet's pen.

The Morden Angel

*A monologue of the plaster bust of an angel who presides
over poetry readings in The Morden Tower, Newcastle.*

(for Connie Pickard)

My sideways smile
means I'm wearing
this joke of my being
like a punishment.

A child of baroque
imagination, I could have
risen! In cloudy theatrical surroundings,
say, with a pipe on a ceiling,
or burdened with a wreath of pineapples,
my squint might not have
disadvantaged me.

But here, where the spirit of
Art, one winter,
snagged the smooth career
of my creator, I came
into my little kingdom
crooked.
          If it was a
muse he needed,
why did my creator make me dumb?
I am full to the lips
with iambic pentameters.
In couplets I might have
inspired him – though
what's come to my attention
as verse in these late days
he wouldn't have believed!
Especially my wings
are worrying. Ought they
to beat like a cherub's
or flutter like Cupid's?
They pin me to the wall
like a target.

It's from trying to
fly away from this wall
or back into the wall
that my temper suffers.

Here come those poets again,
their inelegant wails!
If only my wings would work.
If only my smile could talk.

Re-reading Jane

The Memorial to Jane Austen in Winchester Cathedral reads: In memory of JANE AUSTEN, youngest daughter of the late Rev George Austen, formerly rector of Steventon in this county. She departed this life on the 18th July, 1817, after a long illness supported with the patience and the hopes of a Christian. The benevolence of her heart, the sweetness of her temper, and the extraordinary endowments of her mind obtained the regard of all who knew her and the warmest love of her intimate connections. Their grief is in proportion to their affection. They know their loss to be irreparable, but in their deepest affliction they are consoled by a firm though humble hope that her charity, devotion, faith and purity have rendered her soul acceptable in the sight of her REDEEMER.

To women in contemporary voice and dislocation
she is closely invisible, almost an annoyance.
Why do we turn to her sampler squares for solace?
Nothing she saw was free of snobbery or class.
Yet the needlework of those needle eyes...
We are pricked to tears by the justice of her violence:
Emma on Box Hill, rude to poor Miss Bates,
by Mr Knightley's *were she your equal in situation –*
but consider how far this is from being the case
shamed into compassion, and in shame a grace.

Or wicked Wickham and selfish pretty Willoughby,
their vice pure avarice which, displacing love,
defiled the honour marriages should be made of.
She punished them with very silly wives.
Novels of manners? Hymeneal theology!
Six little circles of hell, with attendant humours.
For what do we live but to make sport for our neighbours
And laugh at them in our turn? The philosophy
paused at the door of Mr Bennet's century;
The Garden of Eden's still there in the grounds of Pemberley.

The amazing epitaph's 'benevolence of heart'
precedes 'the extraordinary endowments of her mind'
and would have pleased her, who was not unkind.
Dear votary of order, sense, clear art
and irresistible fun, please pitch our lives
outside self-pity we have wrapped them in
and show us how absurd we'd look to you.
You knew the mischief poetry could do.
Yet when Anne Elliot spoke of *its misfortune*
to be seldom safely enjoyed by those who
enjoy it completely, she spoke for you.

John Keats, 1821–1950

Keats was Miss McKinney's class, 12th grade English,
and we could tell she loved him
by the way she scolded us. 'Why is it
you young, spoiled people never look?'

Poetry was what we learned 'by heart'.
I can still see it, that clammy, Coke-stained textbook's
Ode to Autumn. I think I half believed I was him,
the spirit of Keats come back, in me, to Michigan.

Devoid of thatch-eaves, lambs and granary floors,
Ann Arbor had its river. I hymned the sallows under
violent-coloured maples. Crickets I remember,
and how the fierce gnats' wailing was oracular.

At the Grave of Ezra Pound

*Venice is an excellent place to come to from
Crawfordsville, Indiana.*
(Pavannes and Divagations)

Cimmerian? Anyway, a swart day.
Its silence immense, unfinished.
The leaden water pleated itself
As our boat drew close to the quay.

We passed through the aisle of bambini,
(White stones with coloured photographs,
Flowers in tender urns,
The pebbles washed, the graves shut and tidy)

And found the poet from Crawfordsville
In a dank, shady plot,
EZRA POUND, drilled into lichened rock.
Readable but not believable.

No *sylva nympharum* shone
Around him, tremulously clear.
No goddess of fair knees, no cave of Nerea,
No marble-leaved 'pleached arbour of stone'.

Olga alone, faithful and morose,
Shared his bracket of sour undergrowth
Where someone had knelt to plant the myrtle
Covering them both.

Whatever he might be writing
Wrathfully against our age
Moulders unheard, unwanted
On that tangled page.

Aletha, goddess of sea-farers, defend him.
'He fished by obstinate isles.'
In the gloom, what further betrayals
Gather the dark against him?

* * *

Dreaming of Immortality in a Thatched Hut

(after a painting by Chin Ch'ang-T'ang)

Drowsing over his verses or drifting
lazily through the sutras,
he blinked in the hazy August silence
through which a blind stream bore on
and the locusts endlessly sawed, performing mistakes
and catching themselves up again like nervous musicians.

Soft rain dropped on the padded dust at nightfall,
dawns poured revelations over the peaks
until, as he slept, he could see it all –
the graceful ascent from the shelving eaves of the hut,
an ease of detachment, the flowing out of his sleeves,
that slow half sorrowful movement of regret
as he rose with the steadying mists about his knees,
away from the rocks and the stunted, gripping pine,
and the books stacked neatly out of the way of the rain.

The Exhibition

(for Alasdair Gray)

The exhibition is of
    all the exhibited people
        gathered together at the exhibition.

How pleasing. Everyone is at ease.
    The canvases are amiably walking around
        choosing faces which are

cut out of smooth brown packing paper,
    pasted meticulously in the spaces
        wearing their names.

How can they fail to be flattered,
    these figures who in frames
        stay distressingly apart from one another,

but when meeting themselves on the walls
    are so delighted?
        That woman lying naked on the bed,

for instance, stops
    brooding over her weakness of will
        and admires her thighs.

And the man without shoes, in his necktie,
    approves his cool sense of detachment,
        his power to despatch it and rise.

Yes, it's all satisfactory self-fulfilment –
    admirer and admired so embraced
        there's no place for the past,

though behind both paint and gallery
    you can see that some old city
        is thinning to dissolution.

Distances between shoulder and shoulder,
    eye and eye grow wider as the
        waste lots fill up with workers' rubble:

brokenhearts, hangovers, torn sheets,
    yards of mattress stuffing, bottles,
        cigarette butts, used newspapers.

Enlightened, momentarily spared,
    the invited say 'thank you' and
        go in their separate directions.

Now the pictures, left holding their
    bodies and heads, have no chance of
        changing things at all by making connections.

The Blue Pool

(after the painting by Augustus John)

It is high summer by the blue pool.
Our heroine has left the safe house of her book
to repose on one arm in the shape of a girl
in this hungry man's painting of a blue pool
with a creamy shelf of dry mountains around it,
a tawny bronze tint to the white reflections.
This could be a hot day near a flooded quarry.
The flowing green dress, the moth-starred jerkin,
the dark bobbed hair are all parts of a story,
but its title and substance have no importance.

What is important is the book's colour, which is yellow.
In a child's picture, the sun would be this colour,
and the view would fall away from the sun
like a symmetrical tent from a pole.
But in this adult landscape, the sun's understood;
it's the undefined source of the light.
So the girl and her book have a moony existence –
as the mind indeed has when it ceases to see as
but returns pure reflections from the blue (or brown)
pools of its senses. The girl could not possibly be reading.

She herself is the quick of the paint's observation
which allows her so sweetly to float out away from herself;
where, for once, she is perfectly happy, perfectly whole;
though she still keeps her finger on her place in the book.
The enamelled bright pages must have something in them,
in a minute she's sure to remember.
She is young, too, and wishes the painter were with her.
Soon she'll slip round the blank fearful page of his easel
to look at herself. Will the painting be like her?
She will think, she thinks, of something intelligent to say.

Seven Poems after Francis Bacon

1 *Study for a Portrait on a Folding Bed*

Flesh squirms on the blue folding bed;
ear torn from a head.
He's the pupil of his eye
at the heart of his house of glass.

Afloat in his well, being, why
does a black palette drip
from that lap of aggression? What
nightmare will the egg hatch
that lies – a prediction of
greenlessness – on that dead step?

2 *Study of a Dog*

The last dog
rises and tipclaws out
of the peagreen hoop
which is all that's left of the park.

It's hot on the penthouse roof,
which is all that's left of Monte Carlo.

The shade of the last tree?
On the far side of the motorway.

Is it water the creature wants?
Or that sad little ball
rolled out of the sand trap
onto the burning turf.

3 *Three Figures and Portrait*

Personality, the flesh artist
(and presiding self-portrait),
has perfected his trick of exposing
bodies to money until
they attain metallic putrefaction.

When these hunks of human stuff
harden into fixed forms,
reptilian man schemes in one circle,
mammalian woman in another.

Her gold ring is larger and brighter
than his rink of empire.

That fury in a cage
is their fortunate offspring.

She has sprung fully armed
from their heads,
and she means to hate them.

At present she's
spooling her childhood
in her chittering skull.

4 Seated Figure

Self-placed,
for years he's struggled to achieve it,
a position exactly at the centre
of his invisible frame.

The expensive Kirman
congratulates his shoes.

The rich blue furniture, discreet blue curtain,
push forward his expression of
resourceful authority; farsighted,
he gazes at the future,

though tensely he holds in readiness
shortsighted spectacles, for details.

You can put your trust in me,
says the strong right shoulder.
But the left will not bear weight
or responsibility;
he's had to remove it
to centre the picture on righteousness.

Shift him three inches to the left
and everything's lost.

5 *Portrait of a Lady*

'I did, of course, consent to it.
I've never been interested in flattery.
Character is your forte, Mrs Alstone.
(Dear Motherwell, I think, or was it Hockney?)
Sir Geoffrey warned me in Paris,
You won't want to hang it in your boudoir.
No way, I told him. My scene's
the sex war, not the boud war.

Now look at that right eye.
There I am, you see, my taste, my power.
The mouth is a betrayal.
I've been abused, you know,
for my generosity. I have risked.
I have guessed. I have made good
my investments. You will find my name
among the Friends of the major galleries.
My calling's to be a friend of artists.

That I was wiser than my husband,
with money, was *not* the reason
for our separation. Shall we say
we differed in numerous big ways?
I believe the misery of my mouth
pays for the height of my brow.'

6 *Triptych*

In Hades
by the swimming pool,
seated, he dries
right foot with
right hand.
Torso has slipped
to the floor,
rosy towel.

Drift flesh
copulates with
old imperative
desire.
Womb lies beneath them,
pink bib, nice pad.

Nearly whole
& fixed
& talking,
this experiment,
(fleshing out
adipocerous soul)
has almost
succeeded.

7 *Study for a Portrait of Van Gogh*

I paint the rich and the damned.
They wince and buy me.
He only painted the sun
as poor as himself.

I live in the world of the world,
its rings of interior.
He lived in the circle of his hat
and through its gold weave
gazed at the angels
like grasshoppers in the heat.

I see the white sweep of his wings,
and I paint, paint, paint.

I lay the whole weight of my gift
on his stooped back.

Brueghel's Snow

Here in the snow:
three hunters with dogs and pikes
trekking over a hill,
into and out of those famous footprints –
famous and still.

What did they catch?
They have little to show
on their bowed backs.
Unlike the delicate skaters below,
these are grim; they look ill.

In the village, it's zero.
Bent shapes in black clouts,
raw faces aglow
in the firelight, burning the wind
for warmth, or their hunger's kill.

What happens next?
In the unpainted picture?
The hunters arrive, pull
off their caked boots, curse the weather
slump down over stoups...

Who's painting them now?
What has survived to unbandage
my eyes as I trudge through this snow,
with my dog and stick,
four hundred winters ago?

Hans Memling's *Sibylla Sambetha* (1480)

(for Peter Forbes and Diana Reich)

I had forgotten the weight of her –
the patient gravitas of her
waxed illumination, speaking through
glazed eyes and lips
covertly to us in the future.

Is her energy contained, constrained
by passionate purity?
Or does a veneer of chastity
tame her for necessary marriage?
Her tranquillity is not quite beauty.

Her hands rest, left over right,
on the ledge between trial
and decision. The veil
dropped stiffly from her headpiece
is not the impenetrable veil.

She is someone observed as certain
looking inward, certainly.
Who can tell if her days were happy,
or if vehemence smouldering within
makes visible innocence or venom?

In the Museum of Floating Bodies and Flammable Souls

(for Angela Leighton)

Painters who painted the flights of martyrs for money,
Who filled the drapery of angels with rose-tinted oil,
Had to please rich patrons with trapeze acts of the body,
Since no one can paint the electricity of the soul.

My lady in her blue silk cowl must by now be topsoil;
She swans into Heaven, almond eyes uplifted in piety.
My lord kneels at prayer in a cassock, blade at his heel.
Not a single electron remains of his sin or sanctity.

While in Hell – well preserved in the water church of Torcello –
The wicked receive their deserts. Disembowelled and dismembered,
They are set upon eternally, yet their bodies alone are touched;
Unless souls, flushed out of the flesh, are the flames that torch them.

No wonder evil's so interesting and goodness pitifully dull.
Torture of the body symbolises torture of the mind;
And burning in the bonfires of conscience is hardly confined
To a hell for bad Italians, being damned and being saved as well.

Whistler's *Gentleman by the Sea*

Nature, who for once has sung in tune,
sings her exquisite songs to the artist alone.
J.M. WHISTLER, 1885

He knew himself as Sunday in a hat,
Patrolling borders of a century that
Lectured the waves and watched them shuffling back.

Till paint abstracted him from joy of this,
Cancelled the certainty he must exist,
And made of him a gentlemanly mist.

Where does the ocean end, the man begin?
Rain and the waves debate beneath his skin.
Tides of his pearl-grey blood drag out and in,

While, soothed and veiled, the moody water breathes
Cerulean horizontals through his knees.
Nature persuades all elements to please

When to the artist Nature sings alone.
Then Art advises Nature in its own
Linseed-on-canvas, frame-begetting tone.

Painting It In

(Remembering Lesley Parry)

Wake up at six o'clock. We're out to sea.
Nothing beyond that fence and slatted gate
but a grey wave and plume-like shapes that could be
flaws in the canvas or unmixed pigment in paint.

Stones, blurred poppies, a wheelbarrow full of grass
affirm a foreground. The world must exist out there.
People must be getting up and getting washed,
putting the kettle on, picking up a newspaper.

Somewhere it must matter terribly not to be late,
not to miss the limousine to the airport,
not to be missed when the finance committee votes;
when the training course commences, not be left out.

But somewhere is hard to believe when it's not invented,
when the world blindly refuses to admit detail.
All that's required is pastoral: sheep among stunted
rowans; for background, eroded 'Moelfre' or 'bald hill'.

The thing's been done so many times. Imagine
brushing the lichen's pale quartz over the rocks,
now the shocking pink foxgloves, painting them in,
old-fashioned *belles de joie*, drunk on their stalks.

What if today decides never to take off its veil,
never to palliate art with a grand show
of perspectives up the valley? More likely all we'll
get is light's first lesson, an application of gesso,

a whiteout of air – sweet, soft, indestructible,
the cloud of unknowing reluctant to create the known.
Hills, stones, sheep, trees are, as yet, impossible.
And when things are unmade, being also feels less alone.

After you left
(for Annabel Cole)

that perpetual summer sun became unpleasant.
It had an ozone minus feel about it,
everyone short tempered and too hot.

So when the impacted storm gathered and broke,
we ran to the East window to look out.
The cwm had already spumed its rolling ghost,

Moelfre was muffled, the Rhinogs hidden or eaten,
thunder thundered, lightning fired and missed
us – maiming, I think the electricity grid.

Then welcome rain, provisional, unfriendly.
The sheep stood backward to it, stony still,
looking, or trying to look, invisible.

Nothing electric at *Pwllymarch* presently works.
I'm writing by candlelight. Supper's half cooked
on the fire; the wine is good.

'Happiness shouldn't be so important.'
About four square inches on the canvas –
that's a piece of luck.

Red Hot Sex

Miranda hoists her lips in a grimace.
Her arms are two peeled twigs, her ankles curl.
That dark soft hair and narrow porcelain face?
A sketch, a spoiled first draft of a pretty girl.

She's friendly with Fred, whose electronic chair
(State of the art for men who can't stand up)
Glides around hers, not touching anywhere.
He's spread into his, an egg (soft-boiled) in a cup,

So cheerfully disposed he makes a joke of that.
He's been in a chair since childhood. Awful burden.
Parents worn out in their eighties. Misses his cat.
A brother, whose wife can't cope, talks of a Home.

Here, he's neither home nor in a Home.
Laughing, he makes Miranda laugh. And me.
A heap among heaps, I glance around the room,
Our island of wheelers in a walking sea.

Thanks to the cash of a caring modern state,
We've space and food. It's institution-dreary,
But okay. When strong enough, I paint.
My helpers set me up in the conservatory,

Paint book, water glass, tray, plates of gouache.
Don't laugh when I tell you, all I paint is flowers.
As long as my Minnie Mouse paw can grip the brush
I forget my melting bones – for those few hours.

And once I can't paint? Never think of it.
No, not true, I do. I look around.
The TV's always on, and there they sit,
So many white-faced zombies. Gets you down.

What can you do? Your mind is seared with pain.
The worse your body, the more it seems to fill
Each tortured fold and cranny of your brain.
I haven't given up yet. I never will.

I pity Pete, for one, and sullen Clive
(Miranda hates it when they stare at her)
Who, half the time, don't seem to be alive.
No jokes, no books, no smirking at the paper,

Unless you count that section of *The Sun*
Stuffed in a plastic sack outside the lockers.
Red Hot Sex. Apologetic porn.
If the cover lovers hadn't both been starkers

They could have stepped right out of the TV.
She might have looked as sexy, selling weather.
And what's he fondling? His own vanity!
I wonder if they'd even met each other

Before they posed? Do actors, acting sex,
Feel anything but numb from the neck up?
$X + Y = Zero$. Solve for X.
Oh, thinking's hopeless! So I paint a tulip.

That lipstick red corolla is a show,
A lure, a pit where unsheathed pizzle-anthers
Practise the only sexy act they know;
Or mock-perform it – chancers playing nature's

Bingo, mixing the useless with the worthless,
Setting the lifewheel spinning, with no aim.
That's Mother Nature for you! I'm an artist.
Choosing to paint, I'm chosen. That's *my* game.

The Miracle of Camp 60

*(The speaker is a fictive Italian ex-POW revisiting the Italian Chapel
on the Orkney island of Lamb Holm in 1992.)*

Amici d'arti, amici dei fiori, amici d'amore,
When in our towns they told us *go fight for Il Duce*
we Dolomiti had to go. We were...coscritti, we
had no choice. I wept when I departed from Trento,
my poor mother, my so sad new young wife.
Credi in Dio, we embraced each other as the train
stretched us apart. But then in the deeps of misery
I had some luck. My seat-partner, how do you say,
was Chiocchetti. L'artista Domenico Chiocchetti
of Moena, a man very sensitive...you understand?
And so he saw my tears. With him he kept always –
like this, around his neck – a spiritual picture,
Madonna delle Olive – Our Lady of the Olives,
of our great Italian painter, Nicolo Barabina.
This medallion Domenico let me hold, for hope,
as the train transported us human meats to Roma,
then to Tunis, to Egitto, to fight the war.
See over the altar, the Madonna of Chiocchetti,
Regina Pacis, Ora Pro Nobis. As we prayed many many times
in that desert of death under the stars.
Our prayers were answered when you Britons beat us.
No more did we have to fear the brute Tedeschi.
So we were glad. Not to be prisoners, you understand,
but to be not any longer soldiers, while we were sad
not to go home. We did not know what was happening
in our country, to our families. When we came to Orkney,
we did not know where we were, so far, so... smorta,
this terrible island, not one tree, not one flower.
Only polvere, calcina, cemento...everywhere
filo barbato, all sunshine strangled in it, and huts
we would use for pigs in Italy, to share.

Only Chiocchetti saw... a holy place.
Look, he pointed through the wires, the azure water,
isole, islands, emerald in the sea. He was painting them
already in his head while we worked through rain and wind
to build the barriers. Labour we did not mind.
Better to work than to despair. Even so,
there was too much time to think of home.
Before the war my occupation was giardinere.
I made gardens for the city of Merano.

After I went back, I was the capo. One day on Lamb Holm
I spied among the rocks a small flower, an iris rare
in Italy, and to myself I said, here we could grow piante,
make little beds, walkways, sentieri.

So with some men I went to the Commandante.
Please may we have some seeds. Seeds? He was surprised.
He found us seeds and bulbs, in some months we had iris,
geranio, calendula, lupini, giglio – you say lily?
We made your desert bloom. Now, why not a piazza with a statue?
OK, says Chiocchetti, without marble I carve cemento;
without bronze, I twist barbed wire. Eccola!
The marvel he created. San Giorgio spearing the dragon.
To show the wish of us Italians to exterminate evil.
Into the base we put our names and coins we saved
from home. Our padre, Gioachino Giacobazzi, swung his censer.
We wept for sadness and joy because from memory
we had made in our ugly camp a dream of Italy.

Allora, came winter and the long nights. We found
some space for a teatro. Talented men among us played
harmonica, mandolin. Always we prisoners had the spirit
to make beauty, but up to that time we had no church,
no place of God to celebrate mass. Yet once again
Il padre, Chiocchetti and myself were called to Major Buckland,
'Signori, you are Catholic. Do you not need a chapel?'
That English Major was, I think, exceptional. Under his
traditional reserve beat surely the Italian heart.
A short time and two new huts appeared, placed end to end,
like so – to make one bigger hut.
And now the talent of Chiocchetti became genius.
He picked skilled helpers and they, too, caught fire.
Palumbo, who studied metal-working in America, contrived
from scrap – gracile, delicato – the screen of iron.
And Bruttapasta whose speciality was concrete.
Regard his altar, made out of just cemento. The same for
la facciata, colonne, campanile, pinnacoli, vetri –
painted in all colori, l'arco, i pedimenti. Also, in red stone
la testa di Cristo crocefisso that was moulded by Pinesi.
It was as if, on this far island, by the mercy of God,
we few had been chosen to prepare in a world destroyed
a home for the immortal dove who alone brings peace
to men and women. Regard – on the vault of the sanctuary
in the fresco of Chiocchetti – a dove with angels.

Mi scusate. Excuse me. I am incapable of beholding this place
without tears. War was good to us. We were prisoners
but we were happy, making our chapel beautiful.
Happier than ever again. When the war finished
we had to depart. I sobbed because we had not finished.
I wept again in Merano. La mia madre, morta...my poor wife.
You know what i bruti soldati did to beautiful women.
We could not have children. To forgive myself for joy
while my loved ones suffered – so many suffered –
it was not easy. Chiocchetti did not come home with us.
He stayed to complete his font, and when I met him in Moena –
many many years later – he told me he, too, felt guilty.
But guilt is not right, he said, for art is joy.
Short is our suffering in this life, joy is forever.

Now an old man, I visit again our joyful chapel
to read in your language a prayer of blessed Francis.

Lord, make me an instrument of peace.
Where there is hatred, let me sow love,
where there is injury, pardon,
where there is darkness, light,
where there is sadness...gioia, la gioia.

*　*　*

Journal Entry: Impromptu in C Minor

(Edinburgh, October 1988)

After weeks of October drench,
a warm orange day,
a conflagration of all the trees and streets in Edinburgh.

Let me have no thoughts
in this weather of pure sensation.

Getting into the car is a coatless sensation.
Driving through the traffic
is the feeling of falling leaves.

The Firth, like the sky, is blue, blue,
with sandy brown puffs of surf on the oily beaches.
The sea swell rises and spills,
rises and spills, tumbling its load of crockery
without breakage.

Is a metaphor a thought?
Then let these shells be shells,
these sharp white sails be sails.

Today the pink enormous railway bridge
is neither a three-humped camel nor a dinosaur
but a grand feat of Scottish engineering;
now and then it rumbles peacefully
as a tiny train, rather embarrassed, scuttles across it.

Sitting with pure sensation on the breakwater,
I unhook the wires of my mind.
I undo the intellectual spider's web.

Then I correct myself.
Soon I'm standing in my grid of guilts
hastily reaching for my thoughts.

For there are people out there.
Not abstractions, not ideas, but people.
In the black, beyond the blue of my perception,
in the huge vault where the wires won't reach,
the dead are lively.
The moment I take off my thought-clothes
I expose every nerve to their waves.

What is this sad marching melody?
A spy, a column on reconnaissance,
the theme from Schubert's Impromptu in C Minor.

It is 1943.
In a frame house that has forgotten him,
a dead man is playing the piano.
I am ten years old. For the first time
I watch a grown woman weep.
Her husband, the white-haired Jewish philosopher,
makes shy mistakes in English.
He puts an arm around his wife
and bows his head.

The theme returns years later
to a farmhouse in Vermont.
This time I myself am at the piano,
a puzzled girl I instantly recognise
although she died through more years than Schubert lived
to make room for the woman I am now.

I smile at her ambition.
She doesn't yet know she will be deaf.

She doesn't yet know how deaf she's been.

What is the matter?

This is the matter: deafness and deadness.
The shoe-heaps, hills of fillings, children's bones.
Headlines blacking out the breakfast chatter
        (We go on eating).
Static and foreign voices on the radio
        (We are late for school).

Then silence folding us in,
folding them under.

But here is the melody.

And here, 'our daemonic century'
in which a dead man's dead march
plays itself over and over
on a fine fall day in South Queensferry
in the head of a fortunate (though deaf) American grandmother.

She sits in the momentary sun looking at the sea.

Once there lived in Austria a schoolmaster's son,
shy, myopic, a little stout, but lucky,
for his talent was exactly suited to his time.
Careless of his health in an age of medical ignorance,
he died at thirty-one, probably of syphilis.
A few moments of his life, five notes of it,
fuse with a few impromptu responses,
a few contemporary cells.

They provide the present and future
of an every-minute dying planet
with a helix, a hinge of survival.

Kosovo Surprised by Mozart
(Bernard Roberts playing K. No. 533, 11 April 1999)

Lovely chromatic Mozart, talk to me
in your language of intimate, arithmetical
progression. Perform with this performer.
Hold that diminished seventh's cutting edge
close against the dominant until it
skylarks away from the tonic's expectant
cages to a charmed high of almost
imperceptible *rallentando*, only to
circle back lightly into the right key.

Why does what is known of happiness,
like sadness, find insignia in harmony?
Your genes were a template of musical
grammar from the hour of your birth.
You must have translated straight from
sensation into sound, ignoring the tongue's
barbed wire at disputed borders. How young
you were, how unfinished your work of
spinning tempi into timelessness.

Easy it may be to bless and be blessed
in the *terra cognita* of Pythagoras, but
who lives there long? Young hungry hours can't
help but devour us, hacking from east to west
through this eleventh day, fourth month, last year
of the twentieth century. An uninhabited body is
slashed and displayed on a pole. It's not unusual
for flesh to be pummelled, pistol-whipped,
groin-kicked, machine-gunned under arrest.

For news is the news, and our cameras favour
burying sufferers alive in rewindable footage.
And your spirit? Escaped long ago in a passion
of inky dots. It's for ten live fingers to decode you –
leapfrogging over the rubble, the incurable hospital,
the wreck of the temple, the cries and imploring hands.
We accuse you, Herr Mozart, of not representing our age.
Simplified, rarefied, perfectionist as ever,
punish us in the key of F Major.

Hearing with My Fingers

A house with a six-foot rosewood piano, too grand
to get out the door? *You buy it, I'll play it!*
So now, as in my childhood, the living-room
has become the piano room, exercising,
like a sun, irresistible powers of gravitation.
How to walk past and not be dragged to keys
that free at a touch the souls of the composers?
The piano itself is soul-shaped. Like lovers,
our baby grands lay deep in each other's curves;
players locked eyes across the Yin and Yang of them,
fingering delight in a marriage of true sounds.

How would a living-room live without pianos,
I used to wonder, beginning my before-breakfast
two-hour stint at the Steinway – scales, arpeggios,
Czerny or cheery Scarlatti, progressing through Bach
(stirrings in the kitchen, waftings of coffee and bacon)
to *Scenes from Childhood* that my hands, to my head's
amazement, still remember after forty years' neglect.

If I fancied myself an object of fate's attention,
I'd take for punishment the fog blinding my ears.
What was I doing those waste, egotistical years
when I snatched what I heard and never told the piano?
I wanted a contract with love. I wanted the words!
And now, apparently, my fingers have forgiven me.
Wordless as right and left, as right and wrong,
drained of ambition, gullied with veiny skin,
they want to go back and teach my eyes to listen,
my heart to see...the shape of a Greek amphora,
plum-blossom after Hiroshima, harmony-seeds
growing from staves my clumsy fingers read.

Arioso Dolente

(for my grandchildren when they become grandparents)

A mother, who read and thought and poured herself into me;
she was the jug and I was the two-eared cup.
How she would scorn today's 'show-biz inanity,
democracy twisted, its high ideals sold up!'
        Cancer filched her voice, then cut her throat.
                Why is it
        none of the faces in this family snapshot
                looks upset?

A father, who ran downstairs as I practised the piano;
barefooted, buttoning his shirt, he shouted 'G,
D-natural, C-*flat*! *Dolente, arioso.*
Put all the griefs of the world in that change of key.'
        Who then could lay a finger on his sleeve
              to distress him with
      'One day, Steve, two of your well-taught daughters
                will be deaf.'

Mother must be sitting, left, on the porch-set,
you can just see her. My sister's on her lap.
And that's Steve confiding to his cigarette
something my mother's mother has to laugh at.
        The screened door twangs, slamming
              on its sprung hinge.
      Paint blisters on the steps; iced tea, grasscuttings,
              elm flowers, mock orange...

A grand June evening, like this one, not too buggy,
unselfquestioning midwestern, maybe 1951.
And, of course, there in my grandmother's memory
lives just such another summer – 1890 or 91.
        Though it's not on her mind now/then.
           No, she's thinking of
      the yeast-ring rising in the oven. Or how *any* shoes
              irritate her bunion.

Paper gestures, pictures, newsprint laughter.
And after the camera winks and makes its catch,
the decibels drain away *for ever and ever.*
No need to say 'Look!' to these smilers on the porch,
        'Grandmother will have her stroke,
          and you, mother, will nurse her.'
Or to myself, this woman died paralysed-dumb, and that one
          dumb from cancer.

Sufficient unto the day… Grandmother, poor and liturgical,
whose days were duties, stitches in the tea-brown blanket
she for years crocheted, its zigzag of yellow wool,
her grateful offering, her proof of goodness to present,
  gift-wrapped, to Our Father in Heaven. 'Accept,
    O Lord, this best-I-can-make-it soul.'
 And He: 'Thou good and faithful sevant, lose thyself
     and be whole.'

Consciousness walks on tiptoe through what happens.
So much is felt, so little of it said.
But ours is the breath on which the past depends.
'What happened' is what the living teach the dead,
  who, smilingly lost to their lost concerns,
     in grey on grey,
   are all of them deaf, blind, unburdened
     by today.

As if our recording selves, our mortal identities,
could be cupped in a concave universe or lens,
ageless at all ages, cleansed of memories,
not minding that meaningful genealogy extends
  no further than mind's flash images reach back.
    As for what happens next,
   let all the griefs of the world
    find keys for that.

Arioso dolente: from Beethoven's piano sonata, opus 110,
third movement; introduction to the fugue.

Postscriptum

Now I am dead,
no words,
just a wine
of my choosing.

Drink to my
mute consent,
my rite of
dissolving.

Over my chalk
eyelids and wax skin
let a wild
reticence in.

Not a tear
or false look.
Poems, stay there
in your book.

Should passion
attend me,
let it flow freely
through Messiaen's

End of Time Quartet:
unendurable riddles
for the clarinet,
resolved in a fiddle's

remorseless,
forgiving ascent.

VI

Verses

The Traveller

You'd think that in this foreign place,
More strange with every word and face,
Where taste and touch and sight demand
New habits of the eye and hand,
It would be easy to repeal
The laws by which we know and feel.

I told my head it would be so.
I left my ghosts, I planned to go
And lure from every parapet
Each older, wiser one I met.
Therefore I emptied out my skin,
Or thought I had, to let them in.

I found a town I loved at sight.
(The streets danced deep into the night
And all the cottages were white.)
I found an inn, I found a room
With casements criss-crossed like a loom,
And beams and ivy and a faint
Perfume of wine mixed with the paint.

Unpacked and clean, I ordered tea
And waited for my company.
No one came. The room grew tall.
Outside the rain began to fall
While pieces of a yellow tree
Broke off and smashed like pottery.
I watched them drop, I ate, I rose,
I looked beneath my hair. I froze.
My ghosts were standing there in rows.

(1961)

In Winter

The sooner ends the old man's day
The earlier the child's.
A tree will give its leaves away
But roots grow wild.
The sun's unsure diurnal stay
Quickens the lovers' arms;
But cattle foul mouldering hay
On the tired farms.

The deeper flows the bridal snow
The hungrier the hare;
Days counted minutes shrink but no
Less time is there.
Because the leaning sun is low
The lovers lie at ease,
But in the drunken streets they go
Whose dumb hearts freeze.

Who shakes the gate of Calvary
Is let by Eden in;
The martyr's opportunity
Is the poor ghost's sin.
Though flesh has a divinity,
The lovers in their beds
Mistrust God's consanguinity
And hide their heads.

(1954)

Opera Piece

Why
do these
pretty, thin girls
put on white gloves
for this season when
heat blooms from the cellos,
flies hop to the spider's strings,
when pianos pound for the
public voices of lilacs,
smiling, bowing and
dying under their
huge, plumed
bosoms?

(1960)

Two Quatrains

Lesson

The girls and boys in winter know
That love is like the drifting snow;
It praises everything although
Its perishable breath must go.

Television

Hug me, mother of noise,
Find me a hiding place.
I am afraid of my voice.
I do not like my face.

Ailanthus with Ghosts

Their veins were white
but they still hung on with weak hands.
Their wings were dry,
but they still waved back at the wind,
'Just one more day. Just one more day.'

Then, very quietly, Monday night,
a frost-gun shot them away.
Imagine the whole population of Heaven
(Heaven was the name of the tree)
falling down simultaneously,

dazzling the root in its bed.
'What a beautiful star,' Heaven said.
Or might have if heavens could notice
the difference it makes to an earth
to be thatched with ghosts.

A Ballad for Apothecaries

Being a Poem to Honour the Memory of
Nicholas Culpeper, Gent.
Puritan, Apothecary, Herbalist, Astrologer
Who in the year of our Lord 1649
Did publish *A PHYSICAL DIRECTORY*
A translation from the Latin of the London Despensatory
made by the College of Physicians
'Being that Book by which all Apothecaries are strictly
commanded to make all their Physicke.'

In sixteen-hundred-and-sixteen
(The year Will Shakespeare died),
Earth made a pact with a curious star,
And a newborn baby cried.

Queen Bess's bright spring was over,
James Stuart frowned from the throne;
A more turbulent, seditious people
England had never known.

Now, Nick was a winsome baby,
And Nick was a lively lad,
So they gowned him and sent him to Cambridge
Where he went, said the priests, to the bad.

For though he excelled in Latin
And could rattle the Gospels in Greek,
He thought to himself, there's more to be said
Than the ancients knew how to speak.

He was led to alchemical studies
Through a deep Paracelsian text.
He took up the art of astrology first,
And the science of botany next.

To the theories of Galen he listened,
And to those of Hippocrates, too,
But he said to himself, there's more to be done
Than the ancients knew how to do.

For though Dr Tradition's a rich man,
He charges a rich man's fee.
Dr Reason and Dr Experience
Are my guides in philosophy.

The College of Learned Physicians
Prescribes for the ruling class:
Physick for the ills of the great, they sneer,
Won't do for the vulgar mass.

But I say the heart of a beggar
Is as true as the heart of a king,
And the English blood in our English veins
Is of equal valuing.

Poor Nick fell in love with an heiress,
But en route to their desperate tryst,
The lady was struck down by lightning
Before they'd embrased or kissed.

So our hero consulted the Heavens
Where he saw he was fated to be
A friend to the sick and the humble
But the Great World's enemy.

Nick packed up his books in Cambridge
And came down without a degree
To inspirit Red Lion Street, Spitalfields,
With his fiery humanity.

As a reckless, unlicensed physician,
He was moved to disseminate
Cures for the ills of the body
With cures for the ills of the state.

Who knows what horrors would have happened
To Nicholas Culpeper, Gent.,
If the king hadn't driven his kingdom
Into war with Parliament.

In the ranks of the New Model Army
Nick fought with the medical men,
Till a Royalist bullet at Newbury
Shot him back to his thundering pen.

'Scholars are the people's jailors,
And Latin's their jail, ' he roared,
'Our fates are in thrall to knowledge;
Vile men would have knowledge obscured!'

When they toppled King Charles's head off
Nick Culpeper cried, 'Amen!'
It's well that he died before the day
They stuck it on again.

Still, English tongues won their freedom
In those turbulent years set apart;
And the wise, they cherish Nick's courage
While they cheer his compassionate heart.

So whenever you stop in a chemist's
For an aspirin or salve for a sore,
Give a thought to Nicholas Culpeper
Who dispensed to the London poor.

For cures for the ills of the body
Are cures for the ills of the mind;
And a welfare state is a sick state
When the dumb are led by the blind.

NOTE: In a series of prefaces to this best-selling manual in English (reprinted at least fourteen times before 1718) Culpeper denounced the College of Physicians who secured their monopoly by keeping the secrets of medicine in the Latin language – just as Rome's priests, before the Reformation, had maintained power by preserving the mysteries of the Bible in Latin. Culpeper's translation, he declared, was made 'out of pure pity to the commonality of England...many of whom to my knowledge have perished either for want of money to fee a physician or want of knowledge of a remedy happily growing in their garden.'

When the victory of the Parliamentarian Army was still in doubt, Culpeper was branded by the Royalist *Mecurious Pragmaticus* as an Anabaptist 'who had arrived at the battlement of an Absolute Atheist, and by two years drunken labour hath Gallimawfred the apothecaries book into nonsense, mixing every receipt therein with some scruples at least of rebellion or atheism, besides the danger of poisoning men's bodies. And (to supply his drunkenness and lechery with a thirty-shilling award) endeavoured to bring into obloquy the famous Societies of Apothecaries and Chyrugeons.' Such abuses, all of them unfounded, were levelled by his political opponents. Even during the Cromwellian interregnum, a broadside appeared (1652) entitled 'A farm in Spittlefields where all the knick-knacks of astrology are exposed to open sale, where Nicholas Culpeper brings under his velvet jacket: 1. His chalinges against the Doctors of Physick, 2. A Pocket Medicine. 3. An Abnormal Circle.'

Culpeper's *London Dispensary*, however, together with a *Directory for Midwives* and others of his 79 books and pamphlets, continued to sell in large numbers. In 1652-3, he brought out his celebrated herbal under the title of *The English Physitian: or, an Astrological-Physical Discourse of the Vulgar Herbs of this Nation, Being a Compleat Method of Physick, whereby a man may preserve his Body in Health, or cure himself, being sick, for three pence charge, with such things as grow in England, they being most fit for English Bodies.*

Though Culpeper may have been in some ways a charlatan, his *Dispensary* remained in print into the 18th century and his *English Physitian* continues to be the most celebrated of English herbals even today. Sadly, Culpeper's remedies, praised and prized by the London poor, were not able to prevent his death at 38 (from an old wound received while he was fighting in the Parliamentarian Army) nor the deaths of six of his seven children who predeceased him.

* * *

After the Fall

Adam: Lady,
      I've not had a moment's love
      since I was expelled.
      Let me in.

Eve: Lord,
      I've not had a moment's rest
      since I was a rib.
      Put me back.

At Kilpeck Church
(Hereford, 1980)

This is where God first laughed
    and created Lilith.
It was on the seventh day.
    God should have been resting.
But look at them laughing,
    coupling in this warm stone.

See this little squat god
    left behind by pagan revellers
Who pours from a four-headed
    wrapping of sacred snake
A libation of smiles from a headless
    bowl of body.

Love's sweet red laughter wells up, over-
    flows, splashes on to pillars,
(Where – patient, compassionate – saints
    wade its abrasions in amused sobriety)
Ripples through the wide arms
    of chapel and sanctuary,

Trembles in the unseen bodies
  of the corbel heads (they embrace
In the rafters in invisible ecstasy)
  proclaims their One Joy
Through a chorus of creatures, as each
  clown, sinner, sage,

Lecher, angel, tramp, whore, vampire,
  fish, swallow, phoenix, pig, dog,
Rabbit, hart, lion, goat, ram, demon,
  monster-eating monster, worm-
Devouring worm, dragon-belching dragon
  of the Lamb of God

Celebrates in effigy its
  laud to the goddess Lilith,
To her open, easy womb. Which is
  also the cradle of the round god.
For together they are fountain and well,
  the flame in the stone,

The jungle in the door, this
  Eden where she lounges,
Arranging her hair, persuading
  the intricate lianas of her body
To delight in the apple,
  ensnare the serpent,

Braid into her vine of life
  the Tree of Life – which does
Remain gracefully within it, but apart,
  persistently flowering in the garden
Of itself, in the arc of its self-
  understanding, in the Mind of God.

For on the eighth day
  God departed from Lilith
And turned to the emergency
  created by Adam and Eve.
Meaning to come back, meaning surely,
  to return to her

And to eternal appetite in Eden,
  where Lilith remains, incomplete,
Unfulfilled, waiting with her life-bowl
  empty in her hands, even
As the fat god laughs from her lap
  and the hollow cup runs over.

The Parson and the Romany

A Black Mountain ballad to a Green Mountain tune

A parson went out one stormy day
To visit the sick in his valley grey.
A Romany girl he met on his way
With eyes like the radiant dawn of day,
And she lived in the weather all around, all around,
She lived in the weather all around.

'Oh tell me, parson my love,' she said,
'Where are you going with your sickle head,
Your long black cloak from your shoulder spread,
And your stoop like a monument to the dead,
When you live with the weather all around, all around,
When you live with the weather all around?'

'When you are as old as I, my lass,
You'll learn how the hard years press and pass,
For grief is the text and pain is the task,
And everyone belongs to the weeping class
While we live with the weather all around, all around.
While we live with the weather all around.'

'And what will you do when your time is done,
And you count up your sufferings one by one,
And put them in a sack with the string undone
For inspection by the Lord and his Ghost and Son
As we pray in the weather all around, all around,
As we pray in the weather all around?'

'Are you a demon or a sprite,' he cried,
'Do you speak out of ignorance or of pride?
Look up where the clouds are gaping wide
To show you the pillars of Hell inside,
While you laugh in the weather all around, all around
While you laugh in the weather all around.'

'That's odd,' said the girl, 'for I've just come
From an angel who was sitting by a pillar of the sun.
He blessed me and called me his chosen one
And soon I'll be having a pretty little son
Who will live in the weather all around, all around,
Who will live in the weather all around.'

The parson, he shook off his cloak and hood,
He threw back his head and laughed where he stood,
'Now tell me your name, O my wicked and good.'
'They call me the Lady of Kilpeck wood.'
So they danced in the weather of the sun, of the sun,
They danced in the weather of the sun.
They danced in the weather of the sun all around,
They danced in the weather of the sun.

(1982)

The Theologian's Confession

Turning his last days page by page,
Man is a God-thing, Anselm murmurs,
And God a man-thing made of language.
Three in One. But I? am embers.

Booked by my bracket's final numbers,
I will be lost in the dash between
Proof that confuses and encumbers
And truth so plain it won't be seen.

Carol of the Birds

Feet that could be clawed, but are not...
Arms that might have flown, but did not...
No one said, 'Let there be angels!' but the birds

Whose choirs fling alleluias over the sea,
Herring gulls, black backs carolling raucously
While cormorants dry their wings on a rocky stable.

Plovers that stoop to sancify the land
And scoop small, roundy mangers in the sand,
Swaddle a saviour each in a speckled shell.

A chaffinchy fife unreeling in the marsh
Accompanies the tune a solo thrush
Half sings, half talks in riffs of wordless words,

As hymns flare up from tiny muscled throats,
Robins and hidden wrens whose shiny notes
Tinsel the precincts of the winter sun.

What loftier organ than these pipes of beech,
Pillars resounding with the jackdaws' speech,
And poplars swayed with light like shaken bells?

Wings that could be hands, but are not...
Cries that might be pleas yet cannot
Question or disinvent the stalker's gun,

Be your own hammerbeam angels of the air
Before in the maze of space, you disappear,
Stilled by our dazzling anthrocentric mills.

* * *

Celebrity

When at last I lie down to sleep
with my reputation
serving the name of my dust
like a grinning doll,
I'll no longer need to remember
any occasion
of human indignity and fuss
to explain it all.

No ill-concealed file of my faults
will ever extend this
crotchety itch of becoming
I know as me
beyond the illustrious face
an approving, vicious
future of sorting and smoothing
decides to see.

As in tennis, love means nothing.
My famous matches
are there for the faithful
in lights that stud the court;
with an inrushing wave of applause
that in praising, passes,
along with the cash, and my skilful
wasted art.

(1990)

A Quest

Precocious, in the news at nine or ten,
She hero-worshipped creamy Englishmen,
Doe-eyed like Rupert Brooke, with downy chin,
A type that dies in youth and likes to swim.

An Alpha graduate at twenty-one,
She picked them macho and American,
Big Michelin shoulders with a greasy tan,
Sliced pie from hunk to hips like Superman.

She hit the acid road at thirty, when
Her analyst unearthed a psychic yen
To crumple under hairy, beery men.
Her Id was rampant and bohemian,

But still she married Mr IBM
Whose cash came handy when she scuppered him
And went to Cambridge where she lived in sin
With deconstructed Cath'lic Marxism.

At fifty, menopausal, nervous, thin,
She joined a women's group and studied Zen.
Her latest book, *The Happy Lesbian*,
Is recommended reading for gay men.

(1993)

The Ballad of the Made Maid

My love is rich and talented
And to my bed he came.
'I'll love you till the sea runs red
But marriage is my aim.'
'But I have my career,' I said,
'My lonely road to fame.
I'd sooner lose my maidenhead
Than lose my maiden name.'

'Oh, I'm too highly paid,' he said,
'To waste my time in pain.
If we were honourably wed
I faithful would remain.
Admit me to your honeyed bed
And hear me swear again,
I'll never take your maidenhead
Without your maiden name.'

'Oh, come into my honeyed bed,
My love of narrow brain,
For to be hugged and cuddléd
Is natural as rain.
But I on oestrogen have fed
Since first I learned the game.
There's many had my maidenhead,
But none my maiden name.'

'Oh, woe is me,' the young man cried
And hid his face for shame.
'And all I want's a blushing bride,
A cottage built for twain,
With running hot and cold inside
And roses round the drain.
But since you've lost your maidenhead
You'll never have my name!'

'My love,' I cried, 'a maidenhead
Is easy to obtain.
To take a lover into bed
Is only honest gain.
But if you think I will be led
Into your baited shrine
You'd better find a maiden bred
In eighteen ninety-nine.'

Oysters

The fat man laughed because
the restaurant told him to,
though the oysters that slipped
at atrocious expense
through his pinguid lips
were poisonous,
the hock at his elbow hardly less,
and the lady, too,
so svelte in the crypt
of her basilisk dress,
was dangerous beyond the laughable.
Wasn't that diamond
clipped at her cleavage
an oyster between
white dunes on a beach,
grown luscious on sewage's
steamy tureen
of barely detectable, radioactive garbage?

Cashpoint Charlie

My office, my crouch, is by the Piccadilly cashpoint where
Clients of the Hong Kong and Shanghai Banking Co.
Facilitate my study of legs as they ebb and flow;
Legs, and the influence of sex and wealth on footware.

The human foot – wedge-shaped, a mini torso –
Used to be, like the monkey's, toed for zipping
Fast through jungles. Just how prehensile gripping
Got to be a closed shop for hands I'll never know.

Anyhow, feet are in jail now, shoes' prisoners,
Inviting comparison, ladies, with steel-tipped bullets,
And sadly, gentlemen, with coffins. My tiptop favourites
Are Dr Martens hammer-like hoofs and laceless trainers.

It's a proved fact that the shabbily shod give more.
Like knee-slashed jeans give more than knife-creased trousers.
And shivering junkies more than antique browsers.
What? Thanks to a glitch in the chem lab (not a war)

I'm legless. Or as good as…it all depends
On where you poke and what your count as me.
To "rise" I use a crutch. It helps the money,
And, like my filthy sleeping bag, offends

Your everyday dainty British git just bad enough
To make him pull his Balaclava face
Hard down over his sweet guilt. I make my case:
OK, if you hate me, you have to hate yourself,

And think it steady at him. Nothing's said, of course.
They never meet your eyes, not even the women
Yanking at their big-eyed kids like I was poison,
Then, with a tight look, opening their purse.

It's crazy, but I love them… it …taking the piss.
If that old guy, that Greek philosopher in his barrel,
Could see me now, in my sleeping bag, beside a hole
In a wall that spits out money, he'd be envious.

Skin Deep

Fashion is about eventually being naked.
VIVIENNE WESTWOOD

What a strange animal that has to get dressed
every morning!
Born with the free gift of a skin,
using it mainly to lie down in;
to bathe, to bask in the sun, to beget
in a snug, pungent, soft-sided, creaturely outfit,
love in it, sleep in it, die in it,
but until then
obsessively live with it
under that pesky Damoclesian ur-question,
what on earth shall I wear?

Just there commenced the *pas de deux* that
partnered me
with *What I Really Am*, despite the battering
I daily took from *Please Approve Of Me*.
And whether love depended on
plot or scenery,
gender, nation, colour, class, society,
or simply chattering,
one of me dressed to pacify the audience,
while the other, under my skin,
kept faith within.

Till fashion whispered, 'All you need, dear,
is a naked self.
Stress-free, perfect for summer or winter wear,
stretchable outside and in,
cheap, chic, dependable, off the shelf.'
So out I went and bought the latest thing in skin,
sexy as sin.
Since when (shocking the panicky crowd
that can't tell them apart)
skin wearing skin has been allowed
outside of Art.

Fool's Gold
(A Saturday Night Sonnet)

Girls in their nervous freedom, heeled and painted,
Swarm out in teams – oh, bold pursuit of passion!
Geared for the sexual snatch, they seem acquainted
With all the ways and means of pubic fashion.
Who has not seen them, arm in arm, come rolling,
Midriffs agape but fending off all gazes,
Haughty and cool, forbidding yet controlling;
Each breast inflames us, every hip amazes.
Girls, were these parts for other girls created?
Walking exposed, you shrug aside our doting.
Or has the art of dressing been defeated
By skilfulness in wearing nearly nothing?
    If so, put on your clothes and tease our pleasure.
    Bared flesh is fool's gold, wealth's a buried treasure.

(Modelled on Shakespeare's sonnet, no. 20, but written
of course, to be spoken by a modern young man.)

Prophylactic Sonnets

> *'I have been used to consider poetry as the food of love,' said Darcy.*
> *'Of a fine, stout, healthy love it may. Everything nourishes what is*
> *strong already. But if it be only a slight, thin sort of inclination, I*
> *am convinced that one good sonnet will starve it entirely away.'*
> JANE AUSTEN
> Pride and Prejudice

I

Eyes fall in love before their users dare
Measure the turbulence behind their gaze,
So, without speech or touch, deep looks lay bare
The underside of smooth, well-mannered ways.
In love, this is the transcendental stage
That if prolonged would sweeten all our lives,
No groans, no grapplings, no hormonal rage,
An end to faking husbands and false wives.

For looks subsist on wish-fulfilling dreams
While firm interpretations wait in doubt.
No shared desire is carried to extremes
When neither cares to say what it's about.
Unless those looks were really saying this:
Love flies in safety over time's abyss.

II

If I'm your book and you have found the page
Where, in the epic, randomly we met
In canto sixty-eight (that was my age),
Now look between us at the alphabet:
You at the *m* or *n* of your career,
Hacking, bewildered, through the savage wood,
I at my *x y z*, yet in the clear,
And primed to be your Beatrice if I could.
There to your left, my pages pile asleep
In brutal certainty of what has been,
While on your right, no ploy of plot will keep
That too determined end from looking thin.
When there's no more to read, I think you'll see
How well you knew my book, how little me.

III

O Übermenschen, flex your miracles!
Nature complies but science overcomes.
So greed's technology shows off its skills,
October strawberries and April plums.
Nothing is fixed that won't defer to power.
The planet, oyster-sized and up for sale,
Auctions its primal assets by the hour,
Then fights for cash by electronic mail.
Fame's not reliable, no more is sex.
Women can mate or unmate at a whim,
Yet choose their offspring's genome, pick 'n' mix,
Or make a him of her, a her of him.
Consider, too, this miracle of mine:
Verse conquers love, ten syllables a line.

Four Grim Fairy Tales

1 *Rapunzel*

> *'Rapunzel, Rapunzel, let down your hair!'*

Safe in a turret of the citadel,
She watched him once again attempt the climb.
The prince was bold and she was beautiful.
The tale assumed its Once Upon A Time.
And would have ended with the usual kiss
Had not the twisted cable at her ear
Picked up vibrations contrary to this.
She valued sex, but kids might interfere
With what she was and what she liked to do.
She wanted glory, wanted to be rich,
And as for power – he might want it, too.
Despite appearances, she liked the witch.
Suppose he didn't share her point of view?
She shook her head. He tumbled in the ditch.

2 *Sleeping Beauty*
(for Isobel Cohen)

Beauty fought shy of acting out her name.
Her face was perfect. Nature made her kind.
A quiet, gentle girl, mistrusting fame,
She ached to be distinguished for her mind.
She'd met Prince Charming, knew him for a bore.
His brother, Prince Publicity, was worse.
Did fate have nothing else for her in store?
Then she remembered that convenient curse.
At twenty-one she taught herself to spin,
Not straw to gold, but yarn she learned to make
Out of the woolly talk that penned her in.
Her conscience pricked her. That was her mistake.
For when she woke, a hundred years were gone.
And no successful prince would take her on.

3 *Was Cinderella Ever Happy?*
A Letter to the Editor

Dear Madam, it was interesting to read
That, deconstructed, Cinderella's mind
Resolved her problem of erotic need
Within a class and sexist double bind.
However, I'm afraid I fail to see
Why one audacious, amatory fling –
A cultural norm in every monarchy –
Transformed her shoe into a wedding ring.

So let's hypothesise. She knew the Prince
Resented the entrapment of his role.
He wanted out. He'd told her at the dance
That she, and she alone, could fit his soul.
Once married, was she miserable because
She never really found out who she was?

4 *If Wishes Were Fishes*
(The Fisherman's Tale)

> *Once upon a time a poor fisherman lived with his wife in a*
> *vinegar jug by the sea. One morning he went down to the shore*
> *and caught a beautiful rainbow-coloured fish, but when he pulled*
> *it ashore, it opened its mouth and began to speak...*

I'd hardly hooked it when I heard the fish
Say, clear as any human, 'Spare my life,
And I will give you anything you wish.'
I threw it back, went home and told the wife.
Before I'd grabbed a beer she's up and at me.
'So what'd you ask for?' Well, I couldn't think
Of anything we wanted. 'What?' says she,
'When I'm here all day slaving at the sink?
Go tell that fish I want a proper home,
I want a dishwasher. I want a car.
I want a life that I can call my own.
Fly me to Hollywood, I'll be a star
And wear pink trousers slung around my hips.
I want a diamond toothbrush. Read my lips!'

*   *   *

Giving Rabbit to My Cat Bonnie

Pretty Bonnie, you are quick as a rabbit,
though your tail's longer,
emphasising suppressed disapproval,
and your ears are shorter,
two radar detectors set on swivels
either side of your skull, and your yawn
is a view of distant white spires – not
the graveyard jaw of this poor dead naked pink

rabbit, who like you, was a
technological success, inheriting a snazzy
fur coat, pepper-and-salt coloured, cosy,
and beautiful fur shoes with spiked toes.
You're both of you
better dressed than I am for most occasions.
Take off your shoes and suits, though,
what have you got?

Look, puss, I've bought us a rabbit for supper.
I bought it in a shop.
The butcher was haggis-shaped, ham-coloured,
not a bit like you. His ears
were two fungi on the slab of his head.
He had a fat, flat face.
But he took your brother rabbit off a hook
and spread him on the counter like a rug,

and slice, slice, scarcely looking,
pulled the lovely skin off like a bag.
So, Bonnie, all I've brought us is food
in this silly pink shape – more like me, really.
I'll make a wine sauce with mushrooms, but will you
want this precious broken heart? this perfect liver?
See, protected in these back pockets, jewels?
Bonnie. What are you eating? Dear Bonnie, consider!

Epitaph for a Good Mouser

Take, Lord, this soul of furred unblemished worth,
The sum of all I loved and caught on earth.
Quick was my holy purpose and my cause.
I die into the mercy of thy claws.

Clydie is dead!

Our lar, our little mammal.
Though his last day didn't believe it.
It kept on moving at its usual heartless pace
over and around a hollow cat-space.

We buried him by the toolshed.
The cat flap wouldn't believe it,
so we sealed its chattering mouth.
We seized and scrubbed his feeding bowls
and sent them to a far shelf.

The fact is, nothing in the house could bear it
when Clyde dropped out of himself...
who waxed loquacious on the subject of roast meat
and cat's rights, who took favours
from my fingers at mealtimes as just deserts,
who always kept his dress-shirt spinnaker-white
while extending an urgent tongue to his tabby parts;
who reserved for himself, every morning,
a place on a lap, whereon for a while he might
subdue a human; upon whose face
the cat-painter's brush had slipped a little
applying the Chinese white; for which he received
in compensation, huge Indonesian eyes –
polished jet in a setting of crinkled topaz;

whose tail was so long he could wrap himself up in it;

who could fill with his length, without exertion,
the entire shelf over the radiator;
who was adept at the art of excretion,
and discreet as to the burying of personal treasure.

Dear, wise Clyde, who after tyrannical Bonnie died,
thrived in her absence, Hadrian after Domitian,
you will never again rule us by vocative law,
or pull back the bedclothes at six with a firm paw,
or bemoan the indignities of travelling by car,
or flourish an upright tail on crepuscular walks,
no, nor compile statistics on the field mice of Wales.

Pwllymarch was your chief estate,
you whom Oxford made and Cambridge unmade,
though Hay-on-Wye and Durham made you great.
Much travelled, valuable, voluble Clyde,
who said so much, yet never spoke a word,
          requiescat.

Where the Animals Go

The beasts in Eden
cradle the returning souls of earth's animals.

The horse, limp cargo, craned down to the terrible quay,
is butchered into a heaven of his own hoofed kind.

The retriever mangled on the motorway, the shot
Alsatian by the sheepfold, the mutilated black-faced sheep –
they rise like steam, like cumulus, crowding in together,
each into the haunches of its archetype.

The drowned vole, the pheasant brought down with his fires,
the kitten in the jacket of its panicking fleas,
flying souls, furred, feathered, scaled, shelled, streaming
upward, upward through the wide thoughtless rose empyrean.

God absorbs them neatly in his green teeming cells.

There, sexed as here, they're without hurt or fear.
Heaven is honeycombed with their arrivals and entries.
Two of each butterfly. Two of each beetle.
A great cowness sways on her full uddered way.
All kinds of cat watch over the hive like churches.
Their pricked ears, pinnacles. Their gold eyes, windows.

* * *

VII

Border Crossings

Talking Sense to My Senses

Old ears and eyes, so long my patient friends,
For you this silicon nerve and resin lens.
Guides when I heard and saw, yet deaf and blind
Stumbled astray in the maxes of my mind,
Let me assist you now I've lived to see
Far in the dark of what I have to be.

Shunted outside the hubbub of exchange,
Knowledge arrives, articulate and strange,
Voice without breath, light without sun or switch
Beamed from the pulse of an old awareness which
Tells me to age by love and not to cling
To ears, eyes, teeth, knees, hands – or any thing.

On Going Deaf

I've lost a sense. Why should I care?
Searching myself, I find a spare.
I keep that sixth sense in repair
And set it deftly, like a snare.

What I Miss

is some hexagonal white seal
like a honey cell.
Silence I miss:
the hand on the fiddle
muting the vaulted arrogance
it raises;
the crowded hush
of the conductor's lifted wand,
then the chorale
walking with little empty breaths
though air it praises.

My air is noises
amplified by an ugly pink
barnacle in my ear.
All the music I hear
is a tide dragging pebbles
to and away in my brain.
Sphered, the harmonies fall,
mutate, abort. Emptiness
is like rain
in my insomniac city,
ceaseless and merciless.

(to Elon Salmon)

* * *

In the Orchard

Black bird, black voice,
almost the shadow of a voice,
so kind to this tired summer sky –
a rim of night around it –
almost an echo of today,
all the days since that first
soft guttural disaster
gave us 'apple' and 'tree'
and all that transpired thereafter
in the city of the tongue.

Blackbird, so old, so young, so
happy to be stricken with a song
you can never choose away from.

Melon, meaning melon

Seeds I scrape away from this quartered melon
are really what the melon is about.
Yes, but I think meaning is about
not being melon, not being edible flesh or fruit,
but being human, complicitous in meaning's making.

A spider has wound her silky trap
around the dictionary I'm cracking open
to look up the word, 'complicitous'.

'Being an accomplice, an associate in crime.'
I am associated with the crime, then,
of separating this melon from the purpose it was made for,
of giving it a meaning all my own.
What a glorious Galia melon,
summer-ripe and delicious! I gobble it up,
lick my fingers, toss away the rind.

This dictionary, old and shabby, has been helping
spiders, for a summer, to be good purposeful spiders.
But when I look up 'melon',
it does not help me to be a good purposeful person.
It will not even tell me what a melon's like to taste.

Terrorist

One morning I despaired of writing more,
        never any more,
when a swallow swooped in, around and out
        the open door,
then in again and batlike to the window,
        against which
beating himself, a suicide in jail,
        he now and then collapsed into
his midnight iridescent combat suit,
        beautiful white markings on the tail.

Inside his balaclava, all he knew
        was something light and airy he had come from
flattened into something hard and blue.
        Thank God for all those drafts I used to
scoop, shove or shovel him to the transom,
        open just enough to let him through.

Off he flew, writing his easy looped
        imaginary line.
No sign of his adventure left behind
        but my surprise
and his – not fright, though he had
        frightened me, those two
bright high-tech bullets called his eyes.
        What they said was
'Fight and fight and fight. No compromise.'

Late

Haunting me at midnight,
a harvester fly, as if
mating with its shadow on the
white ceiling, tells
horror stories about angels.

Its faceless dance has no
individuality. Describe
the identity of that harvester fly?
You can't conceive of such a thing.

Frantic oarlike wings and
six long jointed legs –
awkward to carry –
make a star of it.

For love of light
it immolates its body. No,
it dies in the spider's net –
a root now in the undersoil
of being, not being.

To write of this is the art
of someone who will not
arrive at selflessness,
the fly's, the spider's.

But look at my generosity,
for am I not the one
who provides the ceiling?
And the word for ceiling?

Is there anybody there?
In the fan of stars
opening beyond the ceiling?
In the bloated spider,
in the knot that's now the harvested fly?

A Luxury

No, trilobites didn't
discuss
the future of fossils.

Pterodactyls
formed no
theology of flight.

Did Triceratops ever
lie awake
miserating all night,

or vainly believe that
pills, prayers
or a psychoanalyst

could make everything
wrong
go right?

I'm questioning
the weight
of the human cortex

and what it costs
per life
to ship its freight.

Why, among billions
of killer zooids,
do hominids alone

look in upon
themselves
and curse their fate?

It's not as if pets
and parakeets
and collared turtle-doves

(their dreamy summer
syncopated moan)
and sonic self-locating bats,

and great cetaceans,
iridescent porpoises –
or even head lice,

worms and scuttling feeders
under tombstones –
existed without purposes.

More that the creatures,
lacking our rig
of impudent imagination, miss

(besides our self-propelling genius)
our luxury
of self-destructiveness.

All might have been
explained had
vegetarian Eve before her fall

been true to God's
or Darwin's picture,
or even true at all.

When chance made us
blind chains of protein
built us to advance

by interlacing
with our hardware
something like a dance.

Two steps forward,
two steps
back, and every gain

we grab from nature
in her coin
we have to pay for.

O Time that knows no
soon or late,
be quick, when cycling through us

the cerebral mix
that makes us great
tells nature to undo us.

Christmas Comfort and the Green Man

Go cut for me
Those blood red berries from the holly tree
Before the blackbirds take them!

> Not I, said he.
> Let that bespoke display of berries be,
> The poor birds need them.

> Oh, don't cut down
> The fruiting rafters from their winter home,
> For what would feed them?

Go axe the firs,
And bring those dainty Christmas trees indoors
Before the north winds break them!

> Oh no, he cried,
> Let weather decorate their boughs outside
> With snow and ice.

> They hate to be
> Bowed down with chains of tinsel finery
> And crawling lights.

I came to cheer
The coldest, darkest corner of the year
With news of Christ.

For love of Him
I choose your greenest, sweetest pines to trim
And sacrifice.

> But I was here
> Before the angels taught you not to fear
> The God you trust.

> And I will stay
> To watch the captive angels lift away
> From waste and dust.

> I will be here
> When stars depart and night melts into day.
> I will! I must!

It looks so simple from a distance...

The way lives touch,
touch and spring apart,
the pulse synaptic,
local, but its stretch
electric – as when cities
lose themselves in velvet
under winking planes,
binding black hostilities
with gold chains.

Graves with Children

In summer
Our children swarm over us
Into their weather.
The thresh of bare foot over foot
Erases our names.
Our stories no longer
Are violent enough to allure them.
They take no interest
In the heavy freight of our toys.
Careless, irreverent,
They rise out of your stone,
My stone;
Disappear through chinks
Of impassable light and noise.

There's wind in the grass,
Rain on the moss.
Now silence, winter –
Those unanswerable girls and boys.

Two Countries

In this country,
with its effortless water,
its sea swung effortlessly
from long ropes in the hills,
its sky changing as the weather
turns, and clouds break
on the spokes of the sun,
our discontents screen thinly
what is easy and profitable.

What richness do we not have?
Pigs hatch from apples.
Cows ooze like sacks.
Children can be picked whole as cabbages
from our orchards and haystacks.
Our only frustration, such a strange one,
that we are forbidden
to visit the people of
of that country.

Oh, we have heard how
in that country, rain is sweat.
the fields scant as a map's,
how there is plenitude of mouths only,
how corpses are crops
and murder more casual than sleep.
Which one of us
covets their starved babies
and cratered villages?

Yet somehow, because of them,
we are not at ease with ourselves.
We are good people.
We work diligently.
We would like to make sacrifices.
Something that is
not quite pity
broods over our lakes
and sours our huge loaves.

The Watchers

How wise of our enemy to rely upon the watchers.

Wired without nerves, controlled from tall
Skeletons of electromagnetic steel,
They are dangerous without risk to themselves.
They envisage no distinction, anticipate no destruction.
They are not alive.
Yet they have ears and eyes
No rustle escapes, no flicker misses.

They hover at a level above breathable air,
But are also near.
In our shoes and curtains.
In our pillows. In our spoons.
Even when we say nothing, what passes in our brains
Is traced in encephalogram by their ticking.
We are aware of them when we make love.

And because they are unapproachable through anguish,
Inaccessible to madness as to argument,
We are more afraid of them than of the holocaust.
Yet, hating and fearing them as we do,
It is curious how often we are exhilarated.
It's as if we had acquired new souls.

Have we forgotten how to be bored?
Are we delivered forever from loneliness?
Are we worthy, we wonder, of the marvel of such attention?

From the Primrose Path

Sunset, Primrose Hill, 1986

Effulgence, or copper polyphony!
Where once one cough from the Lord
produced in a vermilion corona
Gabriel with a fiery sword
leaping from the hot heart of punishment.
Now it spills over Regent's Park
a phenomenon of city-vapour, light,
and a catalyst of human perception,
smelting for this rare, Marylebone ceiling
a luminous ore.

How well Nash's domes suit the smooth-bellied
mosque and planetarium – those Muslim minarets,
our narrow Victorian steeples.
Even the Telephone eyesore
gets on in a flat silhouette, leaning
on a spectacle nobody thinks to pay for;
as tonight, on the footpath to Baker Street,
where a flash of high baroque evidence
checks us, I noting chill in the wind, you
Concorde, manned serpent gliding in azure,
eyeing the continents.

A Cradle of Fist

(A hijacker speaks)

'Solidity is a shifting desert,
air is energy,
as the world's clock watches
with its glass eye, *me*,
ticking the tempo of my pulse.

Almighty Word,
allow me to locate myself
in your cradle of fist.
Appoint me first
among the righteous.

Uproot what in me is
unblessed, bestial, sexed,
and let holiness
purge my spirit
of women and weakness.

I would, in the cockpit
of your purpose
be Azrael's talon
plundering, laying waste
the viper's nest.

Send me the clean veil
of the faceless
that I may kill
without conscience the featureless,
eyeless unfaithful.

And when I live again,
golden in the flower
of your will,
reveal to my mother
the face that is mine in Heaven.'

New York Is Crying

New York is crying. I didn't hear screaming, just dead, dark silence.
TYRONE DUX, New York policeman, quoted in
The Observer (London), 16 September 2001

Halfmast New York is crying for her children.
Her firemen, her policemen, her bagwomen,
Her smart investment analysts, her crooks,
Her execuwives in Gucci scarves and pantsuits,
Her TV chatterers and glossy-skinned presenters,
Her cleaners, waitresses and fast food cooks,
Her manicured secretaries and stubby-fingered punters,
Crying because they didn't die or scream.

Her preachers, her evangelists, her health cranks,
Her good-time girls and crack-addicts, her muggers,
Her Italian-Irish-Jewish politicians,
Her lawyers, paralegals and illegals,
Her internet whiz-kids and computer freaks,
Her trouble-shooters, paranoids, beauticians,
Deli proprietors, winos, hot musicians,
Dames with purple hair and crimson poodles...
Listen to them crying, but not screaming.

Is that Walt Whitman? Yes, but he is crying.
Hart Crane, in tears, is haunting Brooklyn Bridge.
Wystan, Dr Williams, mr cummings,
Miss Moore, Miss Bishop, look, they have come flying
In clouds of etymology, but crying.
Even John Astor and Henry Frick are trying,
Under the brassy marble of their monuments,
To sympathise with people who are dying.
Old Teddy Roosevelt, high on your moral horse,
What bracing words can dignify such crying?

But now a Mayor with a bedside manner,
And now a President in shining armour
Weep in the lens light of a billion eyes.
They want the world to notice they are crying.
Tears shall be sown in steel like dragon's teeth.
A crop of planes will pulverise the skies
While terrorists in terror cringe beneath.
Downtown, the bagel man on Chambers Street
Plasters his cart with frantic stars and stripes.

One wild-eyed Rasta with a bongo beats
Implacable voodoos under pulsing lights.
Flowers in the chainlink barrier are dying.

The ghostdust sours and settles with its smell
Of sulphurous flesh, stench of a Polish pit
Old Zbigniew Mirsky, eighty, knows too well;
One sniff, and his tower of hope falls into it.
The architect, America, was lying.
And here's the paper shop of Nizam Din
Locked behind shattered glass. No one's buying
His colourful books or letting strangers in.
The hole in New York is a hole in a belief
That desperately needs to hide itself in grief...
Professor X is lecturing, not crying.
Now, desert scenes and bursts of golden fire.
Those ragged children scuttling here and there
Are very small and far away, but crying.

Toy

Little space-age doll,
your cheerful plastic face
has lost its cool.
It looks too small
in the slippery baggage
of your outer soul.
Your moon-walk legs
are welds of tubelike mail.
Your pachydermatous build
is out of scale.
Monstrous equipment
sprang from that tiny head –
creator jammed, *enfin*,
in the created.

Killing Spiders

Wales, April 2004

I am the enemy of spiders.
I descend with my vacuum cleaner
To exterminate them utterly.
I lay their kingdoms waste.
Nor do I spare their children.

Though they are miracles of life
and can hang by eight legs
spinning elegant death camps
straight from their bodies,
I am better equipped than they are
with my ten hinged fingers
and my great big brain.

Of course, I live far above them,
enormously high in the sky.
Which is why I disdain them.
I don't know how it feels to be spidery,
or how they think by instinct.

Yet sometimes in the wake
Of my hoovering wrath
I feel a pinch of pity for them.
If they could master reasoning
They would honour me and praise me.
They would call me Yahweh.
And name me for the murderer I am.

As I Lay Sleeping

(for Carol Rumens)

Out of the afterlife behind my eyelids
Arrived the offer of a plush hotel.
Yes, there it was, as we were driven past it,
High on a green embankment, white and big.
It had to be Russian. Where else does marble curl
In tufted layers like a powdered wig?
Geraniums blazed in tubs and hanging baskets.
Not for us. We had too many kids,

But where? I'd swear I was alone with you.
The sun set in some oil-polluted stream,
And we were floating there or wading through
Its tessellated fragments when the dream
Revealed the awful place assigned to us:
An eighteen-storey highrise with a view
Into a gulf or gullet – an immense abyss.
The children crowded to the edge of this,

Then one by one they held their hands together,
The way you hold them out to dive or pray,
And off they peeled. One body, then another,
The little stony fledglings fell away.
A dream, I thought, I shouldn't be afraid.
Why was I sure the truth would be more
Beautiful and lethal? Was it war?
No, it was only daylight. But it stayed.

Photographing Change
(for Ernestine Ruben)

How can it be that empty, intangible age
    is stronger than we are?
Fuelled by the sun, it sky-writes 'begin here'
on the eastern, left hand corner
    of a turning page
every morning when, expectantly awake,
we use up hours that taste and feel alike.
    So why are days so differently
the same? Think, days will happen after you
and I no longer need to plan them sensibly,
    or bring to mind a few
urgent forgettable things we have to do.

Think, too, of the split second when a finger
    triggered this snapshot,
shooting time dead. Only when it won't
recur can 'that wonderful time' be caught
    on sepia flypaper.
So the old rapscallion visits his wedding
fifty years after the marriage ended in
    pained, unphotographed divorce.
And the dressed up, smiling guests don't know
    of course,
how long they'll be arrested for. 'That's...who?'
'I can't remember what her name was now.'

Is it an either-or game? Keep your face
    and lose your name,
or lose face by attending to the stream
that keeps you inconsistently the same
    through time and place?
Try photographing change. Try stones, try
trees. Bearded with lichen, they are streaming by,
    free of Plato's petrified ideal.
One wave laps into another, the foam-white
struggle of the brook is its appeal.
Let a river be invented by a stroke of light
that anneals it as it vanishes from sight.

VII

In Memoriam

Sonnets for Five Seasons

(i.m. Charles Leslie Stevenson, 1909-79)

This House

Which represents you, as my bones do, waits,
all pores open, for the stun of snow. Which will come,
as it always does, between breaths, between nights
of no wind and days of the nulled sun.
And has to be welcome. All instinct wants to anticipate
faceless fields, a white road drawn
through dependent firs, the soldered glare of lakes.

Is it wanting you here to want the winter in?
I breathe you back into your square house and begin
to live here roundly. This year will be between,
not in, four seasons. Do you hear already the wet
rumble of thaw? Stones. Sky. Streams. Sun.
Those might be swallows at the edge of sight
returning to last year's nest in the crook of the porchlight.

Complaint

'Dear God,' they write, 'that was a selfish winter
to lean so long, unfairly on the spring!'
And now – this too much greed of seedy summer.
Mouths of the flowers unstick themselves and sting
the bees with irresistible dust. Iris
allow undignified inspection. Plain waste
weeds dress up in Queen Anne's lace. Our mist-
blue sky clouds heavily with clematis.

'Too much,' they cry, 'too much. Begin again.'
The Lord, himself a casualty of weather,
falls to earth in large hot drops of rain.
The dry loam rouses in his scent, and under
him – moist, sweet, discriminate – the spring.
Thunder. Lightning. He can do anything.

Between

The wet and weight of this half-born English winter
is not the weather of those fragmentary half-true willows
that break in the glass of the canal behind our rudder
as water arrives in our wake – a travelling arrow
of now, of now, of now. Leaves of the water
furl back from our prow, and as the pinnate narrow
seam of where we are drives through the mirror
of where we have to be, alder and willow
double crookedly, reverse, assume a power
to bud out tentatively in gold and yellow,
so it looks as if what should be end of summer –
seeds, dead nettles, berries, naked boughs –
is really the anxious clouding of first spring.
...'Real' is what water is imagining.

Stasis

Before the leaves change, light transforms these lucid
speaking trees. The heavy drench of August
alters, thins; its rich and sappy blood
relaxes where a thirst ago, no rest
released the roots' wet greed or stemmed their mad
need to be more. September is the wisest
time – neither the unbearable burning word
nor the form of it, cooped in its cold ghost.

How are they sombre – that unpicked apple, red,
undisturbed by its fall; calm of those wasp-bored amethyst
plums on the polished table? Body and head
easy in amity, a beam between that must,
unbalanced, quicken or kill, make new or dead
whatever these voices are that hate the dust.

The Circle

It is imagination's white face remembers
snow, its shape, a fluted shell on shoot
or flower, its weight, the permanence of winter
pitched against the sun's absolute root.

All March is shambles, shards. Yet no amber
chestnut, Indian, burnished by its tent
cuts to a cleaner centre or keeps summer
safer in its sleep. Ghost be content.

You died in March when white air hurt the maples.
Birches knelt under ice. Roads forgot
their way in aisles of frost. There were no petals.

Face, white face, you are snow in the green hills.
High stones complete your circle where trees start.
Granite and ice are colours of the heart.

Dreaming of the Dead

(i.m. Anne Pennington)

I believe, but what is belief?

I receive the forbidden dead.
They appear in the mirrors of asleep
To accuse or be comforted.

All the selves of myself they keep,
From a bodiless time arrive,
Retaining in face and shape

Shifting lineaments of alive.
So whatever it is you are,
Dear Anne, bent smilingly grave

Over wine glasses filled by your fire,
Is the whole of your life you gave
To our fictions of what you were.

Not a shadow of you can save
These logs that crackle with light,
Or this smoky image I have –

Your face at the foot of a flight
Of wrought-iron circular stairs.
I am climbing alone in the night

Among stabbing, unmerciful flares.
Oh, I am what I see and know,
But no other solid thing's there

Except for the terrible glow
Of your face and its quiet belief,
Light wood ash falling like snow

On my weaker grief.

Waving to Elizabeth

(for Elizabeth Bishop)

For mapmakers' reasons, the transcontinental air routes
must have been diverted today, and Sunderland's stratosphere
is being webbed over by shiny, almost invisible spider jets
creeping with deliberate intention on the skin-like air,
each suspended from the chalky silk of its passing. Thready at first,
as if written by two, four, fine felt nibs, the lines become cloudy
as the planes cease to need them. In freedom they dissolve. Just
as close observation dissipates in the wind of theory.

Eight or nine of them now, all writing at once,
rising from the south on slow rails, slow arcs, an armillary
prevented by necessity from completing its evidence,
but unravelling instead in soft, powdery stripes, which seem to be
the only clouds there are between what's simply here as park,
house, roof, road, cars, etcetera, and the wide, long view
they must have of us there, if they bother to look.
They have taken so much of us up with them, too:

Money and newspapers, meals, toilets, old films, hot coffee.
Yet the miles between us, though measurable, seem unreal.
I have to think, 'Here it is, June 19th, 1983.
I'm waving from a waste patch by the Thornhill School.'
As perhaps you think back from your trip through the cosmos,
'Here where I love, it is no time at all. The geography
looks wonderful! This high, smooth sea's more quiet than the map is,
though the map, relieved of mapmakers, looks imprisoned and free.'

A Dream of Stones

(for Norman Nicholson)

I dreamed a summer's labour,
loss or discovery,
had brought me, on the sand,
to a nest of stones.
What shall I do with these stones
that shine too weakly to be gems,
that might be seeds?

Stones are to build with,
but here there is tidal sea,
bare sand and sea.

Why, since these stones
look anxious to be used,
should they not be planted?
There are no trees here.
Maybe there are trees
coiled inside the smoothness
of the stone seeds.

I am pocking the soil with my heel:
here, here, here, here.
Into each footprint, a glimmering pearl.

They will not be counted,
these seeds, these hopes, these
possible offerings from impossible language.
They resist being tears.

I tell them to you now
as if they were gifts
too alive to be left unburied
under common years.

Red Rock Fault

This is the South-West wind
the North-East breathes and knows;
that lifts linoleum under kitchen doors,
that bends thorned trees one way on the moors,
that hooks back little white knots of the Irthing
in shaggy impermanent weirs
by the empty farm at the river's turning
where spiders make nets for the silted windows
and machinery rusts in the byres.
Fran, has it been two years?

I see you again in your boy's coat
on that sudden and slithery hill of stones
where we ducked from the wind one afternoon
when slant light cut and shone
through glass-white arcs of October grass.
It was just by the Red Rock Fault
where limestone meets sandstone, lass.
You carried your love of that rushy place
in the candle of your living face
to set in the dark of your poems.

And now we have only the poems.
While snow-light, water-light winters still
will come to that ridge of Roman stones,
Spadeadam, Birdoswald, high Whin Sill,
where so many trees lose uncountable leaves
to this wind – one breath from uncountable lives.
Shrill clouds of gathering jackdaws, starlings,
storm an enormous sky.
That huge split ash by the ruined steading –
Cocidius, life-keeper, live eye.

Willow Song

I went down to the railway
But the railway wasn't there.
A long scar lay across the waste
Bound up with vetch and maidenhair
And birdsfoot trefoils everywhere.
But the clover and the sweet hay,
The cranesbill and the yarrow
Were as nothing to the rose bay
    the rose bay, the rose bay,
As nothing to the rose bay willow.

I went down to the river
But the river wasn't there.
A hill of slag lay in its course
With pennycress and cocklebur
And thistles bristling with fur.
But ragweed, dock and bitter may
and hawkbit in the hollow
Were as nothing to the rose bay,
    the rose bay, the rose bay
As nothing to the rose bay willow.

I went down to find my love.
My sweet love wasn't there.
A shadow stole into her place
And spoiled the loosestrife of her hair
And counselled me to pick despair.
Old elder and young honesty
Turned ashen, but their sorrow
Was as nothing to the rose bay
    the rose bay, the rose bay,
As nothing to the rose bay willow.

O I remember summer
When the hemlock was in leaf.
The sudden poppies by the path
Were little pools of crimson grief.
Sick henbane cowered like a thief.
But self-heal sprang up in her way,
And mignonette's light yellow,
To flourish with the rose bay,
    the rose bay, the rose bay,
To flourish with the rose bay willow.

Its flames took all the wasteland
And all the river's silt,
But as my dear grew thin and grey
They turned as white as salt or milk.
Great purples withered out of guilt,
And bright weeds blew away
In cloudy wreaths of summer snow.
And the first one was the rose bay,
    the rose bay, the rose bay,
The first one was the rose bay willow.

Dinghy

Though you won't feel again
    the jib sheet
scalding your hand, or coil
    it again
around the cleat,
    or be able to read
from the shiver
    of a sail
the precise crisis –
    timing the rudder,
coming about,
    reaching at high tilt,
hauled tight
    against the slapping river –
your discontinuedness
    is not yet felt.

All around you
    the life you built
is tacking habitually
    in skilful directions,
swimming your sea,
    climbing your mountains.
But you're left out.
    and grief fills
the leaf-shape of a
    toy boat
far on the horizon;
    while you still weigh
upon these Welsh hills
    alight with your look
of patient inquiry –
    more accurately, dear John,
the attentive
    courtesy of that look.

Cambrian

Here is one more fiery
    sunset for you
not to share
    with the ravens who
rebuild every winter
    their bulky stack
on the ice-cut rock.

Without you,
    the nest will be there
as *Gareg Lwyd*
    will be there –
two eyries folded
    in the lap
of what nineteenth-century
    geologists
used to call *grauwacke*.

Of Murchinson's quarrel
    with Sedgwick
and how they changed that,
    disputing Silurian layers
on the Cambrian map,
    we might have talked
by your Christmas fire,
    we two and you,
while outside, unprovoked,
    the wind blazed higher,
renewing its quarrel
    with everything they drew.

Poem for Harry Fainlight

(d. 1982)

Tree, a silence
voiced by wind.

Wind, breath
with a tree's body.

Axe the bole,
plane the boards.

Here is Art,
the polished instrument,
casket and corpse.

Dum Vixi Tacui
Mortua Dulce Cano

The harp's motto
will do for the harpist's apology.

But your poems, Harry,
those Welsh oaks
stunted by the wind's scream?

They were always
transforming your wrong life
into their live silence.

The harp's Latin motto: *'When alive I was silent.*
In death I sweetly sing.'

Nightmares, Daymoths

A glass jar rattles its split peas and pasta.
Those cysts look innocuous, but they weave
through the kernels, hatching into terrible insects.
Something's on the floor there,
buzzing like a swat wasp.
A belly like a moist rubber thimble
sucks and stings my finger. *Ach*,
my heel reduces it to sewage.

String the creatures up, then.
Hang them on the Christmas tree.

They glisten there like fish, softly
lengthening into milliners' feathers.
See, they are only moths, paper moths or horses,
not even paper but the Paisley curtain
sifting ashy patterns from the winter light.

Order, they order, *order*.

The flame gropes for a fire.
The dream asks meaning to patch its rags.
The flying words want paper to nest in.
Six colours rake the white reach of the rainbow.
Even the smallest hours crawl by with a number.

These letters are marching straight into an alphabet:
X Y Z, not to infinity.

Letter to Sylvia Plath

(Grantchester, May 1988)

They are great healers, English springs.
You loved their delicate colourings –
sequential yellows, eggshell blues –
not pigments you preferred to use,
lady of pallors and foetal jars
and surgical interiors.
But wasn't it warmth you wanted most?

These Grantchester willows keep your ghost,
young and in love and half way through
the half-life that was left to you.
The Cam still crawls through patient grass,
preserving ephemerals in glass.
A bull thrush shouts from a willow thicket,
Catch it! Catch it! Catch it! Catch it!
Catch what? An owl in a petalled dress?
The gnarl at the root of a distress?

Dear Sylvia, we must close our book.
Three springs you've perched like a black rook
between sweet weather and my mind.
At last I have to seem unkind
and exorcise my awkward awe.
My shoulder doesn't like your claw.

Yet first, forgiveness. Let me shake
some echoes from old balled eyed Blake
over your grave and praise in rhyme
the fiercest poet of our time –
you with your outsized gift for joy
who did the winged life destroy,
and bought with death a mammoth name
to set in the cold museum of fame.

Your art was darkness. No, your art
was a gulping candle in the dark.
In the beginning was a curse:
a hag, a drowned man and a nurse
hid in the mirror of the moon
unquietly to work your doom.
A dissolute nun, you had to serve
the demon muse who peeled your nerve
and fuelled your energy with hate.

384

Malevolent will-power made you great,
while round you in the Sacred Wood
tall archetypal statues stood
rooted in air and in your mind.
The proud impossibles loomed behind,
pilasters buttressing a frieze
of marble, moonlit amputees.

Sylvia, I see you in this view
of glassy absolutes where you,
a frantic Alice, trip on snares,
crumple and drown in your own tears.
You were your cave of crippled dreams
and ineradicable screams,
and you were the pure gold honey bee
prisoned in poisonous jealousy.

The gratitude and love you thought
the world would give you if you fought
for all your tears could not be found
in reputation's building ground.
O give the mole an eagle's soul
and watch it battling in its hole.

Because you were selfish and sad and died,
we have grown up on the other side
of a famous girl you didn't know.
The future is where the dead go
in rage, bewilderment and pain
to make and magnify their name.

Meanwhile, the continuous present casts
longer reflections on the past.
Nothing has changed much. Famine, war
fatten your Spider as before.
Your hospital of bleeding parts
devours its haul of human hearts,
excreting what it cannot use
as celluloid or paper news;
eye for eye and tooth for tooth,
bomb for bomb and youth for youth.

Yet who would believe the colour green
had so many ways of being green?
In England, still, your poet's spring
arrives, unravelling everything.
A yellowhammer in the gorse
creates each minute's universe;

a blackbird singing from a thorn
is all the joy of being reborn.

Even in Heptonstall in May
the wind invites itself away,
leaving black stone to compromise
with stitchwort, dandelions and flies.
Tell me, do all those weeds and trees
strewing their cool longevities
over the garden of your bed
have time for you, now you are dead?

Behind the pricked-out drape of night
is there a sheet-white screen of light
where death meets birth to reconcile
the contradictions of your will?
Perfection is terrible, you said.
The perfect are barren, like the dead.

Yet life, more terrible, maunches on,
as blood-red light loops back at dawn,
seizing, devouring, giving birth
to the mass atrocity of the earth.
Poor Sylvia, could you not have been
a little smaller than a queen –
a river, not a tidal wave
engulfing all you tried to save?

Rather than not be justified
you sickened in loneliness and died,
while we live on in messy lives,
rueful or tired or barely wise.
Ageing, we labour to exist.
Beyond existence, nothing is.
Out of this world there is no source
of yellower rape or golder gorse,
nor in the galaxy higher place,
I think, for human mind or face.

We learn to be human when we kneel
to imagination, which is real
long after reality is dead
and history has put its bones to bed.
Sylvia, you have won at last,
embodying the living past,
catching the anguish of your age
in accents of a private rage.

Hot Wind, Hard Rain

The joy of the rowan is to redden.
The foxglove achieves the violence of its climb.
This summer gale flattens the flower
    and deforms the tree.
The dog trots at a queerer angle
    to the disused railway.
The tabby seizes the fledgling blown to the midden.
From the river, gaseous with weed, a reek of decay.

Hot winds bring on hard rain, and here in Durham
    a downpour tonight will probably allay
whatever has got the willows by the hair,
shoving light under their leaves
    like an indecent surgeon.
Now light's in every particle of air,
acetylene wind that blows too hard and clear.
Who sifts the saving from the killing terrors,
    O my dear?

The Name of the Worm

(The speaker is a 90-year-old Jewish doctor who is dying of cancer.
His niece has brought him some roses.)

(i.m. Richard Cohen)

Oh, hallo, good of you to come. Sorry I can't get up.
You'll find the sherry on the sideboard. I regret
that in my present condition... My dear, how thoughtful.
From your garden? Proper roses, lots of petals,
lots of prickles. *Aber süss*, that sentimental military scent –
speaking as an unsentimental, practically defunct medic.

You know, I never did understand, as a young man,
why poets made so much of roses – roses and women –
till Margaret and I were on holiday in the Austrian Alps.
August 1933. We were engaged but not yet married, since
I had my residency still to do at Bart's. I remember,
yes, a wild, spectacular place south of Brenner.
Fischleinboden. That was the inn. We were happy to be
the only English. Everyone else spoke German, very friendly.
Well, one day, three young men... no, two fit-looking chaps
and a grim official – portfolio stuffed with maps –
moved into our annex. We'd preferred it to the main chalet
as cheaper and more private. It annoyed us, the way
these newcomers assumed we'd want to drink and talk at night,
then in the daytime share their walks. Still, we were polite.
Soon it emerged that they were Nazis, only too
chuffed to meet English youth. *We would be friends with you*,
said the handsome one who spoke English. Turned out he'd been
to Cambridge, worked as a teacher in Berlin.
Passionately in love with English literature,
kept quoting from Shakespeare, knew a bit of Chaucer...
And to prove it one morning, presented Margaret with a rose.
Now Margaret, fair-skinned with auburn hair, was in those
days lovely, but her politics were redder than her hair:
Oh rose thou art sick, and the name of the worm is Hitler
– quick as a flash, making a deep, departing bow –
leaving speechless, still holding his rose, the German who,
drained to the colour of his lederhosen, stared at me.
It was the first time, I think, he'd really looked at me.
Through my thick-lensed glasses, I looked back at him.
White curtains fluttered over the Vinschgau, the sun poured in.
I broke the silence. *Excuse me*, I said, and started after her.
I watched his lips tighten, relax, smile and kiss his rose.
Next time, he said, *when you visit here, it will all be ours.*
Then in bewilderment, *Do you not also long to be a soldier?*

Invocation and Interruption
(i.m. Ted Hughes)

Gigantic iron hawk
coal-feathered like a crow,
tar-coated cave bird,
werewolf, wodwo,

you've flown away now,
where have you flown to?

was how this poem began
before the shade of a voice
fell on my hand.
I was going to invoke
a many-sided Hughes and refer
to his poems and Sylvia's;
it was to be called 'Totem'

when I felt that faint weight
of exhaled disapproval. Was it
disappointment?
No shadow from a shaman-flight,
no daemonic revelation;
just a sad discolouring of the air,
an indefinable pressure.

'Please don't imagine I have
flown anywhere,' said the silence
like a voice in deep water.
'The underworld was always a metaphor,
the life after life in which poets
are remade by their interpreters.
I'm better off here with
Sylvia and Otto, Coleridge and Ovid.
Nothing can hurt us;
we're immune to our reputations.
As for you and the others–
you'd best be getting on
with getting on.

Keep marching, keep trudging
out of the trench and stench of one century
over the wire into another.

The millennium? You're still
in the realm of blood and its thirsty ways,
so keep your head down.
Try to preserve the cave birds
at the bottom of your kit
and Prospero's magic in your hip flask.

Don't sell yourself or your poems
for a mess of verbiage. Oh, yes,
and warn those agribusiness bastards
against abusing the Goddess.
Once riled, she tends to avenge herself
without discriminating between
lovers and rapists.
Take special care of her fish.
Take special care of her thrushes.

And don't tell me who I was!

I'm the dream of a boy
who became a man and a lover
only by doing violence to violence.
I killed the fox that brought me poetry
smoking from the gun.
After that midnight encounter,
I set out for...where I am.
Death was my leader, tormentor,
wife, adversary, friend.
And still I'm, like herself,
an invention of my own imagination.
You'll find me in all my books.
So please, no more poems about me,
grateful as I am for the compliment.
I had the last word first, remember.
I'm going to keep things like this.'

A Parable for Norman

(i.m. Norman MacCaig)

Three vast unavoidable ladies,
Time, Fate and Boredom,
come knocking at your door.

What have you got in that school bag?
You eye Ms Time suspiciously.

A full load of years, says she
in a soothing tone.
Friendships, books, bottles,
a few stones.

And I have to buy the lot? – courtly
through your smoker's cough.

Aye, but you pay by the day, dear,
just out of what you've got.
Smiling, she unpacks an invisible file
and then, predictably, flies off.

Flexing undependable eyebrows,
Ms Fate steps up next,
snapping back the hasps
of a departmental briefcase.

What's this?
A display of bone-framed photographs,
all of your face –
half Rose Street bard
presiding graciously in bars
full of like spirits,

half man of Assynt.
Two mistresses, Suilven and Pollaidh,
loom in attendance,
surrounded by a family of
lovely little wild blue lochans.

Exactly what I ordered,
you compliment her, bowing your thanks.

But finally, the third in the trio,
shapeless and clammy with cobwebs,
yawns her way in.
A perfect host even to the nastiest,
you nod, I've been expecting you.
Sit down if you must,
but don't think you'll make yourself welcome.

Old Mrs Boredom sighs and spreads herself
stickily over furniture and pictures.
If you don't like the feel of me, Norman,
why not take up with my kids?

Such as?

Immemorial Magnificence, for a start.
Or Mystical Real Palpable Otherness.

Ugly and pleonastic, you shudder,
and *un*real into the bargain.

No? Well, there's always Venus,
she's real, you'll agree, and popular.

Toute entière à sa proie attachée?
Spare me, spare me! – as you
gravitate towards your desk
unscrewing your fountain pen.

Mars, then, glorious Mars,
on the bloody side of your imagination.
All the best poets write about him.

Not I, you say dryly.
And down go ten lines of
ultra expensive highland wit
with a bitter sting in the finish.

Looking up, you're surprised.
Your drab interlocutress is gathering her
shadows and herding them briskly
through the door. Ye'll no get
(her Parthian shot)
the slightest citation on Parnassus!

And your family (his countershot)
does not stir the slightest flutter
in my heart. Reflecting, he calls after her,
Don't you have a sister called Peace?
But she's gone. Or she just doesn't answer.

Comet

*(i.m. Lewis Lloyd, 1939–1996, Welsh historian
'who toiled at the quarry face of history')*

Bad days end just like good days,
wrapping themselves with relief in simple extinction,
supper dishes washed and tidily put away,
video rewinding with a soft purr,
bedside light switched on, switched off, as we sink,
in the habit of marriage, into middle-aged sleep.
In this April for-two-steady-weeks-cloudless sky
the new comet's flight-path keeps to schedule,
hurtling mathematically according to his circuit,
but by us deserted in its north-west diamond patch.
Get up in the night, and the corner of your eye
catches it sooner than a searching gaze.

By morning it has set beyond belief,
portent or presence filtered lightly through
spread nets of consciousness,
received, if at all, as subliminal unease.
A beetle pulls to a halt in its trek across kitchen vinyl.
A spider out of the drain fakes *rigor mortis*
on killing fields of wet enamel.
Instinctive. Have you noticed
how a butterfly, starved, just out of its chrysalis
but struck, somehow, by a look, will cancel its programme
of fluttering visits and, locked to a petal,
transform itself into a leaf?

Lives. Terrified of shadows.
Where does time go when memory loosens its orbit
and whirls into the night?
In wild trajectories of broken light,
first this, then that dead face flares and burns out.
Where's the soul of immense Lewis, maritime historian
shadowed by his shadow, now that his blurred bulk,
slurring home at midnight, learned and drunk,
has berthed in the sound harbour of his books?
And still what in him matters is the matter of Wales.
There, blazing back of my eyelids, comets' tails,
indelible Vs grooved in salt water by wrecked prows.

Freeing Lizzie

(i.m. Elizabeth Jane Jones, 1905-1999)

Don't mistake it for a camera snapping day.
Instamatics ought to flash for a family occasion,
but today photography has stayed away;
nothing here for display case or mantelpiece,
though the chapel's packed. Exposed in her high place
in front of the stained brown rail around the pulpit,
the elderly organist struggles to pacify her face.
Like everyone else, she's in black,
and the tremulous hymns she plays – the same strains
over and over – loop themselves around the yellowing
plaster and pale windows like black bunting.
Lizzie, had she been with us, would have worn a hat.
Among the last of a hat-wearing generation,
she would have sat in front, upright, eagerly proper.
What will young Reverend Jones have to say about her?

The organ pauses, recommences; everyone rises.
Like spontaneous applause, the first sung hymn
thunders from the pews, peal after peal of Welsh voices.
Self-conscious in ties and suits, Iddon, Gwynfor,
Hefin, Meirion, Aled, Alun bear the coffin,
bumping it gently through the chapel door,
down the side aisle to a raised bier by the platform.
Three ministers, one handsome with silver hair, close in.
They offer a kindly confident, protective power.
Except for a spray of pink roses, the box is bare.
Can it be Lizzie who is shut in there?

Failing to make himself small, the largest grandson stands
cramped by the wall next to a less lofty cousin.
They can't think what to do with their hands.
We who don't speak Welsh, who listen with our eyes
and can't think what to do with our tears,
take comfort. Right words are being said in the right way.
It could be these family faces, these rows of afterlives,
are meeting and merging somewhere with a crowd of others.
Would Lizzie's strong-handed forebears have stayed away?
Parents, grandparents, great aunties in pre-war frocks
must be pouring out of the bronze age seams of the valley,
hastening to help Lizzie out of that box!

There was a song Lizzie liked about a ruined girl
who drowned herself for love in her father's well.
An unmarried aunt at Nant Pasgan used to sing it,
milking the cows at evening, and Lizzie could hear it still –
'a very sad song' – floating out from the ruins of the barn
when we drove her 'home'. It was her only visit.
And that was all the sadness we had from Lizzie.
Beautiful, drownable girls have ballads to live in.
Plain ones can't be picky. They have to marry who comes.
Yet, in God's hands, a marriage's ups and downs
can be the wellspring under the rock that founts a river.
So it was, at least, with Lizzie, who when her brother died
– their hope, their heir, the most beloved one –
gave up her only son (it was a Bible family) to the farm.
'Llawer o ferched, dim mab, a heb etifedd i gadw'r tir.'
The pain of it! But then she had daughters
who married and had sons and daughters, and those
daughters' daughters have sons, and so now, so then…

A pause. A prayer introduces the last hymn,
then the blessing. We shuffle out, heads, eyes down,
which may be why no living soul sees Lizzie,
up and among us, free, smiling at everyone.
Look, look, she's everywhere! Relief leaves us blinking,
chaffing, thanking Reverend Jones, *'gwasanaeth hyfryd,'*
deciding which relatives will ride with whom.
For the ceremony of the cemetery is to come;
Lizzie's bones have to be tucked in with other bones.
Meanwhile, Lizzie's gone ahead to the Cadwgan.
It's going to be a treat of a tea: salmon, beef, cucumber sandwiches,
sausages on frilly sticks, canapés, satays, vol-au-vents,
five kinds of cake besides the bara brith and fruit scones,
yes, and an eighteenth – or twentieth? – great-grandson
who will have to be shown off, chuckled over, noisily passed around.

'Llawer o ferched, dim mab, a heb etifedd i gadw'r tir': 'Many daughters, no son,
without an heir to keep the land.'
gwasanaeth hyfryd: a good service.

The Writer in the Corner

Remembering Paul Winstanley

After long dying, short death.
One snip of the scissors,
One scoop of the palette knife,
The most ordinary nothing in the world,
That's the end of life.

Breathing still, still telling the story,
Wanting to believe there *is* a story,
They pour fresh flowers into the pit
Just before the bulldozer's
Earthen canopy slides over it.

How beautifully the church bells sing
To the crowd in black.
The widow lifts embroidered linen
To her kohl-rimmed eyes.
The canopy won't roll back.

There. They have dispersed.
The priest pays a visit to the toilet
Before he slips into his sky-blue Toyota.
A spray of gravel. He's off to celebrate
The bright day, the pure relief of it.

The upset cemetery, too, seems relieved
Now the bulldozer has understood it.
The driver and his mate light up,
Climb down, begin by habit
To decorate the ugly earth with wreathes.

They take no notice of the unshaved man,
Bald as the Sahara, dressed for youth
But long past it, scribbling in microscopic hand,
'What we live is the story,
What we write has to be the truth.'

Passifloraceae

(i.m. Gordon Brown)

And then Gordon was so beautiful,
    not what we usually say of men;
Of him we do. Didn't everyone admire
    that glimmer of elusiveness
Shining through? Poetry's guardian angel,
    spirit of the Tower,
But ordinary, too. Cry, now, for the indefinable
    loneliness of fact.
There is always a reason to refuse reason,
    then choose to act.
The gorgeous corolla of the passion flower
    huddled in its sack
Chooses or doesn't choose a minute or an hour
    to unclench, fold back,
Reveal to its secret sharers the marvel
    of a story,
Esoteric and erect amid wild, predictable
    filaments of glory.

Gordon Brown, a much loved friend and poet, drowned himself in March 2000.
For many people in Newcastle and Durham he represented the spirit of Morden
Tower where he initiated and arranged poetry readings over many years.

TWO POEMS FOR NERYS JOHNSON

Portrait of the Artist
in an Orthopaedic Halo Crowned with Flowers

She lives next door to dying
In a shack of bones,
A gorgeous spirit furnishing
That worst of homes.

A votive flame, she celebrates
The air she burns.
A flowering halo subjugates
Her crown of thorns.

Her eyes – amontillado
In the brimming glass –
Look straight into the Angel's.
But he will not pass.

Passing Her House

The house she nested in
became her,
unfurled around her
like a summer tree.
You can't pass by
that much desired but
costly new conservatory
without imagining she
still presides there,
tortured for hours
in her sadistic wheelchair,
but working quietly
among her pots and jars,
as if her brush were
walking through,
not painting flowers.

Was there some pheromone
her need unconsciously
released that drew
the needy to her? Who
came to care stayed
to be cared for. In Durham
she was queen-
creator of the hive's
heart, collector of humour's
nectar, conjurer
of sunlight out of gloom.
Her tools of rule
by telephone
were other people's lives;
they loved her for
not leaving them alone.

Those ziggurats of red
defiant shoes,
that dyed bright copper hair.
She laid her champagne tastes
for piquant news,
for waterlight and strawberries,
for art that makes necessity
its gesso, love that make
necessity its pleasure
over the private badlands
of her agonies.
How long, carissima,
before the house you were
forgets you?
Before I pass
forgetting to remember?

Variations on a Line by Peter Redgrove
(for Penelope Shuttle)

'A wind blows through the clock.'
Washes its spinning mesh of brass
with the same salt
that files down whorls in the whelk's shell,
slipper shell and spindle shell.

It's wind whistling through the clock
that licks away the blue plastic eyes
of the lost doll clotted with slime;
that also shapes jewels
made of ruby bright bottle glass
and heavy footballs of mortar-crossed brick.
The beach is smoothed to simplicity
by repeated beatings, and by a silicon tick

through which the wind blows,
bowling its weight along the shore
where waves of surf report on waves of shale,
a lacy froth of unresolved dispute
between the tides of water and the tides of rock.

A spider's curtain flutters
from bric-à-brac inside a sheep's skull
scrubbed with sand. What's more persistent
than a spider in a sheep's skull? A woman, knitting,
taking refuge from the wars of the beach
in a pleasant parlour, a perfectly-regulated clock.

Listen to the wind blowing through her,
through her knitting, through her poems
scrubbed of anxiety. Think of her saying quietly,
'I know what he means, it's comfort to me,
the everlasting breath of God I hear
sweeping through the clock.'

Think of the breath that's been trapped
in the clock, locked up in coal seams,
imprisoned in deep pockets hacked from rock
under slate black weather in slate black Wales.

Or maybe the wind is the voice of the clock
wailing to cohorts of lichened stone
built to hold fast the tribal hills,
telling tales, telling tales through the wind's mouth
that has blown out those makers like candles.

Think of the breath of the English poets
funnelled through England's Pleistocene fells,
scribbling in foam on the Lakes.
How long can a line last
that is writ on water? Or with ink on paper?
Or with fingertips on computer?
Compare it to the writing of ice on rock,
to the sea erasing, millimetre by millimetre
mud books and fossil prints
from tall crumbling shelves along the shore.

Think of the spirits blowing through the clock,
shouting, 'death shall have no dominion',
as death swirls them out, delighted, on the tide.
Think of the sillion shine of Hopkins' mind,
of Wordsworth's mortal immortality,
its clock still ticking, its bell
still tolling, as the years tumble over him,
not asleep between births,
but waking when the world's breath blows through him.

And singing, as your ashes were singing, Peter,
in September, on Maenporth Beach,
as the waves swirled them out in rhythm with the tide,
and the wind told the clock to greet them.

INDEX

Index of titles and first lines

Poem titles are shown in italics, first lines (some abbreviated) in roman type. Initials in square brackets denote the books where poems were first collected. The texts follow those of *The Collected Poems 1955-1995* rather than the earlier collections themselves, with some later corrections and amendments.

ABBREVIATED BOOK TITLES

Living in America (1965)   LA
Reversals (1969)   R
Travelling Behind Glass (1974)   TBG
Correspondences (1974) C
Enough of Green (1977)   EG
Minute by Glass Minute (1982)   MGM
The Fiction-Makers (1985)   FM
Winter Time (1986)   WT
The Other House (1990)   TOH
Four and a Half Dancing Men (1993)   4DM
The Collected Poems 1955-1995 (1996)   CP96
Granny Scarecrow (2000)   GS
A Report from the Border (2003)   RB
New poems (2003-05)   NP
Uncollected poems   UP

A Ballad for Apothecaries [GS], 327

A blunder rectified... [C], 275

A Cradle of Fist [RB], 363

A daughter's difficulties as a wife... [C], 211

A Dream of Stones [FM], 376

A family blunder... [C], 208

A glass jar rattles its split peas and pasta, 383

A grey undecided morning, 75

A Hot Night in New York [RB], 41

A house with a six-foot rosewood piano, too grand, 317

A lean season, March, for ewes, 71

A Letter from an English novelist... [C], 233

A Letter to God on hotel notepaper from Ethan Amos Boyd [C], 228

A London letter... [C], 229

A Love Letter... [C], 237

A Love Sequence [WT], 276

A Luxury [GS], 356

A Marriage [RB], 180

A memory kissed my mind, 138

A mother, who read and thought and poured herself into me, 318

A musk of kittening, 144

A New Year's message to myself... [C], 224

A north wind light this morning, 80

A Parable for Norman [GS], 391

A parson went out one stormy day, 332

A Prayer to Live with Real People [FM], 84

A Present [GS], 75

A prodigal son... [C], 204

A Quest [CP96], 336

A Report from the Border [RB], 27

A Riddle for Peter Scupham [NP], 291

A River [R], 47

A Sepia Garden [4DM], 162

A successful American advises his sons studying abroad... [C], 216

A Summer Place [EG], 38

A Surprise on the First Day of School [GS], 131

A touch of spring, 103

A Tourist Guide to the Fens [RB], 58

A Tricksy June [4DM], 168

A vigorous letter from a salesman of the Lord... [C], 226

'A wind blows through the clock,' 399

A worried father writes to his daughter at Oberlin College... [C], 222

Aberdeen [CP96], 110

About Crying [MGM], 263

Adam: Lady, 330

After a long drive west into Wales, 279

After Her Death [LA], 172

After long dying, short death, 395

After the End of It [EG], 142

After the exhilaration of the peaks, 142

After the Fall [MGM], 330

After weeks of October drench, 313

After you left [4DM], 307

Aged by rains, 115

Ah Babel [MGM], 289

Ailanthus with Ghosts [FM], 326

Alive in the slippery moonlight, 173

'All Canal Boat Cruises Start Here' [TOH], 144

All day, all night, 276

All in the spell of the short days, 235

All saints and all souls, 89

American Rhetoric for Scotland [UP], 106

Amici d'arti, amici dei fiori, amici d'amore, 310

Among others it is the same. It is repeated, 146

An Angel [GS], 279

An Impenitent Ghost [NP], 143

And again, without snow, a new year, 110

And even then [TOH], 270

And then Gordon was so beautiful, 396

Ann Arbor [LA], 32

Another day in March. Late, 24

Apology [LA], 172

Arioso Dolente [GS], 318

Arriving in North Carolina after midnight, 38

As I Lay Sleeping [NP], 367

At Kilpeck Church [MGM], 330

At sundown, a seaforce that gulls rode or fell through, 109

At the Grave of Ezra Pound [RB], 295

At Thirteen [TBG], 133

Attacking the Waterfall [RB], 77

Aubade [R], 139

Bad days end just like good days, 392
Ballad of the Made Maid [CP96], 337
Beauty fought shy of acting out her
    name, 343
Before the leaves change, 372
Beloved Mother, 216
Between [MGM], 372
Binoculars in Ardudwy [4DM], 71
Birth. / Impossible to imagine, 121
Black bird, black voice, 353
Black Hole [4DM], 167
Blessed One, 226
Bloodshed cries Ai Ai, 113
Bloody Bloody [4DM], 165
Boating Pool at Night [EG], 108
Branch Line [RB], 57
Broken bleats, 67
Brueghel's Snow [4DM], 303
Burnished [MGM], 65
Buzzard and Alder [MGM], 114
Buzzard that folds itself into and
    becomes nude, 114
By the Boat House, Oxford [EG], 63

Cain [EG], 268
Calendar [TOH], 277
Cambrian [4DM], 381
Carol of the Birds [RB], 334
Cashpoint Charlie [RB], 339
Casual, almost unnoticeable, 59
Celebrity [TOH], 335
Christmas Comfort and the Green Man
    [NP], 358
Cimmerian? Anyway, a swart day, 295
Clasped in its rigid head of hone, 261
Claude Glass [FM], 98
Clouds – plainmen's mountains, 140
Cloven hoof's-bane [RB], 271
Clydie Is Dead! [GS], 346
Cobalt water, 96
Cold [4DM], 114
Comet [GS], 394
Coming Back to Cambridge [TBG], 59
Complaint [MGM], 371
Condensed stillness lit meanly, 273
Condolences of a minister to his bereaved
    daughter... [C], 200
Contending against a restless shower-
    head, 281

Correspondences: A Family History in
    Letters [C], 193
Cramond [TOH], 112
Creeping close and closer as it falls
    away, 291
Curlews long gone from the valley, 77

Darling, 244
'Dear God,' they write, 'that was a
    selfish winter, 371
Dear Kay. So... a summer, 194
Dear Lord, 228
Dear Madam, it was interesting to read,
    344
Dear Ruth, 231
Dearest Father, 257
Dearest, 237
Demolition [FM], 88
Dinghy [4DM], 380
Distractions, considerations, 286
Don't mistake it for a camera snapping
    day, 393
Don't think, 137
Dr Animus, whose philosophy is a table,
    28
Dreaming of Immortality in a Thatched
    Hut [LA], 296
Dreaming of the Dead [FM], 374
Dreaming or dying? The room as usual,
    247
Drought [EG], 142
Drowsing over his verses or drifting, 296

Earth Station [MGM], 68
East Coast [EG/CP96], 108
Ebb day, full tide, 108
Eden Ann Whitelaw to her sister Kay
    Boyd in London [C], 194
Effulgence, or copper polyphony!, 362
Elegy [TOH], 178
End of a summer's day... [C], 247
England [R], 44
Enormous, this fragment of July, 108
Enough of Green [EG], 117
Epigraph from Reversals [UP], 121
Epilogue: Kay Boyd to her father,
    Professor Arbeiter [C], 257
Epitaph for a Good Mouser [FM], 346
Equisetum, horsetail, railway weed, 86

Eros [CP96], 155
Everywhere up and down the island, 56
Eyes are too close to Nature to be nice, 98
Eyes fall in love before their users dare, 341

False Flowers [GS], 156
Feet that could be clawed, but are not, 334
Fen People [R], 47
Fire and the Tide [EG], 108
Fire struggles in the chimney like an animal, 108
Five Poems of Innocence and Experience [TBG], 151
Flesh squirms on the blue folding bed, 299
Fool's Gold [NP], 341
For bungalows, 48
For mapmakers' reasons, the transcontinental air routes, 375
For weeks the wind has been talking to us, 76
Forgotten of the Foot [FM], 86
Four and a Half Dancing Men [4DM], 128
Four Grim Fairy Tales [NP], 343
Fragments: Mrs Reuben Chandler writes to her husband during a cholera epidemic [C], 214
Freeing Lizzie [GS], 395
From an Asylum... [C], 239
From an Unfinished Poem [FM], 19
From My Study [4DM], 90
From the Men of Letters [MGM], 289
From the Motorway [TOH], 56
From the Primrose Path [NP], 362

Gannets Diving [FM], 22
Generations [TBG], 150
Gigantic iron hawk, 389
Girls in their nervous freedom, heeled and painted, 341
Giving Rabbit to My Cat, Bonnie [MGM], 345
Go cut for me, 358
Going Back [GS], 33
Granny Scarecrow [GS], 169
Graves with Children [EG], 359

Green Mountain, Black Mountain [RB], 182
Gull, ballast of its wings, 123
Gulls think it is for them, 125

Habits the hands have, reaching for this and that, 82
Hadrian's [4DM], 162
Halfmast New York is crying for her children, 364
Hands [FM], 173
Handsome as D'Artagnan, 151
Hans Memling's Sibylla Sambetha [4DM], 304
Harvard [LA], 37
Haunted [RB], 181
Haunting me at midnight, 355
He and It [MGM], 269
He knew himself as Sunday in a hat, 305
He moves off at dawn, 152
Hearing with My Fingers [RB], 317
Here in the snow, 303
Here is one more fiery, 381
Hi yi hee yippee!, 128
Hills? Or a high plateau scissored by rivers? 83
Himalayan Balsam [MGM], 66
Hot Wind, Hard Rain [TOH], 387
Household Gods [FM], 85
How can it be that empty, intangible age, 368
How in this mindless whirl of time and space, 127
How lucky we are, 289
How uneasily I live, 147
How wise of our enemy to rely upon the watchers, 361

I am the doctor, 131
I am the enemy of spiders, 366
I believe, but what is belief?, 374
I call for love, 155
'I did, of course, consent to it, 301
I don't know why at all, 109
I dreamed a summer's labour, 376
I had forgotten the weight of her, 304
I have grown small, 167
I laid myself down as a woman, 132

I lift the seven months baby from his crib, 127
I must have been there, 261
I paint the rich and the damned, 302
'I think I'm going to have it,' 124
I thought you were my victory, 123
'I want you forever and ever,' I want to say, 141
I went down to the railway, 378
I'd hardly hooked it when I heard the fish, 344
I'm an old woman who wants to die, 168
I've lost a sense. Why should I care?, 351
Icon [TOH], 266
If I Could Paint Essences [MGM], 24
If I'm your book and you have found the page, 342
if not necessary, is essential, 137
If Wishes Were Fishes [NP], 344
In flood, familiar footpaths and, 275
In Hades, 301
In March [LA], 125
In Middle England [R], 48
In Passing [RB], 288
In sixteen-hundred-and-sixteen, 327
In summer, 359
In the House [R], 146
In the house of childhood, 153
In the Museum of Floating Bodies and Flammable Souls [NP], 304
In the Nursery [TOH], 127
In the Orchard [EG, 70], 353
In the Tunnel of Summers [FM], 26
In the unbelievable days, 172
In the Weather of Deciduous Souls [NP], 118
In this country, 360
In this picture I preside. I usher in, 264
In truth, beloved brother, 208
In Winter [LA], 324
Incident [GS], 134
Innocence and Experience [GS], 132
Inquit Deus [TOH], 270
Instead of your letter, 141
Intervention of chairs at midnight, 139
Inverkirkaig [TOH], 113
Invocation and Interruption [GS], 389
is some hexagonal white seal, 352

isn't 'making' love, 145
It appeared to be an inn for actors, so our boss, dedication page
It hazes over, 33
It is high summer by the blue pool, 298
It is imagination's white face remembers, 373
It is late, but as usual, 62
It looks so simple from a distance... [NP], 359
It's best, if you can, to love your children, 160
It's not when you walk through my sleep, 181
It's too big to begin with, 272

Jarrow [WT], 99
John Keats, 1821-1950 [GS], 294
Journal Entry: Impromptu in C Minor [TOH], 313
Journal Entry: Ward's Island [TOH], 42
Keats was Miss McKinney's class, 12th grade English, 294
Killing Spiders [NP], 366
Know this mother by her three smiles, 150
Kosovo Surprised by Mozart [GS], 316

Landscape without regrets whose weakest junipers, 30
Language raked tribute from her screen all winter, 80
Late [4DM], 355
Late October. It is afternoon, 124
Leaving [GS], 82
Lesson [LA], 325
Let me not live, ever, without fat people, 84
Letter to a mother from a Confederate soldier... [C], 218
Letter to Sylvia Plath [TOH], 384
Level Cambridgeshire, islands, 58
'Life is what you make it,' my half-Italian, 36
Like threading a needle by computer, to align, 101
Like winter in the hills, the heft of their, 72
Little Paul and the Sea [TOH], 128

Little soul, gentle and fickle, 162
Little space-age doll, 365
Living in America [LA], 30
Lockkeeper's Island [MGM], 62
Long summer shadows calm the grass, 177
Lord, have mercy upon the angry, 268
Lost [4DM], 168
Love [LA], 137
Love Stories and a Bed of Sand [GS], 275
Lovely chromatic Mozart, talk to me, 316

Made up in death as never in life, 173
makes no difference to the flowers, 282
Making Poetry [FM], 17
Maxims of a Christian businessman… [C], 221
May Bluebells, Coed Aber Artro [RB], 81
Melon meaning melon [NP], 353
Meniscus [EG], 267
Midnight air's unbreathing steam, 41
Might be human, 290
Miranda hoists her lips in a grimace, 308
Moonrise [GS], 23
Morning [R], 285
Mostly feeling pity, 104
Mother, 239
Mother, I have taken your boots, 172
Moving from day into day, 26
Mrs Lilliam Culick, divorcée, to Dr Frank Chattle, 244
Musician's Widow [FM], 159
My dear Eliza, 202
My dear father, 204
My dear sons, 216
My love is rich and talented, 337
My office, my crouch, is by the Piccadilly cashpoint where, 339
My sideways smile, 291
My wretched daughter, 200

Naming the Flowers [WT], 282
Negatives [4DM], 273
Neither city nor town, its location, 32
New York [R], 41
New York Is Crying [RB], 364
Nick Arbeiter writes poems on the road to Wyoming after a funeral in Vermont [C], 252

Night Thoughts and False Confessions [TOH], 147
Night walking the dog through the hollow village, 102
Night Walking with Shadows [TOH], 102
Night Wind, Dundee [CP96], 110
Nightmare, Daymoths [TOH], 383
Nightmare in North Carolina [LA], 38
No Greek self-pitying hetairos in blue-rinse curls, 81
No time, no time, 148
No, trilobites didn't, 356
Nor do I wish to prolong this tired debate, 275
North Easter [TOH], 100
North in the mind, ragged edged, stubborn ribbed, 106
North Sea off Carnoustie [EG], 22
Not my final face, a map of how to get there, 170
Notes to a father from a young man gone West… [C], 217
November [FM], 89
Now I am dead, 320
Now that I've been married for almost four weeks, Mama, 211
Nucleic crystals, pursed in the invisible, 271

O Übermenschen, flex your miracles!, 342
Of course I love them, they are my children, 150
Oh, hallo, good of you to come. Sorry I can't get up, 388
Old daughter with a rich future, 110
Old ears and eyes, so long my patient friends, 351
Old Scholars [TBG], 153
Old Wife's Tale [GS], 155
On Going Deaf [GS], 351
On Not Being Able to Look at the Moon [R], 262
On the last day of the poetry festival, 42
On Watching a Cold Woman Wade into a Cold Sea [FM], 158
One morning I despaired of writing more, 354
Opera Piece [LA], 325

Orchid-lipped, loose-jointed, purplish, indolent flowers, 66
Our lar, our little mammal, 346
Out of the afterlife behind my eyelids, 367
Overnight it climbs like a snail, 69
Oysters [GS], 338

Painters who painted the flights of martyrs for money, 304
Painting It In [4DM], 306
Passifloraceae [RB], 398
Passing Her House [RB], 399
Path [EG], 115
Pennine [MGM], 83
Personality, the flesh artist, 299
Phoenicurus phoenicurus [GS], 73
Photographing Change [NP], 368
Phu-eet! Phu-eet! Mr unresting redstart has something to be, 73
Pity / the persistent clamour of a song thrush, 74
Pity the Birds [GS], 74
Plants she loved, all growing things, 159
Poem for a Daughter [MGM], 124
Poem for Harry Fainlight [FM/GS], 382
Poems from Cwm Nantcol [various], 71
Politesse [4DM], 138
Portrait of a Lady [TOH], 301
Portrait of the Artist in an Orthopaedic Halo Crowned with Flowers [RB], 399
Post Scriptum [GS], 320
Posted [EG], 141
Precocious, in the news at nine or ten, 336
Pretty Bonnie, you are quick as a rabbit, 345
Professor Arbeiter to his dead wife [C], 250
Prophylactic Sonnets [RB], 341

Questionable [RB], 156

Rapunzel [NP], 343
Red Hot Sex [RB], 308
Red Rock Fault [FM], 377
Remember how in Edinburgh, 112
Re-reading Jane [FM], 293
Respectable House [EG], 266
Resurrection [EG], 116

Reversals [R], 140
Ruin [EG], 40

Safe in a turret of the citadel, 343
Salter's Gate [4DM], 97
Saying the World [CP96], 18
Seated Figure [TOH], 300
Seeds I scrape away from this quartered melon, 353
Self-placed, 300
Seven Poems after Frances Bacon [TOH], 299
17.14 Out of Newcastle [NP], 104
Shale [FM], 83
She feels it like a shoulder of hair, 260
She knows how to fold, 128
She lives next door to dying, 397
She must have been about, 134
Sierra Nevada [LA], 30
Siskin [TBG], 176
Skills [GS], 101
Skin Deep [RB], 340
Sleeping Beauty [NP], 343
Small bird with green plumage, 176
Small Philosophical Poem [MGM], 28
Snow. No roofs this morning, alps, ominous message, 114
So we struck across the mountains, 217
Sole to sole with your reflection, 273
'Solidity is a shifting desert, 363
Somewhere nowhere in Utah, a boy by the roadside, 32
Sonnets for Five Seasons [MGM], 371
Sous-entendu [R], 137
Spring Again [NP], 103
Spring comes little, a little. All April it rains, 25
Spring Poem [RB], 80
Spring Song [FM], 88
Stabilities [R], 123
Stasis [MGM], 372
Steep path to where the wheatfields' yellow, 108
Still Life in Utah [LA], 32
Stone-age, stone-grey eyes, 168
Stone Fig [TOH], 161
Study for a portrait of Van Gogh [TOH], 302
Study for a Portrait on a Folding Bed [TOH], 299

Study of a Dog [TOH], 299
Suicide [GS], 134
Summer [EG], 108
Suppose I had paused a few seconds, 288
Surprised by spring, 116
Swifts [MGM], 25

Take, Lord, this soul of furred unblemished worth, 346
Talking Sense to My Senses [TOH], 351
Tears flowed at the chapel funeral, 169
Television [LA], 325
Temporarily in Oxford [EG], 61
Terrorist [4DM], 354
Thales and Li Po [EG], 268
Thales, out scanning the stars for truth, 268
that comes to pieces in your hand, 83
That daffodil trumpets its *gaudia*, 100
that perpetual summer sun became unpleasant, 307
That twilight skyline, for example, 78
The Affair [TBG], 152
The beasts in Eden, 348
The Bench [EG], 108
The blank days, 277
The Blue Pool [FM], 298
The Circle [MGM], 373
The Crush [TBG], 151
The Dear Ladies of Cincinnati [LA], 36
The Demolition [TBG], 152
The Doctor [EG], 131
The Editor regrets that he is, 236
The Exhibition [EG], 296
The exhibition is of, 296
The fat man laughed because, 338
The Fear of loneliness, the wish, 287
The Fiction Makers [FM], 20
The Figure in the Carpet [MGM], 290
The Fish Are All Sick [MGM], 111
The fish are all sick, the great whales dead, 111
The Foundations of Belief, 221
The Garden [MGM], 260
The Garden of Intellect [LA], 272
The girls and boys in winter know, 325
The Grey Land [LA], 261
The Holly and the Ivy [MGM], 130

The house she nested in, 397
The idea of event is horizontal, 19
The Inn, dedication page
The joy of the rowan is to redden, 385
The last dog, 299
The Lighthouse [EG], 109
The line between land and water, 47
The Loss [R], 173
The Man in the Wind [MGM], 111
The Marriage [TBG], 151
The Minister [EG], 175
The Minister's wife, in confidence, to a beloved sister during a January storm [C], 202
The Miracle of Camp 60 [GS], 310
The moon at its two extremes, 267
The Morden Angel [WT, TOH], 291
The Mother [R], 150
The Mudtower [EG], 110
The Name of the Worm [GS], 388
The Other House [TOH], 153
The Parson and the Romany [CP96], 332
The Poetry Review [C], 236
The Price [EG], 287
The Professor's Tale [4DM], 160
The room is silent except for the two hearth spirits, 85
The scene they play, 266
The sea is dark, 22
The Short and the Long Days [C], 235
The Sirens Are Virtuous [EG], 265
The snow melts, 125
The sooner ends the old man's day, 324
The Spirit Is Too Blunt an Instrument [R], 122
The Suburb [R], 148
The sumptuous tackiness of the motel, 143
The Sun Appears in November [EG], 18
The sun is warm, 88
The Takeover [R], 149
The Theologian's Confession [GS], 333
The Three [MGM], 264
The train is two cars linking, 57
The Traveller [LA], 323
The Unaccommodated [RB], 72
The Unhappened [R], 261
The Victory [R], 123
The Watchers [R], 361

411

The way lives touch, 359
The way that wintry woman, 158
The wet and weight of this half-born English winter, 372
The White Room [GS], 177
The Wind, the Sun and the Moon [RB], 76
The Women [LA], 46
The world is the world, 270
The worm in the spine, 170
The worst time is waking, 250
The Wrekin [GS], 69
The Writer in the Corner [RB], 397
The young fig tree feels with its hands, 161
Their veins were white, 326
Theme with Variations [TBG], 286
Then I spent a long time, 50
There is crying about crying, 263
There may be a language in which, 270
There may be a moon, 262
There was no hole in the universe to fit him, 134
There, in that lost, 97
They are already old when the fen makes them, 47
They are great healers, English springs, 384
They are not what you think, 265
They belong here in their own quenched country, 63
They give you a desk with a lid, mother, 131
They have blown up the old brick bridge, 88
They have lived in each other so long, 152
They have written it, 153
They were to have been a love gift, 156
They will fit, she thinks, 151
This [WT], 145
This addiction, 41
This hot summer wind, 179
This House [MGM], 371
This is the South-West wind, 377
This is where God first laughed, 330
This world is not *it*, he felt, 269
Though I did not intend, 109
Though not altogether unsuitable, my daughter, 222
Though you won't feel again, 380

Though you won't look at it, 162
Three Figures and Portrait [TOH], 299
Three poems for Sylvia Plath [TOH], 383
Three vast unavoidable ladies, 391
Through dawn in February's wincing radiance, 64
Time to go to school, cried, 278
To My Daughter in a Red Coat [LA], 124
To Phoebe [RB], 127
To witness pain is different form of pain [GS], 170
To women in contemporary voice and dislocation, 293
To Write It [EG], 287
Toy [NP], 365
Transparencies [MGM], 135
Travelling Behind Glass [TBG], 50
Tree, a silence, 382
Trinity at Low Tide [4DM], 273
Triptych [TOH], 301
Tumuli, not hills. Cold earthheaps, 68
Turning his last days page by page, 333
Two Cambridges... [C], 231
Two Countries [R], 360
Two Love Poems [R], 140
Two Poems and a Rejection Slip... [C], 235
Two poems for Frances Horovitz [FM], 377
Two poems for John Cole [4DM], 380
Two poems for Nerys Johnson [RB], 399
Two Quatrains [LA], 325
Two weeks aboard the 'General Wayne', 214
Two years ago, 233

Under Moelfre [RB], 77

Variations on a Line by Peter Redgrove [NP], 401
Vermont Autumn [C], 235
Vertigo [GS], 28
Visits to the Cemetery of the Long Alive [4DM/GS/RB], 162

Wake up at six o'clock. We're out to sea, 306
Walking Early by the Wye [MGM], 64
Walking out of Hay in the rain, imagining Blake, 65

Wanted [EG], 141

Wars in peacetime don't behave like wars, 27

Was Cinderella Ever Happy? [NP], 344

Washing My Hair [RB], 281

Washing the Clocks [4DM], 278

Waving to Elizabeth [FM], 375

We have come to the end of a summer in this gold season, 235

We have seen ghosts of the once green peacocks, 37

We were the wrecked elect, 20

We're going to need the minister, 175

'Well then, goodbye,' she said coldly, 155

Well, they're gone, long gone, 40

West, man, West, 252

What a strange animal that has to get dressed, 340

What am I to do? Where am I to go? 149

What I Miss [TOH], 352

Whatever it is we share with folds of rock, 77

When at last I lie down to sleep, 335

When my mother knew why her treatment wasn't working, 180

When she laid a light hand on his elbow saying, 156

When the camel is dust it goes through the needle's eye [4DM], 179

When trees are bare, 18

Whenever my father was left with nothing to do, 178

Where have you been? she said, 130

Where the Animals Go [FM], 348

Where they will bury me, 61

Which represents you, as my bones do, waits, 371

While my anxiety stood phoning you last evening, 23

Whistler's Gentleman by the Sea [GS], 305

White pine, sifter of sunlight, 182

Who I am? You tell me, 165

Who's Joking with the Photographer [RB], 170

Whose Goat? [MGM], 67

Why / do these, 325

Why don't you Vermonters call October, 118

Why Take Against Mythology (1) [RB], 78

Why Take Against Mythology (2) [RB], 79

Why, love, do you persist, 79

Willow Song [FM], 378

Winter Flowers [EG], 109

Winter Time [WT], 96

With My Sons at Boarhills [EG], 125

With the hot sun palming my back, 90

Without false pride, 224

Without Me [RB], 80

Without nostalgia who could love England, 44

Women, waiting for their husbands, 46

Woodsmoke, 133

Worth keeping your foot in the door, 266

Would want to paint them, 99

You gave and gave, 142

'You have to inhabit poetry, 17

You I embrace, 140

You know it by the northern look of the shore, 22

You know that house she called home, 38

You lie in sleep, 285

You must always be alone, 287

You'd think that in this foreign place, 323

Your letter arrived with its letters, 229

Your time with me ends with August, and now, 135

your tower allures me, 289